D0936850

DISCARD

The Human Side of
Advanced Manufacturing Technology

WILEY SERIES IN PSYCHOLOGY AND PRODUCTIVITY AT WORK

Series Editor
David J. Oborne

The Physical Environment at Work
Edited by D. J. Oborne and M. M. Gruneberg

Hours of Work—Temporal factors in work scheduling
Edited by Simon Folkard and Timothy H. Monk

Computers at Work—A behavioural approach
David J. Oborne

Psychology of Work and Unemployment
Gordon E. O'Brien

The Human Side of Advanced Manufacturing Technology
Edited by T. D. Wall, C. W. Clegg and N. J. Kemp

Further titles in preparation

The Human Side of Advanced Manufacturing Technology

Edited by

Toby D. Wall and Chris W. Clegg
MRC/ESRC Social and Applied Psychology Unit,
University of Sheffield, England

and

Nigel J. Kemp
Thorn EMI, Development Centre Sigma,
Swindon, England

JOHN WILEY & SONS
Chichester · New York · Brisbane · Toronto · Singapore

Library of Congress Cataloging-in-Publication Data:

The Human side of new manufacturing technology.

(Wiley series in psychology and productivity at work)
Includes indexes.
1. Manufactures—Technological innovations.
2. Manufacturing processes—Automation. I. Wall,
Toby D. II. Clegg, Chris W. III. Kemp, Nigel J.
IV. Series.
HD9720.5.H85   1987   331.25   86-32554
ISBN 0 471 90867 3

British Library Cataloguing in Publication Data:

The Human side of the new manufacturing
technology. — (Wiley series in psychology
and productivity at work)
1. Labor supply — Effect of technological
innovation on 2. Technological innovations
— Social aspects
I. Wall, Toby D. II. Clegg, Chris W.
III. Kemp, Nigel J.
331.7'67   HD6331
ISBN 0 471 90867 3

Typeset by Geometra Phototypesetting, Chichester, West Sussex
Printed and bound in Great Britain by Anchor Brendon Ltd,
Colchester, Essex

Contributors

JOHN BESSANT — *Innovation Research Group, Department of Business Studies, Brighton Polytechnic, Brighton, Sussex, UK*

BERNARD BURNES — *Department of Management Sciences, University of Manchester Institute of Science and Technology, Manchester, UK*

MELVIN BLUMBERG — *Department of Computer and Decision Systems, Fairley Dickinson University, Florham-Madison Campus, New Jersey 07940, USA*

JOHN CHILD — *Management Centre, University of Aston in Birmingham, Gosta Green, Birmingham, UK*

CHRIS CLEGG — *MRC/ESRC Social and Applied Psychology Unit, Department of Psychology, University of Sheffield, Sheffield, UK*

MARTIN CORBETT — *MRC/ESRC Social and Applied Psychology Unit, Department of Psychology, University of Sheffield, Sheffield, UK*

THOMAS CUMMINGS — *Department of Management and Organization, University of Southern California, Los Angeles 90089-1421, USA*

MIKE FITTER — *MRC/ESRC Social and Applied Psychology Unit, Department of Psychology, University of Sheffield, Sheffield, UK*

NIGEL KEMP — *Thorn EMI, Development Centre Sigma, Swindon, UK*

GERALD NADLER — *Department of Industrial and Systems Engineering, University of Southern California, Los Angeles, California 90089-1452, USA*

GORDON ROBINSON — *Department of Safety Sciences, School of Engineering, University of Southern California, Los Angeles, California 90089-1452, USA*

SHEILA ROTHWELL — *Henley, The Management College, Henley-on-Thames, UK*

PETER SENKER — *Science Policy Research Unit, University of Sussex, Brighton, Sussex, UK*

TOBY WALL — *MRC/ESRC Social and Applied Psychology Unit, Department of Psychology, University of Sheffield, Sheffield, UK*

PAUL WILLMAN — *London Graduate School of Business Studies, Sussex Place, London, UK*

Contents

Editorial Foreword to the Series

The various volumes within this *Psychology and Productivity at Work* series have been produced for a particular type of reader: anyone who is interested in, and has the job of, improving the productive output of work. The format of the series, which contains edited, single- and multi-authored volumes, helps greatly in this endeavour. Thus the various aspects of this multifaceted problem of working efficiency can be addressed in a number of different ways and from different viewpoints. The list of titles already produced or in preparation illustrates this.

Pleasingly, psychology's important contribution to the world at work has been recognized for some years now. In areas as diverse as personnel selection and training, equipment evaluation and design, and organizational structure and functioning, psychology and psychologists are rightfully recognized as being fundamental to the increase in efficiency.

Unfortunately, this recognition is sometimes slow to occur, and this is particularly true when new areas of technology emerge. The usual pattern is for technologists to develop advanced systems, only to find that they exceed the capacities of people to use them.

Generally, it is only then that the importance of understanding the human side is realized, and the value of psychological expertise is recognized. In this book a number of eminent authors have illustrated well the various areas in which psychology will play a crucial role in humanizing advanced manufacturing technology.

The book has a clear relevance to anyone with an interest in the significance of psychology to our everyday economic and social lives.

David J. Oborne

Preface

It is widely held that we are in the midst of an Information Technology Revolution heralding the dawn of the Information Age. Certainly, enormous national and international political and financial support has been given to promote research, development, and the use of new computer-based technologies, including advanced manufacturing technology. Unfortunately this money, expertise and debate has been focused almost exclusively on the technical aspects of the 'revolution', with scant systematic regard paid to the human side of the technologies.

This book is based on the straightforward premise that the human side of advanced manufacturing technology is important for the people, companies, and countries concerned. We hope it makes a contribution, however small, in concentrating minds and efforts in this direction.

To our patient contributors we offer our thanks, and in particular we acknowledge the help given by June Staniland at the MRC/ESRC Social and Applied Psychology Unit in Sheffield in supporting us throughout all stages of preparing this book.

TDW, CWC, NJK
June 1987

The Human Side of Advanced Manufacturing Technology
Edited by T. D. Wall, C. W. Clegg, and N. J. Kemp
© 1987 John Wiley & Sons Ltd.

CHAPTER 1

The Nature and Implications of Advanced Manufacturing Technology: Introduction

TOBY WALL AND NIGEL KEMP

Today's £400 microcomputer has all the information-processing and control capacity that relatively few years ago would have required a mainframe computer costing tens or hundreds of thousands of pounds. This change has been brought about by recent advances in microelectronics, particularly the development of the powerful, robust yet very low-cost silicon chip. The dramatic reduction in the cost and size of computers, coupled with increased reliability and tolerance for varied environmental conditions, has opened up vast new areas of application. This is leading to the development of a whole range of associated technologies, such as those for data sensing, information display, and materials handling, which bring an ever-increasing number of domestic, office, manufacturing, and other processes within the ambit of information technology applications. It is this potential that has led many to the view that we are in the midst of a 'second industrial revolution' (Halton, 1985), and to refer to the 'microelectronics revolution' or the 'information technology revolution' (Forester, 1985).

That we have reached this stage in the development of information technology is no accident. Nor is technical progress likely to stop in the near future. Marbach *et al.* (1985), and Feigenbaum and McCorduck (1985), document the immense resources that have been poured into this area over the past 20 years, and the billion-dollar programmes now under way to create 'fifth-generation' technologies both in Japan and the United States. European countries have also responded to the challenge both individually (e.g. the Alvey programme in the UK of the Department of Trade and Industry) and collectively (e.g. the European Community's ESPRIT programme).

Naturally, there is a big gap between development at the leading edge of new technology and its practical application. Such is the case with the current 'revolution'. Thus at present the penetration of information technology into everyday domestic and working life is very small compared with its potential. This lag occurs for several reasons. Potential users are not fully aware of the possibilities, associated interfacing technologies have to be developed, skills required for its use are not available, the investment needed is not always readily to hand, and numerous other factors impede immediate application. Nevertheless, it is clear that even today's information technology is being adopted at an accelerating rate.

The brief and recent history of the 'information technology revolution' bears witness to the military, political, and economic forces that have shaped and sustained its development. In many ways history repeats itself. As for previous technologies, from the internal combustion engine to nuclear power, early development is driven by a narrow set of objectives, and wider social considerations take a back seat. Questions of the human and social consequences of the technology lie dormant, and their influence over the developmental process is most notable by its absence. Yet information technology clearly has wide-ranging social implications. The growth of data bases opens up the horizons for computer crime and fuels legitimate fears about loss of personal privacy. New materials and information handling applications offer the possibility of freeing people from some tedious and dangerous jobs, but create the spectre of higher unemployment and perhaps other more boring and closely monitored work. The use of expert systems for medical, legal, and other purposes introduces fundamental issues about responsibility for advice offered. Advances in telecommunications offer the prospect of influencing patterns of work, with a greater number of people working from their own homes. There also arises a whole new set of safety and industrial relations issues. The possible manifestations seem almost limitless.

The prospect of a technology with such pervasive socioeconomic implications raises questions of how best it can be exploited, and what dangers are inherent in its use. Answers, of course, will not be easy to find, especially as the technology itself is developing so rapidly and is manifest in so many forms. Nevertheless, answers should be sought if one is to aim to protect and enhance the quality of life. And the sooner these questions are addressed the greater the opportunity to influence the development process itself. As Forester observes with regard to the wider implications of information technology (1985, p. xvii):

> No doubt society will survive, but what kind of society is emerging is not clear. The debate on the future of industrial society has become somewhat sterile, with labels like 'the post-industrial society' and even 'the technetronic society' being bandied around with little thought given to their true meaning or analytical value. But we are certainly headed somewhere, and the future shape of society is still, to some extent, negotiable. We all have the right to debate and shape the kind of society we want to live in.

AIM OF THIS BOOK

The aim of this book is to debate some of the questions about the social and psychological dimensions of information technology. To consider this new generic technology and its societal implications as a whole is to bite off more than one can chew. Understanding is more likely to be promoted if one identifies particular areas of application in settings about which much is already known. In this way one takes on a more homogeneous set of applications and can consider them against a relatively well-mapped-out territory. This brings enquiry down to more manageable proportions.

Our objective in this book reflects the above strategy. It is to take a modest bite within the more general area of the human side of information technology. We consider its application in the important arena of the manufacturing industry, and particularly in relation to new forms of computer-based technology used directly in the manufacturing process. As such the focus is on what has become known as 'advanced manufacturing technology' (AMT), and our perspective ranges from its implications for the individual at the level of the job through to its organizational ramifications.

To approach our objective we gathered together authors who are recognized authorities on different aspects of manufacturing organization, who represent alternative disciplinary backgrounds, and who are currently involved in research and consultancy into AMT. We asked each to consider the human implications of this new technology within his/her area of expertise. Four of these authors come from the United States, and eleven from the United Kingdom. They cover such diverse disciplinary perspectives as sociology, psychology, and engineering. Their contributions form the core of this book, and provide a challenging and provocative account of the state of the art. As a result the book should be of interest to academic and research staff and their students from a variety of social and engineering science backgrounds who wish to keep abreast of this emerging area of enquiry. It should also be of value to those in industry currently working with or planning to introduce AMT, such as engineers, production managers, personnel and industrial relations specialists, project managers, and trade union officials.

The remainder of this chapter sets the scene for those which follow, and is in five parts. First we make a brief comment to clarify our use of terminology in an area currently overendowed with labels. Second, we describe the nature of AMT, and the main forms in use. This is followed by a consideration of its current penetration within manufacturing organizations. In the fourth section we review some of the early thinking on the work and organizational implications of AMT. Finally, we introduce each of the chapters which follow.

A QUESTION OF TERMINOLOGY

New areas of enquiry and technical development give rise to new terms. This is natural, and necessary for those involved in the area to communicate with one another. In the early stages, however, a wide variety of new labels is typically generated, as individuals and groups working towards different applications and from divergent standpoints coin diverse terms. This can lead to a certain degree of confusion. The same terms are sometimes used to denote different ideas and artifacts, and at the same time different labels are used to cover the same concept or class of application. It takes time for usage to settle down to a more limited and agreed set of terms.

The area with which we are here concerned clearly shows this tendency. Among the many terms used to refer to technological developments based on the silicon microchip in general are 'new technology', 'microelectronic-based technology', and 'information technology'. Similarly, particular areas of application of this generic technology have given rise to different terms. Thus, with regard to manufacturing applications 'new manufacturing technology', 'microelectronic-based manufacturing technology', 'computer-aided manufacturing', and 'advanced manufacturing technology' are among those current in the literature.

One could debate at length the respective merits of these terms and the limits or inclusiveness of their application. For our present purposes, however, little benefit would arise from so doing. For the sake of consistency of presentation we have adopted two which seem to be emerging as the most commonly accepted and inclusive. 'Information technology' (IT) we use to cover modern computer technology with the capacity to store, manipulate, retrieve, and distribute information. 'Advanced manufacturing technology' (AMT) we use to refer to the application of IT to manufacturing processes, and this is discussed in greater detail below. We have used our editorial prerogative to ensure this consistency is maintained throughout individual contributions to the book.

THE NATURE OF ADVANCED MANUFACTURING TECHNOLOGY

Two forms of application of information technology to manufacturing can be distinguished (Sharlt, Chang and Salvendy, 1986). The first comprises direct applications. These are generally taken to include: computer numerical control (CNC) (and its precursor, numerical control (NC), direct numerical control (DNC), robotics, automated guided vehicles (AGV), conveyor control, and automated storage. Here a distinguishing feature is the use of computer technology to control machinery. The information storage, manipulation, and retrieval capabilities of IT are used to distribute information for the control of other equipment which physically transforms or transports materials, or assembles components. This allows the same piece of machinery to carry out a wide range of different operations simply by changing the program. In many respects the IT component replaces the human operator. Typically the computing element in such advanced manufacturing technology is proportionately smaller than in other applications, and the associated machinery much bigger and more costly.

Indirect applications of IT form the second group. They cover production planning and scheduling, inventory control, production control, and factory management systems. These all provide facilities for storing, manipulating, analysing, and in other ways using data to support the management of production. The computer element is typically large and associated equipment used mainly to produce visual displays and hard copy of relevant information. In effect these are particular examples of more general office applications where information handling, not machine control, is the core task.

Our focus in this book is primarily on the direct forms of application, for which we use the term advanced manufacturing technology (AMT). As we shall describe later, these are currently most commonly found as 'stand-alone' technologies. However, it should be recognized that an important feature of such applications is that, with a common information processing base, they have the potential to be combined into more comprehensive production systems. For example, in an engineering setting requiring the machining of metal, the material can be passed from one CNC machine to another to complete the required series of operations entirely through the use of conveyors, robots, and AGVs, with the whole sequence under the control of information processing technology. This directs not only the performance of each individual machine, but also the movement of materials between machines. By using different programs a wide range of components can be made. Such a computer co-ordinated combination is referred to as a flexible manufacturing system (FMS). Moreover, because direct applications also use the same core information technology it is clear that such integration could be further extended, and be tied into production planning, production control, product design (through computer-aided design (CAD) systems) or other computer-based systems. This level of integration is often referred to as computer-integrated manufacturing (CIM). It is this potential that gives rise to the vision of the fully automated factory of the future. This possible integration of direct and indirect applications of IT in manufacturing tends to blur the distinction between them. Our use of AMT includes FMS and CIM, both of which encompass direct applications of information technology.

The nature of AMT can be further clarified by considering its history. This can be traced back to the development of NC machine tools in the late 1940s and during the 1950s. The major driving force behind this initiative was the United States Air Force, whose objective was to improve upon quality and consistency in the making of complex parts for modern weapon systems (Noble, 1979). Traditionally such parts were made by skilled operators working from drawings and using hand-controlled machine tools (lathes, milling machines, grinding machines, etc.). The accuracy and quality of the product was under human control, and naturally was variable in the context of the increasingly fine tolerances required. The idea behind the NC machine tool was to achieve greater consistency of product by replacing the human operator with a mechanism which would always 'operate' the machine tool in exactly the same way. A machine tool was built whose operations could be electronically controlled through a series of instructions coded onto a paper tape. Thus, once the tape had been correctly programmed, each component in a given batch could be made to exactly the same specification, and often much more quickly than by human control; and by building up a library of tapes, a whole range of components could be made in the same way.

A major drawback with NC machines, however, was that the preparation of the paper tapes was a complex and time-consuming business. Specifying the precise movements of cutting edges and materials in three-dimensional space, while taking account of cutting speeds and the range of other factors involved, is no easy task.

In practice the preparation of paper tapes required specialist programmers using costly mainframe computers. This limited the more general use of NC technology, especially in manufacturing settings where precision was less at a premium than in the aerospace industry (Wall *et al.*, 1984).

The advent of cheap and reliable microprocessors in the 1970s altered this situation. The hard-wired NC controller was replaced by computer-based control devices and the result is the computer numerically controlled machine tool. The built-in computer control allows a whole range of programs to be stored and edited directly. Basic programs are still typically produced off-line (on now cheaper computer technology), although more recent models allow for direct input of machining data. Moreover, CNCs now come equipped with automatic tool-changing, which allows them to be used with less manual support for a greater range of operations. Originally conceived within the context of metal cutting, CNC technology has been adapted to a range of other operations, such as computer board assembly.

A key feature of CNC machines is that their controllers, being based on computers, can communicate with other computers and computer-based control devices. This opens up the possibility for developing multi-machine production systems. With this common control technology, CNC is the natural building block in a progression towards CIM or the factory of the future (Voss, 1984). The first step in this process is direct numerical control (DNC). With DNC a number of CNC machines are organized into a cell, using the principles of group technology. They are controlled by a central computer (rather than locally) which downloads the required programs to individual machines. When automated materials handling (e.g. robots) and transportation devices (conveyors, AGVs, etc.) are added and co-ordinated through centralized control, then the system becomes an FMS. Finally, when all the above technology is integrated with system-wide production control, inventory and other systems, full computer-integrated manufacturing is achieved.

In general the history of AMT is one of a progression from the automation of individual machine tools previously dependent on highly skilled operators (NC, CNC), through integration among such machines (DNC), towards much higher levels of integration involving large-scale monitoring and controlling systems (FMS, CIM). All this becomes possible because of the development of a generic, robust, and cheap core information technology. In practice, however, much of this history has yet to be written, as we discuss in the following section on the diffusion of AMT.

THE DIFFUSION OF AMT

The penetration of AMT into manufacturing is uneven, mainly because of its differential applicability to alternative modes of production. Considering manufacturing as a whole, three broad areas may be distinguished (cf. Tarbuck, 1985; Towill, 1984). The first is process industry, as represented, for example, by chemical and aluminium process operations. This area is characterized by dedicated capital-intensive plant specifically designed for high-volume conversion of a limited range of materials. It has a long history of making use of highly automated monitoring and control systems based on (mainframe) computer technology. This has been economically viable because of the highly integrated nature of the technology which allows for a centralized computer facility representing only a very small proportion of the overall cost. There is only limited scope for the application of current forms of AMT in such settings.

The second area of manufacturing is concerned with mass production and assembly of discrete components, as exemplified by the motor industry. This is characterized by high volume output of standard products made with dedicated machinery and transfer lines. There is already a high degree of automation in mass production, usually achieved through mechanical control devices such as cams, timers, and counters. Such 'hard automation' is highly inflexible relative to the 'soft automation' enabled by computer control, but when large quantities of identical parts are required over long periods of time, flexibility is not a major advantage, and such technology is of proven economic effectiveness. Whilst stable markets persist for given products, 'hard automation' will remain viable as a core technology. Nevertheless, AMT is being used for certain aspects of production (e.g. paint spraying and spot welding by programmable robots); and should AMT prove successful elsewhere, it may itself become a spur to a reorientation of mass production industry towards customized products and more frequent design changes which the flexibility of AMT renders more easily achievable.

The final area of manufacturing is that of batch production, which represents a large proportion of all manufacturing activity in industrialized countries. Bessant and Haywood (1985), for example, estimate that up to 70 per cent of all components in the engineering sector are made in batches of less than 50; and Gerwin (1982) suggests that batch production accounts for over 35 per cent of the manufacturing base of the United States. Although batch production is usually considered in the context of engineering establishments, it should not be forgotten that it is also prevalent in many other areas such as the clothing, plastics, ceramics, and woodworking industries.

AMT has evolved largely in batch manufacturing, and it is here that it is likely to be of most immediate benefit. This is because it offers the promise of high quality, accuracy and repeatability of product, increased machine utilization, reduced manufacturing lead times, reduced inventory, lower labour costs, and quicker response to new product design (Bessant and Haywood, 1985; Sharlt *et al.*, 1986). In effect, AMT offers the potential advantages of automation in an area where previously automation was not an economic proposition. Thus, with AMT the focus of this book, batch production is the arena with which we are mostly concerned; though the lessons learned in this context may become increasingly relevant to other areas of manufacturing.

Current empirical evidence on the diffusion of AMT is less than systematic and comprehensive, but nevertheless suggests that its penetration into industry is not yet high. CNC machine tools, for example, accounted for less than 5 per cent of the machine tool population in Britain in the early 1980s (Metal Working Produc-tion, 1983), although by value they represented one-third of all machine tool sales (*Financial Times*, 15 February 1983) and because of their speed and levels of utiliz-ation they account for much more than 5 per cent of the work carried out. Similarly, the number of robots in British industry was only of the order of 1200 in 1982 (Tarbuck, 1985). In general, penetration of such technologies is higher in other advanced industrialized countries. Thus comparative figures suggest there are 0.32 robots per 1000 shopfloor employees in the UK, 0.43 in the United States, 1.46 in Japan and 2.0 in Sweden (Attenborough, 1984). Worldwide there are probably only 150 to 200 FMSs in use (Bessant and Haywood, 1985) with Japan leading the way, followed by the United States and Europe.

From the limited evidence on current diffusion, therefore, there is little support for the notion of an 'information technology revolution' in manufacturing. An 'evolu-tionary' process (Bessant, 1982) is, however, evident. The rate of uptake of AMT is accelerating, and this trend is predicted to continue. Child (1984) reports market growth rates per year estimated at 51 per cent for industrial robots between 1981 and 1986, and Marsh (1984) estimates an annual rate of 30 per cent for the period 1984 – 1990. Similarly, the growth in the market for CAD/CAM systems generally has been calculated at over 40 per cent a year (Charlish, 1985). With governments worldwide promoting the use and development of AMT, and individual organizations gaining experience of IT more generally and now appointing specialists to advise on how its manufacturing potential can be exploited, such predictions do not seem unrealistic.

In short, AMT is not yet the primary technology for the vast majority of manu-facturing organizations, even for those in batch production. What diffusion has occurred to date has been predominantly of stand-alone CNC-based and robotic systems, with more integrated applications such as DNC and FMS being few and far between. CIM remains a futuristic concept. Nevertheless there are strong reasons to believe that the penetration of AMT will accelerate, and that the question being asked by those in industry is not whether to adopt this new technology, but how and when.

SOME EARLY VIEWS ON THE HUMAN SIDE OF AMT

One of the earliest concerted attempts to provide an analysis of the human and organizational implications of advanced manufacturing technology was by Braverman (1974). Working from an explicitly Marxist perspective, he argued that the effect of such technology would be to deskill shopfloor jobs. He made his point in the following way:

> So far as the machine operator is concerned, it is now possible to remove from his area of competence whatever skills still remain after three quarters of a century of 'rationalization'. He is now definitely relieved of all the decisions, judgment, and knowledge which Taylor attempted to abstract from him by organizational means. The true 'instruction card'—Lillian Gilbreth's 'self-producer of a predeter-mined product'—is at last fully revealed in the program tape (p. 202).

The nature of this deskilling process was illustrated by Braverman, as it was by Shaiken (1979, 1980), by considering the effects of NC machine tools in precision engineering. This industry is characterized by the production of small batches of metal parts made to very fine tolerances. Traditionally these are produced by skilled machinists working on general-purpose machine tools. The machinist has the responsibility of translating plans into the finished product. The skill to do this is learned over many years. It involves knowledge of the required cutting speeds of different metals, choosing the appropriate cutting edge, and controlling the machine to achieve the cuts at the correct place, to the specified depth, and in the right sequence. Often, when new parts are designed, the machinist is consulted to determine if and how it can be made. The general-purpose machine tool provides the mechanical power, but the machinist retains the knowledge and the real time control.

The introduction of numerical control, and indeed computer numerical control machine tools can radically affect such work. The mechanical aspect of the equipment remains essentially unaltered, but now its operation is under the control of a program. Decisions on how to machine a given part are pre-recorded and embedded into the program. This defines precisely the sequence, location, and depth of the cuts to be made. In effect, the knowledge and skill required to make the part has been permanently captured in the program. The program controls the entire machining cycle without the need for human intervention.

Other forms of advanced manufacturing technology have the same characteristic. Robots, for example, often include a facility to be programmed by copying a human operator. A skilled paint sprayer, for instance, can guide a robot arm with a paint spray attachment through the movements necessary to complete a given product, and this will be recorded on its program. The whole sequence can then be reproduced on demand.

It is thus clear how advanced manufacturing technology in general, by virtue of its capacity to be programmed, can remove skill from traditional jobs by wresting direct control over the production process from the shopfloor employee. It can leave the erstwhile skilled operator merely with loading, monitoring, and unloading tasks. Computer control provides the opportunity to deskill the kind of jobs which, because of the skill and range of product involved, had before been protected from the deskilling effects of traditional technology. It also provides the opportunity to increase control over a wide range of other types of shopfloor, and indeed office, work.

The capacity of advanced manufacturing technology to move control over production out of the hands of shopfloor operators is not in question. For this to result in deskilled shopfloor jobs, however, also requires that the skills which the technology absorbs are not replaced by others. Braverman argues, therefore, that replacement will not occur. The historical trend to deskill shopfloor work will mean managements will capitalize on the opportunities new technology offers, and divide the new computing, program editing, maintenance, and other required skills among groups of specialists, and out of the hands of the machine operators:

There is no question that from a practical standpoint there is nothing to prevent the machining process under numerical control from remaining the province of the total craftsman. That this almost never happens is due, of course, to the opportunities the process offers for the destruction of craft and cheapening of the resultant pieces of labor into which it is broken. Thus, as the process takes shape in the minds of engineers, the labor configuration takes shape simultaneously in the minds of designers, and in part shapes the design itself. The equipment is made to be operated; operating costs involve, apart from the cost of the machine itself, the hourly cost of labor, and this is part of the calculation involved in machine design. The design which will enable the operation to be broken down among cheaper operators is the design which is sought by management and engineers who have so internalized this value that it appears to them to have the force of a natural law or scientific necessity (Braverman, 1974, pp. 199–200).

The deskilling perspective on advanced manufacturing technology is thus founded on two related factors. The first is the opportunity the technology offers to separate control from the execution of work on the shopfloor. The second is the assumption that management, in pursuit of cost reduction and control, will take advantage of this to deskill jobs.

Braverman's analysis was necessarily based on early forms of advanced manufacturing technology. Many commentators, however, without necessarily accepting Braverman's ideological base, have carried the analysis forward to the newer forms of AMT. Cooley (1984), for example, from an examination of CNC machine tools and computer-aided design (CAD) systems, argues they tend to deskill operators. He states more generally:

It is possible to so design systems as to enhance human beings rather than to diminish them and subordinate them to the machine . . . [but] it is my view that systems of this kind, however desirable they may be, will not be developed and widely applied since they challenge the power structure in society. Those who have the power . . . are concerned with extending their power and gaining control over human beings rather than with liberating them (p. 204).

Recent work on 'human-centred systems' (Corbett, 1985; Rosenbrock, 1983, 1985) also reflects the general concern about how advanced manufacturing technology may pave the way for simplified jobs. Those working from this perspective are trying to develop new technologies which by design encourage placing control in the hands of the operators.

The simplification argument, however, has not remained unchallenged. Jones (1982) observed that 'there are grounds for rejecting a unilateral motivation and capacity to deskill on the part of capitalist management' (p. 179), and that such simplification will 'vary in accordance with differences in, and interrelationships between, trade union positions, product markets and pre-existing systems of management control' (p. 182).

Recent empirical studies suggest Jones's conclusion is well founded. Moreover, the work of Buchanan and Boddy (1983), Clegg, Kemp and Wall (1984), Kemp and Clegg (1987), and Sorge *et al.*, (1983), shows how advanced manufacturing technology can be, and has been, implemented in ways which do not deskill. Even the same forms of AMT have been found to be associated with both deskilled and enriched shopfloor work, depending on the decisions made about their implementation. There is also reason to believe that as the technology becomes more complex, moving towards flexible manufacturing systems to computer-integrated manufacturing, implementations in ways which simplify operator jobs will impair productivity (Blumberg and Gerwin, 1984; see also Chapter 3).

The significance of these studies is not that they negate the deskilling thesis. There is plenty of evidence still to show how many forms of AMT have been used to simplify jobs, and this may be the rule rather than the exception. Rather, the studies make absolutely clear there is choice in how one implements and designs such technology, choice which has implications both for the quality of working life and productivity. The nature of this choice, the factors which affect it, and its ramifications across all aspects and levels of organizational practice and design, is as yet far from clear. But there is a choice. People are not necessarily passive recipients of their own technological artifacts and social structures, but rather can be active creators of their own future. To exercise this choice, however, one needs to articulate and understand the alternatives available.

In a sense this question of choice provides the theme for this book. All the contributions represent an attempt to articulate the alternatives available in the use of advanced manufacturing technology. In this way they provide a basis for understanding and informed choice. They recognize that technology is not neutral, and that it raises certain dangers for the quality of working life. But the main underlying emphasis is a more proactive one: it concerns how one can best exploit the many opportunities offered by advanced manufacturing technology. This is considered from a range of complementary perspectives, as the following outline of the chapters to follow makes clear.

THE CHAPTERS TO FOLLOW

Eight chapters follow, to complete and form the body of this work. They have been structured so that job-related issues precede organizational and broader social issues. There is thus a general progression from one level of analysis to another. In this sense, therefore, the earlier chapters can be seen to inform later chapters as we move from a micro- to a macro-level of analysis. However, the chapters have also been written to stand in their own right. Each considers a separate substantive area and relates this to the use of a type, or several types, of advanced manufacturing technology. What this necessarily entails is that there is a degree of overlap amongst the chapters in their considerations of similar technological forms. Rather than delete these discussions, we have preferred to allow them to stand so that each chapter can be read as a thorough integrated and self-contained review of a specified area.

In Chapter 2 Gerald Nadler and Gordon Robinson discuss issues concerned with the planning, design, and implementation of AMT. They draw attention to the need to extend the planning and implementation process beyond a focus on technological and engineering matters, to one which incorporates operational and management issues. They identify shortcomings in traditional approaches to the introduction of technology, and offer seven principles to help improve the process.

Thomas Cummings and Melvin Blumberg (Chapter 3), discuss the implications of AMT for the design of work. They locate their discussion within a sociotechnical systems theory perspective and consider the interrelationships among individuals, the job, the work group, and the organization. That is, they examine features of the social system and consider the degrees of match or mismatch of this with the technical system. Their discussion is illustrated by way of case studies which focus on CAD systems, FMS, and robotics. In concluding, they emphasize the systemic nature of work design and present implications of the use of AMT for managers and researchers.

In Chapter 4 Sheila Rothwell considers the nature of selection and training for AMT. The chapter begins with a discussion of the major concepts in the area, and the traditional methods used. The author then examines the selection and training of operators, craftsmen and technicians, supervisors, computer specialists, professional engineers, and managers within the context of AMT. Evidence is drawn from a wide range of case studies and shows the inadequacies of most current approaches to selection and training. The chapter concludes with a consideration of alternative approaches to and requirements for AMT.

Bernard Burnes and Mike Fitter (Chapter 5), examine the nature of control over AMT systems. Specifically, they are interested in the supervision of these new technologies. Thus, they consider the changing requirements for the roles and the content of jobs for supervisors and first-line managers. In reviewing the literature they show the changing nature of supervision which has moved from a concern with 'man-management' to one of 'system regulation'. They argue that there are choices to be made concerning the way in which control is exercised, and that this will determine to an extent the demand for supervision and the content of supervisory jobs.

John Child (Chapter 6) presents a detailed review of organizational design for advanced manufacturing technology. The chapter begins with a discussion of distinctive features of AMT. These are its flexibility and potential for system integration. The author then considers both macroeconomic and specific strategic contingencies which influence the design of organizations. In particular, attention is focused on production contingencies relating to product volume and product variety. The second half of the chapter discusses the integration of manufacturing processes and functional groupings with computer-based technologies, the location of control over production processes, and management organization. The review concludes with a consideration of some major issues in organization design resulting from the use of AMT.

In Chapter 7 Paul Willman examines AMT from an industrial relations perspective. Specifically, the author outlines and discusses innovations in manufacturing industry and the institutional background of industrial relations. The nature of industrial relations is examined through a consideration of collective bargaining processes and new technology agreements. It is illustrated by findings from studies set in the motor industry, and by accounts of union organization and bargaining structure. The chapter concludes with an examination of the implementation of AMT and the problems faced by trade unions in influencing this process.

John Bessant and Peter Senker (Chapter 8) outline the societal implications of AMT. They consider the new technologies to be a major driving force for social change, and this is illustrated through an examination of the skill requirements for advanced manufacturing technology. Thus, they discuss the types of skills likely to be in demand, where they will be needed, and the changes in working patterns between present and future manufacturing organizations. Comparative data are presented from the UK, West Germany, and Japan to illustrate national initiatives in attempting to cope with this transition. Problems specific to skill levels in the UK are discussed, and the need to develop long-term policies for managing change is noted.

In the final chapter (Chapter 9), Chris Clegg and Martin Corbett argue that the importance of the human aspects of AMT is often unrecognized in practice. They examine some of the reasons for this, with particular focus on why social scientists have failed to make an impact in this area. They call for the adoption of a research and development strategy incorporating prospective development work to complement traditional retrospective evaluation studies. The authors identify three areas of particular promise corresponding to issues of process, content, and outcome, and argue that social scientists should be sharing their expertise with practitioners from other disciplines by collaborating in multi-disciplinary ventures incorporating technical, cognitive, and social concerns.

REFERENCES

Attenborough, N. G. (1984). Employment and technical change: the case of micro-electronic based production technologies in UK manufacturing industry. Working Paper, Government Economic Service, Department of Trade and Industry, London.

Bessant, J. (1982). *Microprocessors in Production Processes*. London: Policy Studies Institute.

Bessant, J., and Haywood, W. (1985). The introduction of flexible manufacturing systems as an example of computer integrated manufacturing. Final report, Innovation Research Group, Department of Business Management, Brighton Polytechnic.

Blumberg, M. and Gerwin, D. (1984). Coping with advanced manufacturing technology. *Journal of Occupational Behaviour*, **5**, 113−30.

Braverman, H. (1974). *Labor and Monopoly Capital*. New York: Monthly Review Press.

Buchanan, D. A. and Boddy, D. (1983). Advanced technology and the quality of working life: the effects of computerized controls on biscuit making. *Journal of Occupational Psychology*, **56**, 109−19

Charlish, G. (1985). Competitiveness with computers: computer-aided design. *Financial Times*, 27 February.

Child, J. (1984). *Organization: A Guide to Problems and Practice* (2nd edn.). London: Harper & Row.

Clegg, C. W., Kemp, N. J., and Wall, T. D. (1984). New technology: choice, control and

14   *The Human Side of Advanced Manufacturing Technology*

skills. In G. C. van de Veer, M. J. Tauber, T. R. G. Green and P. Gorny (eds), *Readings on Cognitive Ergonomics: Mind and Computers*. Berlin: Springer Verlag.

Cooley, M. (1984). Problems of automation. In T. Lupton (ed.), *Proceedings of the 1st International Conference on Human Factors in Manufacturing*. Amsterdam: North Holland.

Corbett, J. M. (1985). Prospective work design for a human-centred CNC lathe. *Behaviour and Information Technology*, **4**, 201–14.

Feigenbaum, E., and McCorduck, P. M. (1985). Land of the rising fifth generation. In T. Forester (ed.), *The Information Technology Revolution*. Oxford: Blackwell.

Forester, T. (1985). *The Information Technology Revolution*. Oxford: Blackwell.

Gerwin, D. (1982). Do's and don'ts of computerised manufacturing. *Harvard Business Review*, **60**, 107–16.

Halton, J. (1985). The anatomy of computing. In T. Forester (ed.), *The Information Technology Revolution*. Oxford: Basil Blackwell.

Jones, B. (1982). Destruction or redistribution of engineering skills? The case of numerical control. In S. Wood (ed.), *The Degradation of Work?* London: Hutchinson.

Kemp, N. J., and Clegg, C. W. (1987). Information technology and job design: a case study on CNC machine tool working. *Behaviour and Information Technology* (in press).

Marbach, W. D. *et al.* (1985). The race to build a supercomputer. *Newsweek*, July 4th. Reprinted in T. Forester (ed.), *The Information Technology Revolution*. Oxford: Blackwell.

Marsh, P. (1984). The dawning day of the robot. *Financial Times*, 19 December.

Metal Working Production (1983). *The Fifth Survey of Machine Tools and Production Equipment in Britain*. London: Morgan-Grampian.

Noble, D. (1979). Social choice in machine design: the case of automatically controlled machine tools. In A. Zimbalist (ed.), *Case Studies on the Labor Process*. New York: Monthly Review Press.

Rosenbrock, H. H. (1983). Robots and people. *Work and People*, **9**, 14–18.

Rosenbrock, H. H. (1985). Designing automated systems: need skill be lost? In P. Marstrand (ed.), *New Technology and the Future of Work and Skills*. London: Pinter.

Shaiken, H. (1979). Impact of new technology on employees and their organizations. Research Report, International Institute for Comparative Social Research, Berlin.

Shaiken, H. (1980). Computer technology and the relations of power in the workplace. Research Report, International Institute for Comparative Social Research, Berlin.

Sharlt, J., Chang, T. L., and Salvendy, G. (1986). Technical and human aspects of computer-aided manufacturing. In G. Salvendy (ed.), *Handbook of Human Factors*. New York: Wiley.

Sorge, A., Hartman, G., Warner, M., and Nicholas, I. (1983). *Microelectronics and Manpower in Manufacturing*. Aldershot: Gower Press.

Tarbuck, M. (1985). The engineering industry. In P. Senker (ed.), *Planning for Microelectronics in the Workplace*. Aldershot: Gower Press.

Towill, D. R. (1984). Information technology in engineering production and production management. In N. Piercy (ed.), *The Management Implications of New Information Technology*. Beckenham: Croom-Helm.

Voss, C. (1984). Management and new manufacturing technologies. Working paper, Australian Graduate School of Management, Kensington, New South Wales.

Wall, T. D., Burnes, B., Clegg, C. W., and Kemp, N. J. (1984). New technology, old jobs. *Work and People*, **10**, 15–24.

The Human Side of Advanced Manufacturing Technology
Edited by T. D. Wall, C. W. Clegg, and N. J. Kemp
© 1987 John Wiley & Sons Ltd.

CHAPTER 2

Planning, Designing, and Implementing Advanced Manufacturing Technology

GERALD NADLER AND GORDON ROBINSON

INTRODUCTION

The 29 October 1985 NOVA programme (on the Public Broadcasting Service in the USA) on 'Technology at Work' chronicled 'the progress and controversy surrounding the techniques of computer automation now sweeping American industry'. It showed the marvels of computer-aided design, computer-aided process planning, simulation of prototype testing instead of physical product testing, robots in fabrication and assembly, automatic storage and retrieval in huge warehouses, and computer-integrated manufacturing of all parts. It, quite briefly, described all of the manufacturing technologies considered in this book and from which so much improved productivity and competitiveness are expected.

However, several disquieting comments were made during the programme. Unions and various researchers expressed concerns about jobs being eliminated. Several of those being interviewed noted that very few companies have adopted the new technologies; they are not 'sweeping American industry'. Another noted that the new capabilities might serve best as a guide toward which a company might want to move. The programme displayed a 'gee-whiz' view of *general* manufacturing, with nothing about what a company might do to plan, design, and implement a *specific* manufacturing system. The process of converting this (plus all types of) knowledge to useful practice is the most critical problem in the organization.

THE PROBLEM

While the new and continually developing technologies are generally seen as inevitable facts of modern life, there is a great deal of discussion about why these great changes are *not* taking place. Those discussing this issue focus on why some specific technological programme or solution was not used, without explaining why the technological solution did work in certain cases.

We (as well as others, e.g. Downs and Mohr, 1976) believe that this is an erroneous way to look at implementation. By promoting one particular recommendation (e.g. CAD or simulation testing) with scant reference to the myriad of other changes going on in an organization, implementation is reduced to a selling, packaging, or lobbying effort. Typically, one group of people (e.g. engineers) develops a programme or solution intended for another group of people to use. When the second group does not use the recommendation, the first group calls it an 'implementation gap'. The second group might prefer to call it a 'design gap', citing reasons such as lack of resources, poor timing, poor design for operational needs, or the fact that it is politically ill-advised, misunderstood, or too threatening. These reasons are each part of an overriding problem—incompatibility of the proposed system with the other systems and events in the organization. In the face of continuous changes bombarding an organization, a presumed dichotomy between design and implementation increases the likelihood of this incompatibility—and of implementation gaps.

We discuss some myths that have perpetuated that false dichotomy, and suggest some strategies for overcoming these gaps. Since the focus of this book is on practice rather than social theory, we draw primarily on our own experiences and on evidence from case studies rather than on the less conclusive, though vast, literature on diffusion of innovation (see Radnor, Feller and Rogers, 1978).

For years, many have argued that people will support what they help to create. A corollary, that the design and implementation *process* is more critical to the success of an innovation effort than the *product*, has become a cliché, but this may wrongly imply that people simply need some emotional 'ownership' of an innovation in order to accept it. When an implementation failure is blamed on the 'not invented here' syndrome or on 'resistance to change', it implies that the user group lacked the necessary emotional attachment. This attribution is simplistic and condescending. The point is that the design may be wrong! Furthermore, there is no reason to assume that a solution with advanced technology is automatically good!

We see the implementation gap as composed of three psychological gaps: a value gap, a knowledge gap, and a behaviour gap. Each gap can result from certain myths (Wacker and Nadler, 1980), as discussed below.

Value gap

The incompatibility between a proposed manufacturing system and other organization events can stem from a difference in values. Solutions to defined problems are likely to be rejected by those who do not share the definition of the problem. For example, one popular misconception about industrial quality-of-life programmes we call the 'altruism myth': that quality-of-life programmes are for the benefit of the workers—who ought to be grateful—and that the organization benefits from the resultant goodwill. If paternalism or mutual trust permeates the organizational context, then altruism may be a warranted assumption. However, when other organizational events do not occur within these values, then altruism may appear as thinly veiled one-upmanship.

A value gap then exists between the intentions of the designers' and the managers' and operators' perceptions of reality.

In order to avoid value gaps, designers must not expect values to change all at once. Neither should designers treat values as fixed. The target manufacturing technology or system may have to be preceded by structural changes which create value-changing experiences and expectations.

Knowledge gap

The incompatibility between a target manufacturing innovation and other organizational events can stem from a difference in knowledge. Even though they are attracted by the values implicit in a new idea, users may not have enough skill and knowledge to make it work for them. The resulting frustration can cause rejection of the innovation and a retreat to more familiar practices. In a study of the cognitions of food-plant workers organized into five autonomous groups, Wacker (1979, 1981) found that in two groups knowledge of the technical system developed at a slower rate than knowledge of the social system. This created a number of problems for those two groups that did not occur for the other three groups.

Beumier and Coessen (1975) reported the case of a glass company which began several projects aimed at improving organizational effectiveness. Although the projects ended very successfully, knowledge gaps were encountered. They reported

> (i) anxieties and uncertainties with a new strategy, (ii) concern that top management may not appreciate significant departures from the old that the teams proposed, (iii) hesitancy to be so open about what has been so long a part of their career and success, (iv) informal status among organization levels within the team, (v) team euphoria and overidentification with the strategy, and (vi) an 'ideal' is utopia and sometimes suspicious, although most supervisors and managers were very enthusiastic.

One of the myths that contributes to knowledge gaps is the 'know-it-all myth'. This includes the faith that the scientific method is the key to successful change (Nadler, 1978). In reality, social science has yet to produce a reliable technology for the implementation of technological change.

Also contributing to knowledge gaps is the 'cloning myth': that what worked well in one setting is likely to work well in comparable settings. In many cases this is not effective because the purposes to be achieved are not the same (Nadler, 1981). Furthermore, most technological changes are modified as they are assimilated into a system; thus adopting the original design elsewhere is very difficult.

Cloning may occur with the use of outside consultants. A hospital asked a consultant to help it improve its medical records library system (Nadler, 1981). A project team of administrators, service staff, and physicians was formed by the consultant and subsequently designed a well-recognized significant innovation. Eight months later the consultant received an assignment in a similar hospital to improve their medical records library system. Recommending the first hospital's solution is the usual action by such a consultant, but this could be counter-productive. Furthermore, the abrupt announcement of a solution could have stirred waves that could have complicated implementation. The consultant set up a project team and asked them to start from scratch. The team identified somewhat different purposes from those of the first hospital. After the team had progressed, the consultant presented the first hospital's solution. The team borrowed and adapted software, but there were fundamental differences between the two final designs.

Behaviour gap

Job descriptions, organization charts, compensation schemes, and physical layouts all exist primarily to direct individuals' behaviour. When the attempted installation of a manufacturing system is divorced from these organizational mechanisms, a behaviour gap can exist. Very often, problems do not work themselves out under operational conditions. This illustrates what we call the 'snapshot myth': focusing on the before-and-after images of the change without developing an orderly progression of transition steps. In order to do something new we usually have to undo something old. This often affects work habits, social linkages, authority and jurisdictional lines, rewards and incentives, risk bearing and career expectations, resource allocation, and training.

Just as a manufacturing innovation is affected by other aspects of the organization, it can affect them. Often these effects take years to materialize, as people gradually learn the nuances of the changes and modify their strategies, work habits, and interaction patterns. Failure to recognize the evolutionary aspects of institutional innovation we call the 'instant gratification myth'. Proponents of innovations who declare a programme successful, only to see a 'backlash' develop later, are victims of this myth.

THE TIME ISSUE

Systems exist with a 'structure' or 'space' and also in time. The structural aspect of a system—that of a richly interconnected set of subsystems—is now fairly well understood and appreciated at both design and management levels. That the environment in which the organization operates is also an important part of the total system has been learned later, and has become more of a problem as it has become less predictable.

The other systems dimension—time—seems less understood; at least less systematically understood and more difficult to incorporate into specific plans and operations. Possibly an examination of this dimension as it affects planning, design, and implementation will provide a different and useful view.

Problems with 'time' were discussed by Schon (1977) and brought into the industrial organization arena by Trist (1980) in his analyses of the 'turbulent environment'. The implementation 'problem' can also be viewed in the time dimension, as can problems in worker security (their future), middle management's resistance to change (their security and future), and the labour union's search for new roles beyond their traditional, rather 'static' model.

Four issues related to planning, design, and implementation and the human roles therein can be viewed as 'time' processes. This perspective has the potential to clarify problems and thereby might lead to solution directions or the motivation to try new solutions.

Process and product

The processes and products of design must be seen as inseparable. The realities of design and implementation at any reasonably complex systems level, such as a new technology, show an endless cycling of both large and small events in both process and product. From the outside this might look almost random. The distinction between these phases, probably believed in by most designers and too many managers, comes from our focus on much simpler products for our models of the design process. Especially when the human involvement with the new product is fairly straight-forward, the product simply 'arrives' and the processes are over. For example, con-sider the design of a new toaster or electric drill. However, the redesign of even a small department around the 'arrival' of a new computer presents a situation that may best be viewed as not a simple extension of 'toaster' design strategy. It is qualitatively quite distinct. Few engineers have thought this through, and close to none have seen it in their formal design training.

Cherns' 'minimum critical specification' (1977) is one interesting way of look-ing at this problem. He suggests, as one of his ten organizational design principles, that decisions in the design process be held back (in time) as far as possible. Some are actually to be held back until the initial operating phase. The reasons are largely related to the people who will use the resulting 'product', the two most important being the use of their knowledge in the design, and cultivating their 'ownership' of it.

New technology

New technologies—'robots' or office 'automation' with computers—create both excitement and fear. It is often assumed, by both the designer and the ultimate users, that these technologies will simply be bought and installed. Delays in installation and efficiencies far below predictions are, of course, commonplace. Perhaps it would be helpful if more designers understood that there are two substantive and time-consuming design stages standing between the 'arrival' of the new technology and an operating system based on it.

The first design problem is the translation of the technology into a specific technical system. For example, there are, of course, literally thousands of ways a computer (technology) can be configured and programmed as a new technical system in a factory. (One of these thousands is not to use it at all!) Usually this design phase is treated rather trivially and focuses on issues such as general size and costs—probably the easiest decisions. Often the vendor will have made, at least implicitly, most of the design decisions that should be made here—with *his* criteria, not the users'.

The second design stage or problem is the coupling of this technical system to the proposed social system which will operate and maintain it. This socio-technical system must also be designed. Designers are even more reluctant to admit the problems at this level than in the translation of technology to technical systems described above. They have two fond hopes: that 'soon' they will be able to eliminate most of the people, and that those who are left will 'fit in' somehow. Experience with new and complex technologies has shown them wrong on both counts. The more complex the technical system, the more, rather than less, the system depends on the operators to keep it going. The roles for the operators simply change.

It is interesting to note that in suggesting the 'stages' above, a 'time' trap has been laid. The second does not simply follow the first. Nor, for that matter, does the 'discovery' of a new technology necessarily drive the rest. Volvo's 'invention' of a new technology for mass-producing automobiles (Gyllenhammar, 1977) and Shell-Canada's decision to limit the decisions made by automatic systems (Davis and Sullivan, 1980), are two rather dramatic instances wherein the characteristics of the social system suggested the need for new technologies or very different technical systems from that envisaged from a technical or 'engineering' viewpoint alone.

Cultural change

The 'cultural norms' in most organizations are centred on stability. These norms are largely perpetuated by middle management and possibly the unions. Both tend to see their knowledge of, and stake in, the present system as a key to their survival and continued crucial role. Major organizational changes, such as may (should?) take place with the introduction of a new technology, are therefore resisted by these groups, from early conception through final production. This resistance can be highly effective.

For organizational survival in the face of new technologies it is necessary that this energy be directed at protecting continual mechanisms of change, rather than protecting the current state. That is, the cultural norm would be continual search for, and implementation of, new ideas, in both product and production. The unacceptable position for this organization—the one that would violate its norms—would then be not having change, or at least not having a search for change. The Japanese are clearly ahead here (Robinson and Nadler, 1984).

For this to occur, it will be necessary for some rather major issues to be addressed and substantive changes made in most organizations. Individual career paths and security are among the most important. Roles must also be changed, such that change is driven and implemented by these formerly conservative forces, rather than from 'above' or from the engineering groups. Broader participation in planning and economic knowledge is also necessary. There is some evidence that substantive change may be requested by the production groups themselves if they have access to the pertinent economic information (private communication to the authors by managers at several of the more innovative organizations).

Planning, design, and implementation

Perhaps, in order to convey and reinforce the changes in our perceptions of events in time, we should have some basic name changes. Perhaps the words 'planning', 'design', and 'implementation' themselves should be completely decoupled from any substantive process or group or time period. They would still describe 'momentary' activities that continuously cycle during any change process. Perhaps 'change' is the proper overall descriptor. That is, there are no planning meetings, nor design meetings, nor implementation activities. All are change (or potential change) meetings or activities. All will routinely have all three sub-activities mixed richly together. Even the way they interact and unfold will not be predictable in advance, but rather will be driven (hopefully) by systematic methods and goals.

The separation of design, planning, and implementation derives from the historic separation of the people and organizational units carrying out these activities. Management plans; engineering designs; and operating management and supervisors implement. Awkward steps are now being taken by many organizations to blur deliberately these distinctions in their operating, production modes. 'Participation' in its many forms has become popular. If one common form of participation, the quality circle, is examined, however, it may well be noted that it is precisely the continued separation of planning, design, and implementation that are the main forces preventing the QC's potential impact. For example, they often have rather nebulous ties to planning and design skills as well as to implementation authority (Robinson and Peterson, 1983).

Even the activities of 'continued improvement' are usually considered to go on separately, possibly spearheaded by industrial engineers, after implementation of some major change. Another awkward fiction! How can any really important 'continued improvement' be qualitatively distinguished from redesign? Does it not raise planning and implementation issues? The unions would point out the implementation issues if industrial engineering hadn't noticed them! What is the distinction between continued improvement and Cherns' (1977) call for design decisions after production begins—as a part of the main design effort?

Implementation begins with the first rumour of a new technology. Design never stops (another of Cherns' principles). Planning shouldn't stop. We note the successful Japanese are almost perversely fixated on continued improvement. Perhaps it is all change, with both the experts in, and events of, planning, design, implementation, and improvement, all completely interwoven—and unfolding in time.

PRINCIPLES FOR PLANNING, DESIGN, AND IMPLEMENTATION

As noted above, a snapshot view of the future factory is at best incomplete. It ignores continuing developments in technology, such as those that produced the robot, and it encourages debate about the desirability of specific renderings of technological possibilities, forms unlikely to appear in any event, far less to be influenced by the debate.

The design of future factories is the focus here, a topic far more significant than any specific technological possibility, such as the robot, or for that matter any specific picture, such as the totally automated factory. Three issues must be considered:

1. A factory does not appear suddenly in full operational maturity, but rather is continually designed and redesigned, implemented, constructed, and rebuilt.
2. It is not automatically programmed to be improved. Continual energy and direction must be employed if it is to adapt successfully to changing needs and potential.
3. It will never be entirely free of people, never be completely automatic or robotic in this sense.

As a result, there are several principles to be followed in the original or modernized design of a factory (Nadler and Hibino, 1987):

1. Uniqueness

Each manufacturing system, future or present, is unique. Design should not proceed by trying to install a solution from another factory. Even though it may appear, for example, that all hospital technology is identical, there are so many variations in community needs, perceptions, resources, and human involvement, that one cannot assume that even the standard activities—open-heart surgery, food preparation, nursing care patterns—can really transfer easily from one hospital to another. Similarly, simply because General Electric has automated much of its own manufacturing as a showcase, does not necessarily mean that it will succeed in promoting sales of factory automation equipment (Landro, 1982).

2. Purposes

The hierarchy of the factory's purposes should govern all parts of original or modernized design. Current activities are an insufficient, and potentially ineffective, basis for developing manufacturing systems. Merely automating what is now being done can mean doing very efficiently what ought not to be done at all!

3. System after next (Malpas, 1978)

The guide for developing a recommended factory design should be based on what the factory would be if it were possible to start afresh, not on what presently exists. Once the purposes of the factory are identified, one should look toward the most effective solution as the target to govern today's design decisions. Many alternatives—as ideal as possible—should be developed and kept as viable options for as long as possible (Alexander, 1979). Specifying a plant after next should be based on regularity conditions rather than on all possible conditions. Regularity conditions are usually those external factors that occur most frequently—for example, size of population served, most ordered model—or which are considered most important—for example, most delicate model. As irregularities are incorporated into the target guide, as much as possible of the target should remain in the solution. In other words, do not throw away what is good for 85 per cent of the needs simply because the other 15 per cent is not accommodated.

A factory design should accommodate all stakeholders—users, customers, workers, and so on. This means that a manufacturing system will incorporate pluralistic and multichannelled flows or subsystems, each at the appropriate technology level. Thus 25 per cent of the production may be robotic, 35 per cent semi-automatic, 25 per cent job-shop methods, and 15 per cent custom or hand work. In other words, there is no one best way. In addition, factories will need frequent modifications as products, processes, and so on change. What was once robotically produced may need to be changed as sales change or other technology becomes available.

4. Systems

Each factory and subunit should be considered as a system. Each system is specified by eight elements, each one defined by six dimensions. This element/dimension idea of a system is illustrated in Table 2.1. In addition each element in the manufacturing system is itself a system. For example, a robot is considered a physical catalyst in the factory system, but it can likewise be specified in terms of elements and dimensions: the robot's purposes, inputs, outputs, and so on.

5. Limited information

Deciding on data to collect during design is based on three considerations—purposes, ideal systems, regularities—not by the vacuum cleaner approach of collecting all data. Designing a future manufacturing system by thoroughly analysing everything, in order to find out what is wrong with the present system, provides only an inward-looking guide.

6. People design

Those now in, or soon to be in, a factory, should be continually involved in design and modernization. To assume that the automated factory is the last word in design does not recognize the need for continual productivity improvements. Thus productivity circles, workshop groups, and related participatory activities are essential even in the robotic factory.

The specifications of a manufacturing system should include only the minimum number of critical details and controls, regardless of how many robots and automated devices may be present. People who operate in the factory system should be given flexibility in achieving their assigned purposes.

Table 2.1   Solution framework—system matrix*

Elements	Dimensions
Purpose: mission, aim, need, primary concern, focus	Fundamental: basic or physical characteristics—what, how, where, or who
Inputs: people, things, information to start the sequence	Values: motivating beliefs, global desires, ethics, moral matters
Outputs: desired—achieves purpose—and undesired outcomes from sequence	Measures: objectives—criteria, merit and worth factors—and goals—how much, when, rates, performance specifications
Sequence: steps for processing inputs, flow, layout, unit operations	Control: how to evaluate and modify element or system as it operates
Environment: physical and attitudinal, organization, setting, and so on	Interface: relation of all dimensions to other systems or elements
Human agents:** skills, personnel, responsibilities, rewards, and so on	Future: planned changes and research needs for all dimensions
Physical catalysts:** equipment, facilities, and so on	
Information aids:** books, instructions, and so on	

Source: adapted from Nadler (1981), p. 89, fig. 9.3.
*   Each system is specified by eight elements, each one defined by six dimensions.
** Agents, catalysts, and aids help process inputs into outputs without becoming part of outputs.

7. Betterment timeline

A solution should be defined as a change plus a built-in future change. A factory of the future is not itself the solution. It represents merely the change made now, within which a schedule for improvement is also set up.

These seven principles are guides to the design of any kind of factory, not just an automated one. They provide the operational tools for putting into action the three issues noted at the start of this principles section.

A PROCESS FOR PLANNING, DESIGNING, AND IMPLEMENTING

The ingredient which is needed to convert even these effective principles into practice is an integrative, time-based strategy or process. The principles already emphasize that conventional problem-solving concepts are insufficient, especially in relation to the three basic objectives of any planning and design effort (Nadler, 1981), namely: (1) to maximize the quality and effectiveness of the recommended manufacturing system; (2) to maximize the likelihood of implementing the recommendation; and (3) to maximize the effectiveness of the planning and design resources. Conventional approaches focus almost exclusively on the first objective. Without including the other much more human-oriented objectives, the conventional approaches, because they engender the gaps and myths reviewed before, have been a major cause of the slow rate of adoption and the low implementation record of advanced manufacturing technologies.

A time-based PD&I approach rests on some straightforward assumptions. Time is irreversible in the mortal world of seeking to create or restructure a specific manufacturing system. It cannot be slowed down or speeded up and it illustrates negative and positive infinity.

A continuous (rather than discrete) timeline is the fundamental basis for understanding the past, present, or future of any phenomenon. Assume that a straight line in space with an arrow at one end represents a timeline. Any arbitrary point can locate the present, which automatically defines the past and the future. Many models (formulas, pictures, prose, poetry, drawings, or graphs) are symbolic forms abstracting, modelling, or describing the past, present, or hoped-for conditions of the phenomenon of interest.

Each phenomenon description thus far is static. Most contain only a limited perspective about the phenomenon, even omitting knowledge already available about its past and present conditions, but deemed to focus elsewhere. Descriptions of a future are typically predictions of what the static conditions may be or what someone or some group wants the conditions to be in the future. Names and labels are often assigned to such snapshots of the future, such as 'post-industrial society', 'automation', 'autonomous work groups', 'ecological humanism', or 'Marxist communism'.

But everything is speculative after the present, irrespective of the firmness and certainty assigned to the prediction of the future. Yet a specification of a future condition, the current view of the outcomes of planning and design, is still static, a snapshot of the assumed future.

A static snapshot of a future manufacturing system is often inappropriate because it is assumed that each snapshot is 'right', and that the specific organization knows *how* to move from today's snapshot to tomorrow's. How poor this assumption is for future outcomes can be recognized by several reasoning flaws:

1. Those making the prediction adopt a posture of 'selling the solution' rather than seeking to solve a problem.
2. Snapshots assume that merely reaching the status described is *the* solution, and thus omit continuing change and development capability as a part of the future.
3. Snapshots of the future produced in the past have proven to be notoriously wrong—the prediction in the 1950s of automatic factories in the 1970s is patently

wrong. The 1960 snapshots of the rest of the century neglected the energy crisis. The 1970 projections revealed little if any understanding of the impact of inflation. Snapshots of 1980, in the USA, for example, foresaw little of the trade deficit and federal debt.

The only way to comprehend the future (and to achieve implementation of solutions, not just produce snapshots) is on a timeline. A tomorrow, a next week, a next month cannot be ignored by stating that a snapshot of the future will automatically transfer the present to the snapshot conditions. Conversely, what is done tomorrow, next week, next month in developing snapshots of several futures, significantly influences both the nature of the snapshots and the amount of change toward them. Implementation and continued, flexible, and guided effective change (along the timeline), from whatever present condition exists to a more desirable condition of existence, are critical real-world measures of success for planning and design.

The timeline perspective demonstrates how PD&I can integrate the changing realities of the client's or organization's world with the principle of design. The PD&I world works along a timeline in parallel to the client, organizational, or real-world timeline in which the problem or need emerges.

Figure 2.1 shows the overall timeline in the left column. The next column represents the organization's world as it continues to operate over time. The organization remains as the base of operation throughout and beyond the P&D effort, and is the source of decision-making regarding acceptance and implementation of the solution.

Of course, a problem seldom appears as suddenly as the dot indicated by '1' would imply. Some dissatisfactions, desires, poor performances, or uncertainties usually build up to the point where the organization decides something needs to be done, almost always within some time limitations, to create or restructure the manufacturing system.

Figure 2.2 portrays the continuing interactions needed between the organization and P&D worlds at every step and phase. Such interactions are needed even if people from the organization serve on the project team. They become P&D world people as the project proceeds because their perceptions are very likely to be P&D-oriented soon after the project's start. With the major decision-makers' decisions and activities quite probably affecting the performance of the P&D effort, there is a continuing need to keep both perspectives in contact. Responsibility for the interaction falls to the P&D people who must adapt to, and continually seek, this joint interchange of perspectives.

This frequent sharing of perceptions and understanding is greatly aided by considering an effective P&D strategy (a set of phases and steps that incorporate the thought processes 'driving' the effort) based on the P&D principles. Such a strategy as currently developed is portrayed in Figure 2.3. The iterative and flexible nature of an actual effort is not shown: iterative because, as time goes along, the P&D effort may repeat at the then current levels of perception, phases or steps appearing

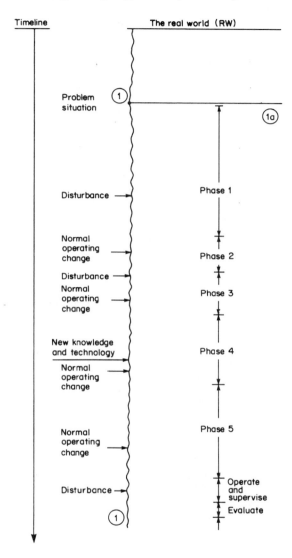

Figure 2.1   P&D scenario—first perspective. Reproduced by permission of John Wiley, Inc., from Nadler (1981).

earlier in the strategy; flexible because a project may develop ideas at (7), say, before measures of effectiveness (5).

The reasoning process of a strategy which focuses on the opportunities offered by a purpose orientation is summarized by phases 1−5 in Figure 2.3, as follows (the principles involved are shown in brackets):

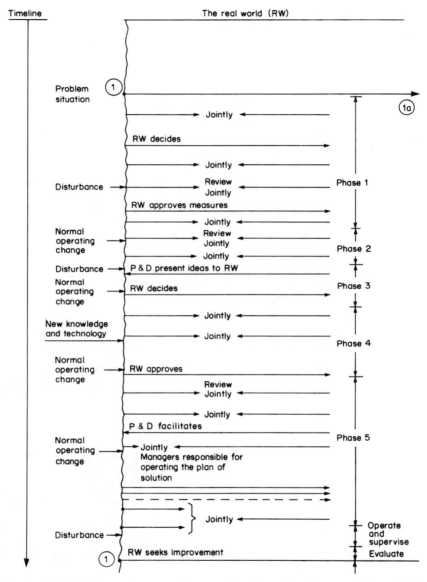

Figure 2.2   P&D scenario—second perspective. Reproduced by permission of John Wiley, Inc., from Nadler (1981).

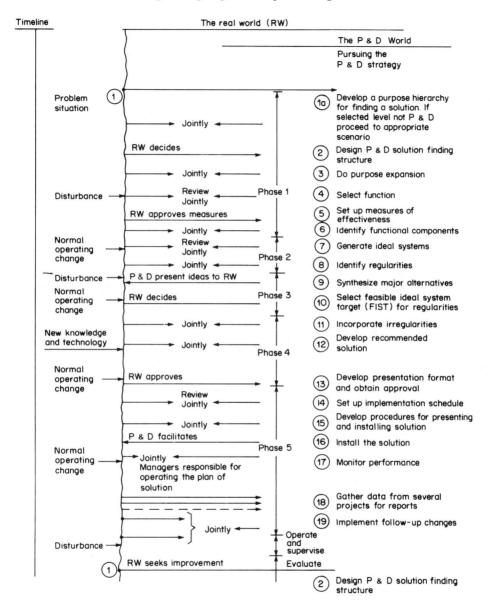

Figure 2.3   P&D scenario—third perspective. Reproduced by permission of John Wiley, Inc., from Nadler (1981).

Phase 1—Develop a purpose hierarchy (array(s) of purpose statements from small to large wherein each larger one describes the purpose of its predecessor) from which is selected the purpose(s) the specific manufacturing system should achieve [uniqueness, purposes]. Measures of effectiveness or conditions that will indicate successful achievement of the purpose are identified for the selected level [people design].

Phase 2—Generate ideas, preferably creative and ideal, that achieve the selected and bigger purposes in the hierarchy [solution after next].

Phase 3—Group and shape ideas into major alternatives from which a feasible ideal solution target is selected. An ideal solution target considers only the regularity conditions (factors that occur with the greatest frequency or are considered most important) [solution after next, limited information, systems].

Phase 4—Detail the workable solution or policy which incorporates all necessary irregularities and exceptions, while staying as close as possible to the target [systems, solution after next].

Phase 5—Implement the workable solution, while letting purposes and the target guide all the minor decisions needed during implementation and in creating a continuing change and improvement attitude [betterment timeline, people design].

Setting up purposes in a hierarchy in *Phase 1* pushes the P&D project immediately into exploring alternative reasons for the effort, expanding the solution space, and selecting the biggest purpose/function which the project can seek to achieve with the 'best' possible solution. Pursuing this right at the beginning of a P&D effort is essential because there is no way of knowing, when starting, whether or not a 'breakthrough' solution can be attained. So the process pushes the project to a level of high potential for ideal results right away by looking at the context described by the hierarchies. This also provides much greater assurance that a purpose which needs to be achieved will be selected, a project will have a worthwhile 'pay-off', avoids working on the wrong problem and establishes proper priorities for various projects and functional components. For example, the president of a company, after months of discussion about the problems of late deliveries, high overtime costs, and poor quality, called an engineer to help design a 100 per cent increase in manufacturing facilities. The engineer used this strategy to discover that the right problem was related to developing manufacturing controls. One *can* design a system to expand capability, but this strategy avoids such hasty errors.

These same strategy ideas are also used to develop the P&D system or planning structure (2 on Figure 2.3). This is the step which also introduces, especially for complex manufacturing projects, an overall protocol of project stages (e.g. need assessment, feasibility study, preliminary design, etc.) and possible adjustments for each stage in the regular guiding pattern described here (e.g. the possibility of developing ideal alternatives before finishing purposes, doing several steps concurrently rather than sequentially with different groups).

Phase 2 focuses individual and group creativity on what is now known to be a needed purpose in its broad context. As many 'ideal' solutions as possible are developed to remove thinking restrictions and widen the choice of alternatives.

Phase 3 shapes the ideas into possible major alternatives. These are developed by playing the *believing game*, which encourages a group or individual to seek specifications for how an idea *can* be made operational. This can raise the questions which need to be answered by data collection, research, learning, and evaluation. Then it is possible to select a feasible ideal system (plant after next) for regularity conditions to serve as a guide for developing a recommendation. The regularity concept fosters creativity by allowing people to consider initially only one set of conditions rather than the many that are usually present.

Phase 4 concerns the necessary exceptions and irregularities while seeking to maintain the good qualities of the target solution. As a result, more workable solutions will be multichannelled and pluralistic, comprising more than one set of steps or flows and even outcomes. Why discard the excellent solution that copes with 95 per cent of the conditions because another 5 per cent cannot directly fit into it? P&D will often result in solutions with three or four integrated channels close to the target. Detailing the solution so it is implementable while incorporating as much as possible of the target still keeps a high potential for obtaining 'ideal' results.

Phase 5 uses the purposes, purpose hierarchy, suggestions for ideal solutions, target, and regularities in making the many, often minor, decisions that are necessary in making a change or installing a solution. The continual interchanges between the P&D world and other members of the client's world (Figure 2.2) make implementation a natural action moving into operating and supervising purposeful activities, rather than a sudden change 'they' (P&D world) impose.

Illustrating these phases for a whole manufacturing system involving new technology would require far too much space. A simple case, however, that highlights the phases, illustrates the thought processes and directions of reasoning proposed here.

This case, from a cardboard carton manufacturing company, shows how the strategy and principles help to avoid (Nadler, 1981) 'doing efficiently that which ought not to be done at all'. The industrial engineering department was asked to analyse the die cutting operation for a corrugated box designed to hold and dispense large plastic storage bags. Because of the complexity of the die cutting required in the box design (see Figure 2.4), the waste was running at 25 per cent and the downtime around 30 per cent.

> Instead of doing studies on the die cutting operation, we worked with the group to make a purpose hierarchy where we continued asking the question, What is the purpose or function? until we arrived at the function: 'Provide the customer with a flexible waterproof container' [see Figure 2.5]. Then backing up we decided to design a system for the function level 'package and dispense plastic bags'.
>
> After developing several ideal systems, we constructed a system matrix in which we identified the necessary constraints and the regularity (i.e. what would normally be expected of the system) for six of the system elements [see Table 2.2].

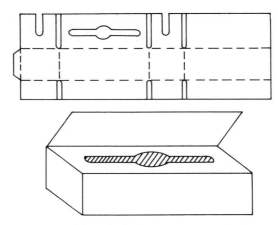

Figure 2.4   Original box design. Reproduced by permission of John Wiley, Inc.,
from Nadler (1981).

Table 2.2.   System design matrix for package and dispense bags

	Constraints	Regularity
Input	Must use corrugated	
Output	Must not damage bag	Storage bags
	Must be easy to open	
	Must dispense only one bag at a time	
	Bag must be easy to grab	
	Package must be attractive	
Sequence	Packaged before reaching store	
Environment	Store	Hardward store and supermarket
Equipment	None	
Human factor	Package must weigh under 25 pounds and easy to handle	

The resulting design consisted of a box that did not require any die cutting and still met the customer's specifications. Therefore, the troublesome die cutting operation was eliminated entirely [see Figure 2.6]. Reproduced by permission of John Wiley, Inc., from Nadler (1981).

As with any real project, iteration occurs and uncertainty exists when following this strategy. But the huge advantage it represents is the positive direction of reasoning that it leads the individuals. Probing the project area with a search for the pertinent (and limited) information about purposes, customer/client/sponsor needs, ideal systems for regularities, system matrix elements and dimensions, and so on, is likely to be far more effective than the conventional dicta to analyse what exists, gather 'all' the

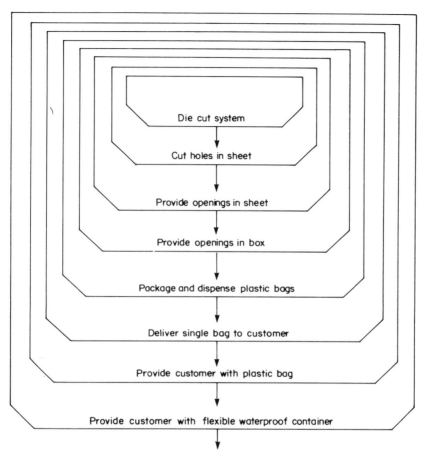

Figure 2.5   Function expansion for box die-cast system. Reproduced by permission of John Wiley, Inc., from Nadler (1981).

information, patch up what exists, rely only on the experts, and find out what the Jones' are doing. Studies of expert and successful engineers and planners verify the essentials of these statements by showing that the experts had characteristics and attributes of practice more closely allied with the former set than the latter (Peterson, 1985).

SUMMARY

Other chapters in this book discuss many issues related to the human perspective of modern manufacturing systems. These human aspects demand that a different approach to planning, design, and implementation be taken if they are to be adequately considered. The human perspectives are reviewed in a recent report of site visits

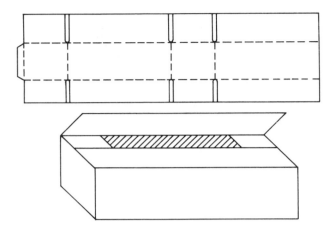

Figure 2.6   Improved box design for package and dispense bags. Reproduced by permission of John Wiley, Inc., from Nadler (1981).

to successful installations of advanced manufacturing technology (National Academy Press, 1986). Approaching the design of an automated factory, for example, with our conventional methods is, in effect, a major contributor to the lack of success in attaining the desired results from both the efforts of planning and design, as well as the outcomes of any automated facilities actually put in place.

The major problem concerns the modes of reasoning surrounding the process of converting all of the high-technology knowledge to useful practice. Several myths and gaps of understanding surround the conventional modes: the value gap, the knowledge gap, and the behaviour gap.

These gaps and myths explain why a different way of planning, designing, and implementing is needed. A time issue shows the inseparability of the processes and products of design, the distinctive yet interrelated stages of designing and coupling the technical system with the required social operating system, and the need to develop a 'culture of change' in the automated factory itself. The words 'planning, design, and implementation' ought to be replaced by a phrase such as 'continuing change'.

Seven principles for planning, design, and implementation (or for continuing change) are available to integrate the gaps and time issues to aid specific development of manufacturing systems: uniqueness, purposes, system after next, systems, limited information, people design, and betterment timeline.

The development of a timeline scenario integrating these principles and laying out specific ways of reasoning to do planning, design, and implementation, are presented. The phases involve determining purposes, developing alternative ideal systems, arranging a solution after next or a feasible ideal system target, developing details which incorporate irregularities, and installing the solution. Integrated with these phases of planning, design, and implementation are the features regarding specifying and presenting the solution specifications, involving people, using appropriate information and knowledge, and arranging for continuing change and improvement.

Although the methods for planning, design, and implementation are continually being modified and are subject to change, they have been used successfully in many applications, including the design of factories and manufacturing systems. Furthe research, especially through the National Science Foundation programme on Design Theory and Methodology, will help in refining and expanding these ideas to make them usable by engineers, planners, and designers.

REFERENCES

Alexander, E. R. (1979). The design of alternatives in organizational contexts: a pilot study. *Administrative Science Quarterly,* **24**(3), 382−404.

Beumier, F., and Coessen, J. M. (1975). *Applications of the PTR Strategy.* University of Louvain, Belgium.

Cherns, A. B. (1977). Can behavioral science help design organizations? *Organizational Dynamics,* **5**, Spring, 44−64.

Davis, L. E., and Canter, R. R. (1956). Job design. *Journal of Industrial Engineering,* **7**, 6−13.

Davis, L. E., and Sullivan, C. S. (1980). A labour−management contract and quality of working life. *Journal of Occupational Behavior,* **1**, 29−41.

Davis, L. E., and Wacker, G. J. (1987). Job design. In G. Salvendy (ed.), *Handbook of Industrial Engineering.* New York: John Wiley.

Downs, G. W., and Mohr, L. B. (1976). Conceptual issues in the study of innovations. *Administrative Science Quarterly,* **21**, 700−14.

Gyllenhammar, P. G. (1977). *People at Work.* Reading, MA: Addison-Wesley.

Kanter, R. M. (1977). *Men and Women of the Corporation.* New York: Basic Books.

Landro, L. (1982). GE promotes factory automation, but some doubt big market exists. *Wall Street Journal,* 21 October, p. 35.

Malpas, R. (1978). Engineering excellence in manufacturing processes. *Engineering* (England), **218**, June, 563−68.

Nadler, G. (1978). Is more measurement better? *Industrial Engineering,* **10**(3), 20−25.

Nadler, G. (1981). *The Planning and Design Approach.* New York: John Wiley.

Nadler, G., and Hibino, S. (1987). *Developing Breakthrough Thinking.* Available from Department of Industrial and Systems Engineering, University of Southern California.

National Academy Press (1986). *Human Resource Practices for Implementing Advanced Manufacturing Technology.* A report by the Committee on the Effective Implementation of Advanced Manufacturing Technology, Manufacturing Studies Board, Washington, DC.

Pellegrin, R. J. (1978). Sociology and policy-oriented research on innovation. In M. Radnor, S. Feller, and E. Rogers (eds), *The Diffusion of Innovations: An Assessment.* Evanstown, IL: Northwestern University.

Peterson, J. G. (1985). Personal qualities and job characteristics of expert engineers and planners. Ph.D. dissertation, Department of Industrial Engineering, University of Wisconsin−Madison.

Radnor, M., Feller, S., and Rogers, E. (1978). *The Diffusion of Innovations: An Assessment.* Evanstown, IL: Northwestern University.

Robinson, G. H., and Nadler, G. (1984). Design of organizations and jobs: sociotechnical principles and Japanese work practice. In *Proceedings of the Human Factors Society,* 28th Annual Meeting, pp. 336−340. Published by Human Factors Society Inc., Santa Monica.

Robinson, G. H., and Peterson, J. G. (1983). Groups at work: a sociotechnical view. In *Pro* ceedings of the Human Factors Society, 27th Annual Meeting, pp. 566–570. Published by Human Factors Society Inc., Santa Monica.

Rogers, E. (1978). Re-invention during the innovation process. In M. Radnor, S. Feller, and E. Rogers (eds), *The Diffusion of Innovations: An Assessment*. Evanstown, IL: Northwestern University.

Schon, D. A. (1973). *Beyond the Stable State*. New York: Norton.

Taylor, J. C., and Wacker, G. J. (1976). Case study report: Paperboard mill. Unpublished paper, Center for Quality of Working Life, University of California at Los Angeles.

Trist, E. (1980). The environment and system-response capability. *Futures*, **12**, April, 113–27.

Wacker, G. J. (1979). The use of cognitive maps in a case study of the evolution of an industrial organization. Doctoral dissertation, University of California at Los Angeles.

Wacker, G. J. (1981). Toward a cognitive methodology of organizational assessment. *Journal of Applied Behavioral Science*, **17**, 114–29.

Wacker, G. J., and Nadler, G. (1980). Seven myths about quality of working life. *California Management Review*, **22**, 15–23.

The Human Side of Advanced Manufacturing Technology
Edited by T. D. Wall, C. W. Clegg, and N. J. Kemp
© 1987 John Wiley & Sons Ltd.

CHAPTER 3

Advanced Manufacturing Technology and Work Design

THOMAS CUMMINGS AND MELVIN BLUMBERG

Modern organizations are showing an increased interest in advanced manufacturing technology (AMT). Driven by recent advances in computers and automated methods, new technologies are rapidly expanding into most functions of manufacturing, including design, fabrication, assembly, planning, and control. They can drastically alter how organizations make products, as well as deal with suppliers, customers, and support personnel. Perhaps most important, AMT can have a profound impact on work design—how tasks are grouped into jobs and allocated among work groups.

Preliminary evidence suggests that the full potential of AMT may not be realized because of lack of attention to work design (Blumberg and Gerwin, 1984; Butera and Thurman, 1984). Organizations adopting the new technologies tend to pay far more attention to their technical aspects than to their work-design features. They tend to view AMT within the framework of existing work designs which may be inappropriate for operating the technologies. Moreover, although considerable research has been devoted to AMT itself, there is a dearth of information about its work design implications.

This chapter examines the crucial relationship between AMT and work design. It explores in a preliminary manner how work can be designed to operate the new technologies most effectively. The first part of the chapter briefly describes the most prevalent forms of AMT used today. The second part presents a work design framework which identifies alternative work designs and key contingencies determining their success. Based on the information in the first two parts, the third part explores how advanced manufacturing technology affects work design. The final section draws implications for creating work designs for the new technologies.

NEW MANUFACTURING TECHNOLOGY

The primary goal of manufacturing technology is to provide organizations with a competitive advantage through enhanced product performance, reliability, quality, and cost superiority. When combined with good marketing and product-support services, manufacturing technology is the basis for market share, growth, and stability of employment. If manufacturing organizations are to compete successfully in today's world economy, the important question is not whether to adopt new technology, but how to accelerate its implementation.

There are essentially two types of manufacturing systems: continuous and intermittent. Continuous production can be either flow processing, as is found in such industries as petroleum, chemical, and paper making, or mass production of discrete items, such as automobiles, refrigerators, or straight pins. Continuous manufacturing systems tend to be highly automated with sophisticated command and control technology.

Intermittent production systems consist of job shop or small batch and large batch operations. Small batch manufacturing typically emphasizes obtaining and filling individual orders for varied products in lots of 100 or fewer per year. These are typically produced using general-purpose machines controlled by highly skilled workers. Large batch operations involve production runs of the order of 100 — 10,000 units per year with frequent product-line changes. Machines are relatively unspecialized and controlled by a mix of skilled and unskilled workers. In contrast to continuous manufacturing, intermittent production generally follows no invariable sequence, remains in process longer, requires general-purpose machine tools with skilled operators and is not highly automated. Because this form of manufacturing represents a high percentage of the manufacturing base in industrialized countries (over 35 per cent in the USA, according to Gerwin, 1982), it is the major target for applications of advanced manufacturing technology.

In this section we briefly describe five forms of advanced manufacturing technology: (1) computer-aided design, (2) computer-aided manufacturing, (3) group technology, (4) robotics, and (5) flexible manufacturing systems. Although in practice these technologies are not mutually exclusive (e.g. flexible manufacturing systems are a form of group technology and can involve the use of robots), we will discuss them separately for ease of presentation.

Computer-aided design

Computer-aided design (CAD) has had three major capabilities: interactive computer graphics, simulation, and data bases. In its simplest form a CAD system is nothing more than an electronic drawing board. In its advanced forms, interactive computer graphics allow engineers and drafters to work in two or three dimensions by means of a light pen. Wire mesh can be generated automatically to perform finite element analysis of structure to simulate a product's reaction to stress. The results of design analysis can be displayed statistically or graphically showing distorted wire mesh or colour stress patterns.

CAD programs are capable of performing geometric transformations enabling designers to rotate the product about any axis, to zoom in for a close-up, or to take a distance perspective. Kinematics capability permits the parts to be placed into motion to check for mating with other parts or for vibration. Data bases are available which provide the capability to retrieve previously designed products and to incorporate elements of them into new products. It is also possible to obtain hard-copy printouts of the drawings with prewritten textual material incorporated.

CAD systems can also generate manufacturing process instructions, tapes, or programs for automatic machine tools, together with bills of materials. Thus the same data base used to design the product may also produce orders to vendors for parts and materials, manufacturing instructions for a nearly unmanned factory, and manufacturing and financial information for other systems.

A recent challenge is to integrate CAD systems with other computer-aided functions. This has led to the development of a computer-integrated manufacturing (CIM) system in which CAD systems are linked via a hierarchically ordered network of computers with other manufacturing and business systems, such as computer-aided process planning and tool design, computer-aided manufacturing testing and inspection, manufacturing resources planning, and financial performance reporting (Hubbard, 1985; Kegg and Carter, 1982).

Computer-aided manufacturing

The modern era of automated manufacturing technology can be traced to the development of record/playback technology by General Electric, Gisholt, and others in the late 1940s, and to the development of numerically controlled (NC) machine tools in the 1950s. Record/playback technology involves the production of a part by a skilled machinist on a specially equipped machine which allows the speed, feed, and cutting motions under operator control to be recorded on tape. Numerical control, however, involves an entirely different philosophy of manufacturing (see Noble, 1980). Rather than relying on the capacity and willingness of human operators to generate optimal movements of the cutting tool, the instructions for NC tools are derived from mathematical equations representing the geometry of the parts to be produced. The equations are translated into a series of discrete instructions coded most commonly on paper or mylar tape. When fed into the machine's electronic control unit, the taped instructions cause the cutting tool to move through the required trajectory.

With the development of compact and reliable microprocessors in the 1970s, it became possible to mount dedicated, stored-program computers directly on the machine tools to perform basic NC functions. These computer numerical control (CNC) tools were able to store and retrieve the information from a number of tapes and permit editing of existing programs to reflect engineering design changes and correction of errors (see Noble, 1980). Early NC and CNC machine tools were able to perform only a single metal-cutting function, such as drilling. Modern machines equipped with automatic tool changers are able to perform a wide variety of functions, such as drilling, boring, tapping, and reaming, without the need for operator intervention or movement of the workpiece to a different machine. These advanced multi-function systems are referred to as 'machining centres'.

Computer numerical control has evolved into direct numerical control (DNC). Here, several NC or CNC machines are organized into a machining group or 'cell' under the real-time control of a central computer. Inputs, bypassing the tape-reader circuitry, are linked directly to the machine control units regulating their operation and accumulating performance data.

Group technology

Group technology is both a facility layout and a philosophy of manufacturing management that attempts to bring the efficiencies of mass production to batch manufacturing. It is a modern approach to work organization that can be applied to both traditional and advanced manufacturing technology, rather than a form of AMT itself. Continuous production systems achieve cost effectiveness not so much by reducing machine time required to produce the parts, but by significant reductions in material handling, set-up time, waiting time, and work-in-progress inventories. Batch manufacturing, on the other hand, is typically organized by function. Parts are processed in lots, then transported to another machine for the next operation. Although this has the advantage of reducing set-up costs, it increases inventory costs because parts may spend days or weeks in transit and waiting. Parts must also be handled many times, increasing the likelihood of damage, and may travel several miles crisscrossing the shopfloor to return to the same functional area many times.

Group technology begins with a recognition that similarities exist in the characteristics of parts involving their shape, weight, size, material, and process requirements. Next, these parts are associated with a group of machines possessing the necessary capabilities for processing them. Simply stated, group technology involves the identification of a 'family' of parts and a 'cell' of machines to process them. Ideally, a part is completed in a cell and there is no duplicate machinery between cells. (See Hyer and Wemmerlov, 1984 for an excellent bibliography and detailed discussion of the formation of group technology cells.) Research suggests that group technology can provide substantial savings in areas such as set-up time, scrap, rework, and both in-process and finished-goods inventory (Hyer and Wemmerlov, 1984).

Robots

A robot, according to the Robot Institute of America (now called the Robotics Industries Association) (1980) is: 'A programmable, multifunction manipulator designed to move material, parts, tools or specialized devices through variable programmed motions for the performance of a variety of tasks' (p. 7).

Robots consist of two major subsystems: a controller and a manipulator. The controller is the mechanism, as complex as a microcomputer or as simple as a cam, which allows the robot to be programmed and guides its motions. The manipulator consists of the electromechanical, hydraulic, or pneumatic base which supports and powers the arm, and the arm itself. In addition to lifting capacity, manipulators are characterized by their ability to move the robot easily through different geometric patterns in three-dimensional space, as well as by their capacity, complexity, and cost. Manipulators are further classified in terms of their effectors. Usually not part of the robot itself, the end effector consists of the rotational devices, grippers, and other tools which the robot uses to grasp, hold, bend, rotate, or press the material being processed.

Robots have been used primarily in manufacturing, particularly for unpleasant, hazardous, or monotonous tasks where worker turnover and product quality tend to be problematic. Major applications include welding, spray painting, material handling, machine loading and machining assembly (Kolpanen, 1984). In the USA, robots have been increasingly applied to industrial training and education (US International Trade Commission, 1983).

Future growth in the use of robots is highly speculative. Realistically, explosive growth of robots would depend on widening the scope of their application through improved technology, and on reducing their cost. If robots are to spread beyond the manufacturing sector, improvements are needed in such areas as proximity, touch, force, and vision sensors, and the ability to respond to spoken command. Also, improved software is needed which will provide robots with the ability to adapt to changes in their environment.

Flexible manufacturing systems

Flexible manufacturing systems (FMSs) integrate most of the technologies just described. They are a natural outgrowth of group technology and CNC/DNC systems combined with automated tool changers, part conveyors, information reporting, and, in more advanced forms, robots for material handling, inspection, or assembly tasks. FMSs typically use one or more central computers for generating operation instructions, routing parts, monitoring activities, and compiling statistics. FMSs can process a wide variety of parts, run in any random sequence. They can also acquire production capacity incrementally, convert production capacity as required by product life cycles, and produce other parts to be specified in the future (Hutchinson, 1976).

Blumberg and Gerwin (1984) extensively studied FMSs, and provided the following description of one in the USA. It was purchased in 1972 for approximately $5 million by the tractor division of a diversified manufacturer. The system, developed to produce six major housings for a new line of tractors, consisted of six general-purpose machining centres, four head indexers, three loading stations, and two computers arrayed over a floor area of approximately 9,000 square metres. The individual housings—approximately 1 metre cubes weighing about a metric tonne each—were manually palletized and loaded on to carts with the aid of a crane and fork lift. Power for the carts was provided by 12 underground tow chains into which a tow pin attached to each cart was inserted. Under control of an FMS computer, the carts were routed to a work station where the palletized casting was transferred to the machine by a shuttle carriage. A DNC computer controlled processing of the casting. Then it was returned to a cart and routed to its next work station, or returned to a loading station. This process was carried on simultaneously for approximately a dozen parts of several families which appear in random sequence at the work stations.

The equipment was run on a two-shift, five-day schedule with an occasional third-shift skeleton crew. The shift crew consisted of a foreman, three loaders, three operators, a tool setter, and a mechanical repairman. Human intervention was required at the loading stations, and at the machines for in-process inspection, reclamping, tool replacements, chip-clearing, and clearing of shuttle-carriage malfunctions.

A more advanced FMS is employed at Fujitsu Fanuc's factory in Japan. It consists of 29 machining cells served either by automatic pallet changers or robots. Palletized workpieces are transported between the work stations and storage areas by computer-controlled, wire-guided carts. At night, NC machining is monitored by a single worker stationed in a control room. Machining availability runs close to 100 per cent, and machine use averages $65-70$ per cent (Usui, 1982; Merchant, 1983; Bylinsky, 1983).

WORK DESIGN FRAMEWORK

This section of the chapter provides a framework for understanding work design. The framework derives from sociotechnical system theory (Trist *et al.*, 1963; Cummings and Srivastva, 1977), and includes designing jobs and work groups for high levels of productivity and employee satisfaction. Because work design ties people to technology, it provides the critical link between the advanced manufacturing technology just discussed and employee behaviour and attitudes.

Sociotechnical systems theory includes two underlying premises. The first is that, whenever people are organized to perform work, there is a joint system operating, a sociotechnical system. This comprises two independent yet correlated parts: a technological part which consists of the tools, machines, and techniques required for task performance; and a social part which comprises the people and the relationships among them needed to perform the tasks. Because the technical and social parts must work together to create a useful product or service, it is necessary to design work to facilitate that interaction. This requires work designs that jointly match technological requirements and people's needs. Such jointly optimized work designs result in high levels of productivity and employee fulfilment.

The second premise is that sociotechnical systems are open systems which exist in the context of a larger environment. The environment provides the system with needed inputs, such as raw materials, and serves as an outlet for system outputs, such as goods and services. Because sociotechnical systems are dependent on their environment, they must create and maintain effective environmental relationships in order to survive and develop. This may require adapting to environmental changes, as well as influencing the environment in favoured directions.

Based on these two premises, work design is aimed at jointly satisfying technological and personal needs, and matching environmental conditions. These technical, personal, and environmental contingencies determine the kinds of work designs that are likely to be most successful. This section first discusses these work-design contingencies, and then describes specific work designs appropriate to various combinations of the contingencies. Specific features of the work context which support the different work designs are also discussed.

Work-design contingencies

Technical factors

Two key technological features can affect work design success: technical inter-dependence, or the extent to which the technology requires co-operation among employees to produce a product or service; and technical uncertainty, or the amount of information processing and decision-making employees must do during task execution (Slocum and Sims, 1983; Cummings, 1978; Susman, 1976). The degree of technical interdependence determines whether work should be designed for individual jobs or for work groups. When technical interdependence is low, and there is little need for employee co-operation, work should be designed for individual jobs. When technical interdependence is high, on the other hand, work should be designed for groups composed of people performing interrelated tasks. The amount of technical uncertainty determines whether work should be designed for external forms of control, such as supervision, standardization, and scheduling, or for employee self-control. When technical uncertainty is low, and employees have to process little information during task performance, work should be designed for external control mechanisms, such as hierarchical supervision and schedules. Conversely, when technical uncertainty is high, work should be designed for employee self-control and decision making.

Personal factors

Researchers have found that at least two kinds of personal needs can affect work-design effectiveness: social needs, or the desire for significant social relationships; and growth needs, or the desire for personal accomplishment, learning, and development (Brousseau, 1983; Hackman and Oldham, 1980). In general, the degree of social needs determines whether or not work should be designed for individual jobs or for work groups. The greater are people's social needs, the more they should be satisfied with group forms of work. Growth needs determine whether work designs should be routine and repetitive or complex and challenging. The greater are people's growth needs, the more they should be attracted to enriched kinds of work offering high levels of autonomy, task variety, and feedback of results.

Environmental factors

The last work-design contingency involves the task environment of the sociotechnical system. Because the system must exchange matter-energy and information with its environment, the nature of the environment should affect how the system is designed to manage those exchanges (Susman, 1970). Specifically, when task environments are relatively stable, exchanges can be programmed and standardized. In this situation work designs should emphasize routine performance. Conversely, when task environments are relatively dynamic and are changing unpredictably, exchanges must be managed adaptively as the circumstances demand. Here, work should be designed for high levels of information processing and decision making, and should emphasize flexible behaviours.

Work designs

The technical, personal, and environmental contingencies affecting work design success can be used to identify four pure kinds of work design suited to different combinations of the contingencies: (1) traditional jobs; (2) traditional work groups; (3) enriched jobs; and (4) self-regulating work groups (Huse and Cummings, 1985). The work designs and relevant contingencies are shown in Table 3.1, and described briefly below.

Table 3.1.   Work designs and contingencies

	Contingencies									
	Technical inter-dependence		Technical uncertainty		Environ-mental dynamics		Growth needs		Social needs	
Work designs	Low	High	Low	High	Low	High	Low	High	Low	High
Traditional jobs	×		×		×		×		×	
Traditional work groups		×	×		×		×			×
Enriched jobs	×			×		×		×	×	
Self-regulating work groups		×		×		×		×		×

Traditional jobs

Historically, the tendency has been to break jobs down into their simplest components and to specify the tasks and work methods of the components. Individual jobholders are expected to do routine and repetitive work, with planning, evaluation, and decision making being delegated to others, such as supervisors, inspectors, and engineers. Although traditional jobs have come under increasing criticism by quality-of-work-life advocates, the contingencies shown in Table 3.1 suggest that, under the following conditions, such jobs can be productive, satisfying, and responsive to environmental exchanges: when technical interdependence and uncertainty are both low; when people have low social and growth needs; and when the environment is stable.

Traditional work groups

These are composed of members performing routine yet related tasks, such as might be found on assembly lines. The group task is typically broken down into simpler, discrete parts, often called jobs. The tasks and work methods are specified for each part, and the different parts are assigned to group members. Co-ordination and control of members' performances and of environmental exchanges are carried out by external control devices, such as supervision and schedules. Traditional work groups are most effective: when technical interdependence is high yet technical uncertainty is low; when people have high social needs yet low growth needs; and when the environment is stable.

Enriched jobs

These work designs provide employees with increased opportunities for responsibility, decision making, and challenge. Individual jobs are designed for high levels of skill variety, autonomy, and feedback about results. The task is also organized so jobholders experience a whole piece of work which has positive significance for others, such as co-workers or customers (Hackman and Oldham, 1980). Enriched jobs are most successful: when technical interdependence is low but technical uncertainty is high; when people have low social needs yet high growth needs; and when the task environment is dynamic.

Self-regulating work groups

Alternatively referred to as autonomous or self-managing work groups, these work designs involve multi-skilled members controlling their own task behaviours around an overall group task. The task forms a relatively self-completing whole, and members are given the necessary autonomy, skills, and information to regulate task behaviours and manage environmental exchanges (Cummings, 1978). The group may help determine production goals, as well as perform such functions as inspection, maintenance, purchasing, and hiring new members. Self-regulating work groups are most effective: when technical interdependence and uncertainty are both high; when people have high social and growth needs; and when the task environment is dynamic.

Work context

Work designs exist in a larger organizational context which can affect whether the designs are implemented and operated effectively. This work context consists of various personnel, measurement, and control practices having to do with the selection, training, compensation, and supervision of employees. To the extent that these practices fit or match the work designs, they are likely to reinforce the kinds of task performances required to operate the designs. Historically, organizations have devised a traditional set of personnel, measurement, and control methods which support and reinforce traditional forms of work design. These practices reinforce repetitive behaviours, with low amounts of decision making and self-control. In order to operate enriched jobs and self-regulating work groups, however, these traditional practices need to be modified. Selection needs to be aimed at employees with high growth and/or social needs, while training programmes need to emphasize multiple skills, complex decision making, and self-control. Similarly, compensation practices need to reinforce both learning and good performance at the individual level for enriched jobs and at the group level for self-regulating work groups, Finally, supervision needs to support employee growth and decision-making.

THE IMPACT OF ADVANCED MANUFACTURING TECHNOLOGY ON WORK DESIGN

So far we have described briefly the advanced manufacturing technology being applied to organizations today, and introduced a contingency framework relating different work designs to different technological, personal, and environmental conditions. Given this knowledge, we can now examine the key interface between the new technologies and the work designs, with particular attention to the kinds of work design necessary for operating the technologies effectively.

Unfortunately, there is little research directly relating advanced manufacturing technology to work design. Most of the relevant literature is at best speculative regarding this key interface, typically offering general predictions or observations about how the technologies are likely to affect employees' work lives, organization strategies and designs, and labour market characteristics (see, for example, Susman and Chase, 1986; Ayers and Miller, 1983; Bylinsky, 1983). The relatively few empirical studies in this area have tended to offer rich case descriptions of the introduction of the new technologies into organizations, with relatively little direct examination of work design effects (see, for example, Argote, Schkade, and Goodman, 1983; Petro, 1983).

In the absence of an extensive body of scientific knowledge relating advanced manufacturing technology to work design, we will first offer some speculations about this linkage. This can be accomplished by examining how the new technologies can be expected to affect three key work design contingencies: technical interdependence, technical uncertainty, and environmental stability. Such information provides a reasonable basis for predicting which work designs are likely to be most appropriate for the contingencies. Then, in light of these predictions, we will review three case studies examining the introduction of advanced manufacturing technology into organizations. We will assess the extent to which the organizations' work designs match the demands of the new technologies, as well as the consequences of that matching. This information should allow us to draw several pertinent implications of advanced manufacturing technology for work design effectiveness.

Advanced manufacturing technology, contingencies, and work designs

Advanced manufacturing technologies can be expected to have a number of effects on the technological and environmental contingencies determining work design success. Knowledge of these effects is necessary to specify the kinds of work designs most appropriate to matching the contingencies.

Technical interdependence

This technical contingency refers to the extent to which the different parts or phases of the technology are interrelated requiring co-operation among employees to make a product or provide a service. In general, advanced manufacturing technology seems to score high on this dimension. Flexible manufacturing systems, for example, integrate the different phases of the manufacturing process, such as design, fabrication, and assembly, into a tightly co-ordinated yet flexible system. Central computers control operations, materials transfer, monitoring, and scheduling. This helps to reduce unnecessary buffer inventories and to shorten lead times between the production of different products. Because the overall flow of production is accelerated and more tightly linked, technical interdependence is greatly increased. Similarly, in computer-aided manufacturing, different CAD systems are linked via a network of computers with other manufacturing and business systems, thus increasing the interdependence among these components.

Technical uncertainty

This dimension involves the amount of information processing and decision making that employees must do during task performance. The new technologies drastically reduce the amount of routine information processing and decision making that employees customarily do. Automated production systems, such as computer-aided manufacturing and flexible manufacturing systems, are generally capable of detecting and correcting many of the variances occurring during operation with relatively little human intervention. There is increased need, however, for employees to manage the unforeseen and non-routine variances that cannot readily be controlled by computers. Such variances can be particularly costly in advanced manufacturing technologies. They can quickly shut down the entire manufacturing system because the different parts are highly integrated; and such variances can result in large amounts of inferior product because of the accelerated speed of production. In order to control non-routine variances rapidly, and as close to their source as possible, employees must process a good deal of information and engage in complex problem solving and decision making in real time. Consequently, they must cope with a high level of technical uncertainty during task performance.

Environmental stability

This final contingency refers to the extent to which the task environment of the manufacturing system is predictable and allows programmed and routine responses. Traditional manufacturing technologies tend to face relatively stable task environments. They are buffered or decoupled from external disruption by such mechanisms as raw-materials and finished-goods stocks. Advanced manufacturing technologies, on the other hand, potentially face more dynamic task environments. The technologies are more tightly coupled to vendors and customers, as well as to staff and service functions in the organization. Thus, unpredictable changes in these external functions can place severe demands on the system's adaptive capacity. Flexible manufacturing systems, for example, have little inventory, and are susceptible to disruption in raw material deliveries and to bottlenecks in the transportation and distribution system. Although many of these external disruptions can be routinely managed, the tighter coupling of the manufacturing system to its task environment requires more timely, novel responses when unpredictable conditions are encountered.

Work designs

The above analysis suggests that advanced manufacturing technologies are likely to result in higher levels of technical interdependence, technical uncertainty, and environmental dynamics. If so, appropriate work designs should be oriented to groups of employees rather than individualized jobs, and to employee self-control and decision making rather than external forms of control, such as supervision. This calls for self-regulating work groups, a conclusion also reached by others examining work design implications of advanced manufacturing technology (Susman and Chase, 1986; Blumberg and Gerwin, 1984).

Such groups are organized around interdependent tasks to facilitate co-ordination of task performance. For example, they might be responsible for a manufacturing cell or an entire shift in a flexible manufacturing system. Members are given the necessary skills, information, and freedom to respond to unforeseen disturbances arising from within the production system and its task environment. They have the multiple skills to deploy themselves as the circumstances demand, and the capacity to detect and control non-routine variances. Group members might rotate between jobs, sharing the burden of the most boring tasks and gaining greater insight of the overall manufacturing process. They might be responsible for engaging with management and service staff in on-line problem solving.

Case studies

Now that we have derived a relevant work design for the contingencies associated with advanced manufacturing technology we can examine three of the few field studies assessing the introduction of such technology into organizations. We are especially interested in whether the organizations responded to the new technologies by redesigning work along the lines suggested here, by introducing self-regulating work groups. If so, productivity and employee satisfaction should be relatively high, particularly if employees have high social and growth needs. On the other hand, failure to design work appropriately should have negative consequences for managing necessary technical interdependencies and non-routine variances arising from the technology and the task environment. Employees should have problems achieving high levels of productivity, and they should experience undue stress and trouble in trying to operate with an inappropriate work design. The three case studies include the introduction of computer-aided design into a drafting department, the application of a robot in a manufacturing plant, and the implementation of a flexible manufacturing system in a tractor factory.

Case 1: Computer-aided drafting

Petro (1983) studied the drafting department of a northern New Jersey manufacturing company with annual sales of £130 million. After an exhaustive search lasting nearly 2 years the company purchased a computer-aided drafting system called CADAM, partly because of its compatibility with the company's mainframe computer.

All decisions regarding the new equipment were made by managers. They communicated with vendors, attended demonstrations, and after the purchase decision was made they decided how to implement the new equipment. Only after the system had been purchased (3 months prior to its installation) were drafters officially advised of the imminent change. Prior to the official announcement, however, word of the purchase had circulated via the company grapevine, raising considerable speculation and fear about job reassignment and layoffs.

According to Petro, the first meeting between management and the company's drafters lasted about an hour, and consisted of an explanation of the CAD system's capabilities and its potential benefit to the company. No actual demonstration was given, nor were potential employee benefits discussed. Management representatives made commitments that there would be no layoffs because of the CAD system. They also stated that the position of CAD operator was considered a lateral move for drafters with no increase in pay over the old system. Management then asked for volunteers to work on the new system. Of 40 drafters present, eight volunteered. Four of those subsequently withdrew. The remaining four were trained by the vendor.

Management's original plan was that all drafting would be done by the CAD operators with the remaining drafters doing set-up and checking tasks. It soon became apparent that the four CAD operators could not service the entire workload. Additional work stations and a second shift were added. At the time of the study, a call for more volunteers had been issued with little response.

In an attempt to determine the reason for the lack of interest in working on the CAD system, Petro interviewed the drafters who refused to volunteer. A typical first response was, 'Why should I go learn a new job with more pressure for no more pay?' When pressed further, the drafters admitted a fear of being unable to master the new job. A typical remark was 'I don't know anything about computers.'

When the drafters were asked how they felt their job status compared with that of the CAD operators, the majority responded that their present status was equal to or slightly above that of the CAD operators. The CAD operators, on the other hand, responded that their new job status was considerably higher than that of their previous job. There also appeared to be friction between the CAD operators and the remaining drafters. Some drafters continued to do drawings manually and even took work home in an effort to show that the new system was less productive than the old method. When management learned of this, reprimands were issued. This exacerbated the deterioration in the required working relationship between the manual drafters and the CAD operators, resulting in a further decline in productivity.

Petro referred to this behaviour as the 'Bunyan syndrome'. Paul Bunyan was a legendary American folk hero and lumberjack who boasted that he could outperform anyone in cutting down trees. According to legend, when power saws were invented, a contest was called. After mighty effort and close results, Bunyan lost and faded from the scene to be replaced by lesser men with better equipment.

Petro also interviewed persons in departments which depended upon the CAD department for the drawings necessary to produce customer orders. Interfaces with other departments were particularly troublesome because the CAD department did not have its own manager to deal full-time with scheduling problems and to communicate with user departments. People in other departments felt animosity toward the CAD system because it affected their ability to meet schedules, yet it afforded no direct way to communicate with 'it'.

When the system was originally purchased it had a dedicated computer and excellent response time. However, the company's information systems department began using the CAD computer for other purposes, and the response time of the system fell, with resulting boredom for the CAD operators and loss of productivity for the drafting department.

Another interesting outcome of Petro's study concerns a different aspect of the CAD system's impact on operator productivity. He found that the CAD system multiplied the effectiveness of all of the workers. However, this productivity effect was greatest for those manual drafters having the highest level of skill.

Finally, Petro found that pay was a major source of dissatisfaction for the CAD operators. Because most of the literature on CAD systems was written by equipment vendors, there was little mention of appropriate pay scales for CAD operators. However, once pay scales from comparable firms became available the salaries in the company under study were shown to be below the norm. Even though management had initially stressed that CAD operators would be paid the same as manual drafters, the operators felt that management would have to change this policy. Older operators appeared willing to accept the situation, but younger ones indicated they were ready to leave when a better offer became available. The dilemma facing management was either to assign drafters to the CAD system rather than depend upon volunteers, or to hire from the outside at a premium salary. In the latter case the firm would have to deal with the problem of salary inequity for existing workers. It would also have to lay off some of the present drafters and thereby break the original commitment not to do so.

Case 2: Robotics

Argote, Schkade and Goodman (1983) studied employee reactions to the application of a robot in a non-unionized manufacturing plant employing approximately 1,000 people. The robot was introduced into a department responsible for grinding and milling bar stock. The department employed 40 people spread over three shifts. The robot was placed at the beginning of a horseshoe-shaped line through which products proceeded sequentially. The robot was used to load and unload two milling machines, and was operated by one person on each shift.

The company informed employees about the robot approximately 1 year before it was installed. Talks were given by the plant manager, notices were placed in the cafeteria, and discussions were held with first-line supervisors. In addition, the company held an open house during which the robot was demonstrated.

Workers were interviewed twice, several months before and several months after the robot was put on line. Interviews were conducted with first-line supervisors, higher-level managers, and production staff and support personnel from other departments.

Implementing the robot involved creating a manufacturing cell consisting of two milling machines, the robot, and an employee. The robot took over the material-handling task previously performed by a human operator. The operator's task changed from largely physical activities to more cognitive monitoring and control activities. This required the development of new skills aimed at problem solving, controlling the interface between the milling machines and the robot, and programming and operating the robot.

The introduction of the robot was stressful for employees. The researchers suggested that this stemmed in part from having to learn new tasks and responsibilities, and partly from operating a new and expensive piece of equipment. There was some evidence of the Bunyan syndrome here too. In the early interviews Argote and her colleagues reported that there was considerable speculation regarding whether an exceptional operator could outpace the robot. In the later interviews, operators appeared resigned to the fact that the robot was faster. As the researchers pointed out, even though operators knew objectively that they were operating the robot, subjectively they still considered themselves in competition with it.

Although the robot did not change the workflow in the department, it did alter some of the interaction patterns. Operators reported that they had less time to talk with their co-workers because they needed to concentrate more on the task. There were also changes in relationships with other departments. Operators had to interact more frequently with support personnel from the engineering and maintenance departments.

Support personnel also felt that their jobs had changed. The robot represented a new level of complexity for maintenance, engineering quality control, and scheduling. The researchers reported feelings of frustration among support personnel. They were not involved in planning for the new robot, and they needed to acquire new skills and procedures.

Pay for the new job classification was also an issue in this case. Management re-evaluated and reclassified the operator's job based on task changes. Although the job was subsequently upgraded, workers felt that the new pay grade was too low for the skills required.

Case 3: Flexible manufacturing system

Blumberg and Gerwin (1984) and their colleagues (Blumberg and Alber, 1982; Gerwin, 1981, 1982; Gerwin and Tarondeau, 1982; Gerwin and Leung, 1980) studied the individual and organizational effects of flexible manufacturing systems in five firms in Europe and the USA. The first phase of the research began in 1979 with semi-structured interviews of managers and staff specialists in such areas as manufacturing, quality control, maintenance, manufacturing engineering, and data processing. These interviews led to more specific questions, and finally culminated in an in-depth survey of foremen and worker reactions to a flexible manufacturing system in an American firm (the same FMS described previously in this chapter, see pp.41–42).

The plan to adopt the new technology was part of a corporate strategy to replace obsolete, single-purpose machinery with more modern equipment needed to produce a new line of farm tractors. The decision to purchase an FMS, rather than some other technology, was made by an *ad hoc* task force from the company's industrial-engineering department.

The FMS went on line in 1972, and was the second one implemented in the USA. After installation a team of highly skilled personnel led by engineers from the manufacturing-engineering department initially operated the equipment. This improved equipment utilization during the break-in period, but created other difficulties when the equipment was turned over to operating personnel.

Blumberg and Gerwin designed a comprehensive questionnaire for measuring several factors which have been shown to affect employee performance, motivation, satisfaction, attendance, and retention. These included variables having to do with task characteristics, personal growth needs, job satisfaction, equitable rules and pay, healthful and safe working conditions, meaningful work, work-related stress, job attitudes, job switching, and aspirations for the future. (See Blumberg and Gerwin, 1984; and Blumberg and Alber, 1982 for a complete description of the measures used.) The research sample consisted of two foremen, two machine repairmen, six operators, six loaders, and two tool setters. All employees were male and worked a two-shift, 5-day schedule. Except for the foremen, all of the employees were members of the United Auto Workers Union.

Questionnaire results were compared with the responses of a normative sample of employees in the machine trades, and a more general sample of employed adults. (See Blumberg and Gerwin, 1984, for details and sources.) These comparisons suggested that jobs on the FMS were not sufficiently enriched in terms of meaningfulness, autonomy, task identity, responsibility, and feedback. Consequently, employee work motivation was low.

The researchers also found that job satisfaction was generally low, although it varied somewhat with occupation. Employees with higher-paid, more challenging occupations tended to have higher job satisfaction. Results for work-related stress indicated that work on the FMS was relatively stressful, especially for two stress factors—inability to use valued skills and likelihood of job loss. Interestingly, foremen felt that employees had too much say about workplace decisions, while employees felt that they had too little participation in decision making.

Blumberg and Gerwin also asked a number of open-ended questions. In response to a question asking what the men hoped to be doing in 5 years, over half responded they would like to be in lines of work having more variety and responsibility. Sixteen of the eighteen employees responded that they felt worried about health and safety, particularly from moving carts and fumes caused by the coolant. They also identified five major problem areas: pay, performance, maintenance, safety, and tooling.

Pay problems centred around the lack of an incentive system. FMS operators were the same pay grade as other machine operators, but could not earn additional money because the equipment set the upper limit to productivity. They were extremely dissatisfied because lower-skilled employees were on an incentive system and frequently made more money than they did. Moreover, once assigned to the FMS, employees were not allowed to 'bid off' to other areas where they could earn incentive pay.

Performance problems resulted from people on one shift not completing work properly, not making needed machine adjustments and tool changes, and not cleaning the equipment and adding coolant. This negligence made work more difficult for the next shift.

Maintenance problems resulted, ironically, from the versatility of the FMS. Because it made many key parts that directly fed the production line, there was little opportunity to take the equipment out of service for needed maintenance. Management was also unwilling to schedule mechanics for overtime on third shift, weekends, or during plant shutdown. Consequently, a number of 'quick fixes' had been installed that made machine operation very eccentric. This angered many of the operators who constantly had to kick or push parts into position when a 20-minute maintenance procedure was denied during working hours.

Tooling problems had to do with disorganization of the tool room, insufficient tooling, and insufficient time to adjust certain tooling properly. Moreover, because tooling as well as spare parts for the FMS were very expensive, management was reluctant to keep sufficient stock on hand.

Blumberg and Gerwin's study suggests that work on the FMS had little potential for motivating people, was not very satisfying, and was stressful. Unfortunately, the work situation also seemed to lack opportunities for extrinsic motivation. Pay, especially the lack of an incentive system, was of major concern to most of the employees. Other factors affecting motivation were job stress, health and safety worries, and frequent equipment breakdown or eccentric operation.

Case studies and work design

The three case studies provide a much-needed empirical examination of the consequences of introducing advanced manufacturing technology into existing organizations. Although the studies involve different kinds of technology and different industries, they offer some strikingly similar observations regarding work design effects.

First, work redesign appeared to receive only scant attention in the organizations. Although there was ample realization that operating the new technologies required learning new skills and behaviours, there was little if any recognition that traditional job designs should be modified accordingly. As suggested previously, the new technologies seem suited to self-regulating work groups. Yet none of the organizations appeared to move in this direction, with the possible exception of the robotics case, where employees' jobs involved more decision making and self-control. In the CAD case the new jobs were treated as equivalent to the existing, traditional drafting jobs. Similarly, in the FMS case, where technical interdependence and uncertainty were highest and where self-regulating work groups would be most relevant, jobs remained fragmented along functional lines—e.g. machine repairmen, operators, loaders, and tool setters. Thus the organizations seemed to respond to the new technologies within the framework of existing, traditional job designs. They showed little appreciation for the need to redesign work in the directions suggested here.

Second, the new technologies resulted in increased interdependence between the organizations' production system and various support, supplier, and user groups. Yet there appears to have been relatively little recognition that such interfaces might require special attention and work redesign. In all three cases, support personnel had problems relating to the new technologies. They had to learn new skills and procedures to service the technologies, and they had to face new demands that affected their ability to function effectively. These external groups were afforded few opportunities to influence either the design of the new technologies or the way they related to them. Moreover, the organizations paid relatively little attention to redesigning work so that employees operating the advanced manufacturing technology could better manage interdependencies with other units. Again, there appears to have been little recognition of the way the new technologies had changed key technical and environmental contingencies, and of the need for redesigning work to account for those factors.

Third, in addition to neglecting the work design effects of advanced manufacturing technology, the organizations also appear to have underestimated the degree to which the work context should be modified to support the new tasks. In all three cases, employees experienced pay inequities in operating the new technology. In the CAD and robotics cases, employees had to learn new skills and perform new tasks, and felt that pay should be adjusted to account for these changes. In the FMS case, the new technology set upper limits on productivity, and thus employees were not able to take advantage of the company's incentive system. Rather than recognizing and resolving pay inequities initially when the technologies were being designed and implemented, the organizations confronted the pay problems only after they had becomed a major source of employee dissatisfaction. Similarly, in all three cases employees experienced stress associated with the new technologies, yet the organizations failed to anticipate and help manage the stress before it became a problem. In the CAD and robotics cases the stress resulted from having to learn new tasks and to make significant changes in work methods. In the FMS case, stress was the consequence of under-utilization of employees' valued skills and of fear of job loss. Rather than take special steps to confront and manage these problems, the organizations seemed to treat the introduction of advanced manufacturing technology as something that could be managed with traditional organizational responses.

Fourth, the three cases show the negative consequences that can result when organizations fail to redesign work and modify the work context to accommodate advanced manufacturing technology. As described above, there was considerable employee dissatisfaction with pay, as well as stress associated with learning new skills and performing new tasks. In the FMS case where employees felt the technology had not sufficiently enriched their jobs, work motivation and job satisfaction were generally low. Employees also felt that there was too little participation in decision making, and that in the future they would like work having more variety and responsibility. In all three cases there was a general dissatisfaction with the way the new technology was linked to external support groups. Thus the negative consequences were not limited to employees directly operating the new technologies, but were also experienced by those indirectly affected by them.

IMPLICATIONS FOR WORK DESIGN

The work design framework and case study analyses suggest a number of practical implications for creating effective work designs for advanced manufacturing technology.

Because there is so little research in this area, the implications should be treated as general guides to work design rather than precise, scientific prescriptions. Clearly there is considerable need for conceptual refinement and empirical exploration in this area.

Work design choices

Choices about work design should take into account those technical, environmental, and personal contingencies determining work design success. Analysis of advanced manufacturing technology suggests that it is likely to result in increased amounts of technical interdependence and uncertainty and of environmental dynamics. If so, the most appropriate work design should be self-regulating groups, where members interact around interdependent tasks and have the necessary skills, autonomy, and information to control technical and environmental variances as close to their source as possible. Such work groups derive from sociotechnical systems theory, and were initially applied in continuous-process technologies, such as oil refineries, coal mines, and weaving mills (e.g. Hill, 1971; Susman, 1970; Trist *et al.*, 1963). Interestingly, advanced manufacturing technology has many of the properties of continuous-process technologies (see Chapter 6, p. 123), particularly tight integration among the different functional parts. Thus, earlier attempts to create work designs relevant for continuous-process technologies seem to have contemporary relevance to advanced manufacturing technology.

Susman and Chase (1986) suggest that designing work for advanced manufacturing technology requires a fundamental choice about whether to downgrade or upgrade the skills of shopfloor employees. A downgrading strategy would relegate most decision making and variance control to managers and support personnel while leaving lower-level operatives to perform whatever simple tasks cannot readily be automated. Although this approach affords management more control over shopfloor personnel, it may increase managerial and staff overhead costs as well as sever the learning loop between those who initially detect variance and those who subsequently correct it. Given these problems, Susman and Chase argue strongly for an upgrading strategy, where employees have the necessary skills and abilities to regulate their own work activities and control variances. Such upgrading is congruent with applying self-regulating work groups to the new technologies. It provides employees with the skills and abilities to operate such work designs.

In addition to upgrading employee skills, applications of self-regulating work groups require attention to key individual differences that affect how employees respond to work designs. Specifically, employees with higher growth and social needs are likely to be most responsive to self-regulating work groups. They would enjoy the challenge and opportunities for development afforded by increased skill use and decision making; and they would like the social contact of working in an interactive work group. Thus, choices about applying self-regulating work groups to advanced manufacturing technology also involve decisions about upgrading employee skills, and about selecting employees with high growth needs and social needs. Such choices have important implications for modifying the work context to support and reinforce self-regulating groups.

Work context modifications

As suggested previously, the larger work context can affect whether work designs are implemented and operated effectively. The organization's personnel, measurement, and control practices need to fit with and reinforce the kinds of task behaviours implied by the work designs. Self-regulating work groups require interactive performances around an overall group task, as well as considerable information processing and decision making during task execution. The following work-context features can be expected to support those task behaviours:

1. Selection practices that are aimed at employees having high growth needs and social needs. This can be facilitated by providing potential recruits with realistic job previews about working in self-regulating groups, and allowing them to voluntarily self-select into such work designs (Cummings and Srivastva, 1977). Although direct measures of these individual differences can also be obtained, they are probably better used for helping people make more informed job and career decisions than for selection purposes.
2. Training programmes that help to provide employees with multiple skills needed to detect and control technical and environmental variances, and social skills necessary to engage in group problem solving.
3. Reward systems that promote learning multiple skills and performing tasks effectively. This might include a skill-based pay system where employees are compensated for the breadth and/or depth of skills they have mastered (Lawler and Ledford, 1984). It could also involve a group-based pay-for-performance system, where the overall group is rewarded for specific productivity gains (Lawler, 1981).
4. Management styles that are oriented to helping group members develop the necessary competence to make work-related decisions and solve complex problems. This leadership role would be highly consultative and include helping the group manage key external interdependencies.

The design process

A final implication of the work-design framework and case-study analyses involves the process by which work designs are formulated and implemented. Organizations have traditionally viewed work design as something that occurs after the technical system has been designed. They have tended to design the technology and then adapt or fit the work design to it. This can severely limit the time needed to develop a fully functioning work design. Self-regulating work groups, for example, take a considerable time to develop. Employees need to gain the multiple skills necessary to operate the technology and the expertise necessary to form an effective problem solving group. These developmental activities may take as long, if not longer, than the time needed to make the advanced manufacturing technology operational. Consequently, work design needs to be considered early in the design process when the new technologies themselves are being designed. This would provide more lead time to develop the work design. It might also result in a better fit between the work design and the technology because both would be designed jointly (see Chapter 2).

In addition to designing work earlier in the design process, organizations need to treat subsequent implementation of the work designs as an evolving process requiring considerable learning and adjustment (Cummings and Mohrman, 1987). In contrast to implementing technology which tends to follow a mechanical – construction process, implementing work designs requires a more developmental process. Work designs generally proceed through a series of growth stages as they develop towards maturity. Employees need to learn new skills and procedures as well as the behaviours required to enact the designs. This learning requires continual feedback about how the new work is progressing. The feedback enables employees to make necessary adjustments in the design, and to their behaviours, as circumstances require. In implementing self-regulating work groups, for example, members may use information about their interactions to make adjustments in how they jointly detect and control variances. This feedback/adjustment cycle continues until the work design is implemented fully. It supports the learning required to implement the work design.

CONCLUSION

Advanced manufacturing technology is increasingly being implemented in modern organizations. These technical advances raise expectations for significant improvements in production and responsiveness to customer demands. In order to achieve the full impact of these improvements, however, organizations need to design appropriate work structures to operate the new forms of technology. The work designs need to be responsive to specific technical, environmental, and personal contingencies associated with the new technologies. Moreover, organizations need to ensure that their personnel, measurement, and control practices support and reinforce the work designs.

Although there is little research on the relation between advanced manufacturing technology and work design, a review of the few empirical studies strongly suggests that organizations may have problems implementing and operating the new technologies. They tend to view these technologies within the framework of existing, traditional work designs. These designs involve relatively narrow job descriptions and external forms of control, and are best suited to technologies having low degrees of uncertainty and interdependence, and to stable task environments. The studies also suggest that organizations tend to underestimate the extent to which the work context needs to be modified to support advanced manufacturing technology, including changes in reward systems, training, and relations with support services. Failure to design work appropriately, and to modify the work context accordingly, can result in poor performance, job dissatisfaction, and increased employee stress.

This chapter proposes that advanced manufacturing technology requires non-traditional work designs and significant modifications in the work context. Specifically, the new forms of technology tend to increase technical interdependence and uncertainty and environmental dynamics. These contingencies call for self-regulating work groups, composed of multi-skilled employees who can jointly control technical and environmental variances. Such work designs are best suited to employees with high growth and social needs, and may require upgrading employee skills and making changes in selection practices, training programmes, reward systems, and management styles.

Clearly, organizations need to attend to work design and the work context early in the design process, preferably when the advanced manufacturing technology is being developed. This will provide more lead time to develop appropriate work designs and to make necessary contextual modifications. It should also increase the likelihood that the work design and the technology will jointly support each other.

REFERENCES

Argote, L., Schkade, D., and Goodman, P. S. (1983). The human side of robotics: how workers react to a robot. *Sloan Management Review,* **24,** 31−41.

Ayers, R., and Miller, S. (1983). *Robotics: Concepts and Applications.* New York: Ballinger.

Blumberg, M., and Alber, A. (1982). The human element: its impact on the productivity of advanced manufacturing systems. *Journal of Manufacturing Systems,* **1,** 43−52.

Blumberg, M., and Gerwin, D. (1984). Coping with advanced manufacturing technology. *Journal of Occupational Behavior,* **5,** 113−30.

Brousseau, K. (1983). Toward a dynamic model of job−person relationships: findings, research questions, and implications for work system design. *Academy of Management Review,* **8,** 33−45.

Butera, F., and Thurman, J. E. (eds) (1984). *Automation and Work Design.* Amsterdam: North Holland.

Bylinsky, G. (1983). The race to the automatic factory. *Fortune,* **107**(4), 52−64.

Cummings, T. (1978). Self-regulating work groups: a socio-technical synthesis. *Academy of Management Review,* **3,** 625−34.

Cummings, T., and Mohrman, S. L. (1987). Self-designing organizations. In W. Pasmore and R. Woodman (eds), *Research in Organization Development,* Vol. 1. New York: JAI Press (In press).

Cummings, T., and Srivastva, S. (1977). *Management of Work: A Socio-Technical Systems Approach.* San Diego: University Associates.

Gerwin, D. (1981). Control and evaluation in the innovation process: the case of flexible manufacturing systems. *IEEE Transactions on Engineering Management,* **EM-28,** 62−70.

Gerwin, D. (1982). Do's and don'ts of computerized manufacturing. *Harvard Business Review,* **60,** 107−16.

Gerwin, D., and Leung, T. K. (1980). The organizational impacts of flexible manufacturing systems: some initial findings. *Human Systems Management,* **1,** 237−46.

Gerwin, D., and Tarondeau, J. C. (1982). Case studies of computer integrated manufacturing systems: a view of uncertainty and innovation processes. *Journal of Operations Management*, **2**, 87−99.

Hackman, J. R., and Oldham, G. (1980). *Work Redesign*. Reading, MA: Addison-Wesley.

Hill, P. (1971). *Towards a New Philosophy of Management*. Epping: Gower Press.

Hubbard, R. (1985). The factory of the future. In *Seminar Notebook: Productivity Improvements; Maintenance; Repair Operations*. American Production and Inventory Control Society, Spring Seminar, 24−26 April, New Orleans, pp. 31−2.

Huse, E., and Cummings, T. (1985). *Organization Development and Change*, 3rd edn. St Paul: West Publishing.

Hutchinson, G. K. (1976). Production capacity: CAM vs. transfer line. *Industrial Engineering*, September, pp. 30−5.

Hyer, N. L. and Wemmerlov, U. (1984). Formation of group technology cells. In *Conference Proceedings, Synergy '84*, 13−15 November, Chicago, USA; and American Production and Invention, Control Society, Falls Church, Virginia, 22046, USA.

Kegg, R. L., and Carter, Charles F. Jr (1982). The batch manufacturing factory of the future. *Technical Paper MS82-952*, Society of Manufacturing Engineers, Dearborn, Michigan 48128, USA.

Kolpanen, E. A. (1984). The impact of robotics on job security and quality of working life. Unpublished masters paper, The Pennsylvania State University, College of Business Administration, University Park, PA, May.

Lawler, E. (1981). *Pay and Organization Development*. Reading, MA: Addison-Wesley.

Lawler, E., and Ledford, G. L. (1984). Skill based pay. Working paper, Center for Effective Organizations, University of Southern California.

Merchant, M. E. (1983). Production: a dynamic challenge. *IEEE Spectrum*, **20**, 36−9.

Noble, D. F. (1980). Social choice in machine design. In A Zimbalist (ed.), *Case Studies on the Labor Process*. New York: Monthly Review Press.

Petro, J. (1983). Management of computer-aided drafting technology: variables that affect system performance. Unpublished paper, Management Research Seminar, MA 690. Fairleigh Dickinson University, Madison, NJ.

Robot Institute of America (1980). Robotics today. *RIA News*, Spring.

Slocum, J., and Sims, H. (1983). A typology of technology and job design. *Human Relations*, **33**, 193−212.

Susman, G. (1970). The impact of automation on work group autonomy and task specialization. *Human Relations*, **23**, 567−77.

Susman, G. (1976). *Autonomy at Work*. New York: Praeger.

Susman, G., and Chase, R. (1986). A socio-technical analysis of the integrated factory. *Journal of Applied Behavioral Science*, **22**, 257−70.

Trist, E., Higgins, G., Murray, H., and Pollack, A. (1963). *Organizational Choice*. London: Tavistock.

US International Trade Commission (1983). Competitive position of U.S. producers of robotics in domestic and world markets. Publication 1475; December.

Usui, N. (1982). Untended machines build machines. *American Machinist*, June, pp. 142−43.

The Human Side of Advanced Manufacturing Technology
Edited by T. D. Wall, C. W. Clegg, and N. J. Kemp
© 1987 John Wiley & Sons Ltd.

CHAPTER 4

Selection and Training for Advanced Manufacturing Technology

SHEILA ROTHWELL

INTRODUCTION

Selection and training for advanced manufacturing technology (AMT) might be expected to have received particular attention from both researchers and practitioners. Yet this has not been the case, despite a widespread debate on the nature of skills required and the extent of deskilling taking place. However, the approach to and definition of skill in Britain generally explains some of the reasons for this 'low-key' approach to selection and training.

The chapter begins by attempting to define some of the major concepts of manpower policies, selection, and training as presented in the textbooks or as commonly understood in practice. This provides a yardstick against which the methods used by companies in the implementation of AMT can be evaluated and the reasons for the differences explored. Evidence of the application of selection and training techniques in organizations is then presented, followed by a discussion of possible alternative approaches that might have been adopted, and of the reasons for the inadequacies found.

A range of recently published research findings will be drawn upon, including the author's Henley research which consists of over 20 case studies on the application of computerized technology in a variety of industries, organizations, and processes. For the purposes of this discussion the material is drawn from the case studies in manufacturing industry, although comparisons are occasionally made with findings from studies in service industry.

The manufacturing applications in the Henley research included: the implementation of automated process control in the factory (mainly in production, assembly, and packaging sections); the introduction of quality and quantity control and testing equipment; automated warehousing; and various materials management systems. Some of these latter systems integrated stock control, production control (including raw materials and work in progress), and order processing systems. They thus had potential for integrating the manufacturing process in significantly new ways, linking warehouse, factory floor, clerical departments, and management offices.

Other major research studies to which reference will be made include that by Warner and his colleagues (Sorge *et al.*, 1983) into the application of CNC machinery; by Cross (1985) on maintenance engineering craftsmen in process industries; and Wilkinson (1983) on microelectronics innovation in batch engineering in the West Midlands. The chapter also draws on research published by various government bodies, such as the National Economic Development Office, Manpower Services Commission, and Department of Trade and Industry.

The concluding section will emphasize the complexity of the rationalities involved in the change process, and their implications for manpower policies.

CENTRAL CONCEPTS IN SELECTION AND TRAINING

Manpower policies

Ideally, every organization should have some overall concept of its 'employment policy' or 'human resource strategy' which stems from its overall business policy, has a long-term orientation and includes but goes beyond both an employee philosophy and a manpower plan (Rothwell, 1984a). It might be expected, therefore, that the techniques of selection and training applied in the introduction of advanced manufacturing technology would derive from such a context.

The essentials of manpower planning consist of the planning and implementation of adjustments to any actual or anticipated mismatch between supply and demand, in a way that is appropriate to the needs of the organization and the existing employees. A range of sophistication is possible, from complex statistical analyses to 'back of an envelope guesstimates'. Computerized data bases and computerized manpower models can aid and simplify the process considerably, especially in facilitating the exploration of alternative ways of achieving or meeting change, rather than the provision of idealistic blueprints for the future which tend to be abandoned at the first shift in reality. While a range of personnel policy instruments exists to adjust mismatches between supply and demand, selection and training techniques are probably the most obvious even if they cannot always be implemented rapidly enough to overcome the time lags inherent in any system which attempts to relate business planning and human resources. Yet unless they are utilized within some overall framework or idea of direction, they become mere 'ad hoc' and reactive responses to what may be assumed, rather than real, needs.

Selection techniques

What sort of selection techniques might be expected in terms of good employment practice? Occupational psychologists have established the basis for a scientific approach to selection (Ungerson, 1983) and many of the techniques used in industry have developed from these. Others, however, have grown up on a fairly 'ad hoc' basis and gradually become systematized, although they have not been subject to rigorous evaluations using reliability and validity studies which may take considerable periods of time. Inevitably, selection processes adopted for new technology are less likely to have met such requirements. Nevertheless, they may well be expected to conform to standards of 'good practice' as set out in personnel texts. These frequently follow the principles of Rodgers' seven-point plan, whereby consideration should be given to the candidates' physical characteristics, attainments, ability, aptitudes, interests, personality, and circumstances (Rodger, 1952). Moreover, the methods used should be technically sound, administratively convenient, and as fair as possible (Higham, 1983).

Preparation of the 'job' and 'person' specification is the initial and often the most difficult part of the whole process, and especially in relation to new technologies. It is, however, critical in understanding why the job exists, what needs to be done and in what way, and thus for deciding the requirements of the person needed to do it in order to meet the organization's needs. It is also likely to be used in the preparation of the recruitment advertisement (if any), as the criterion for other aspects of the selection process, and eventually even for performance monitoring, training, planning, and job evaluation purposes.

While the choice of selection method depends on the vacancy to be filled, the elements of studying the job and the applicants, comparing what each has to offer against the demands of the job, and subsequently following up the selection, are common to all methods (Higham, 1983). They may perhaps vary to a greater degree where selection involves 'transfer' from within, and entails redeployment, although similar principles should still apply.

The planning and administration of sound selection processes are generally assumed to be the responsibility of the personnel function, even if other managers play a part at various stages of the process, and may be the ultimate decision takers. The same is also generally true of training, though to a lesser extent, since training may be carried out by a greater variety of different persons both inside and outside the organization, even if nominally under the 'umbrella' of the personnel department's training plan.

Skills definition and training techniques

Training is defined in the Department of Employment's glossary of training terms as 'the development of the attitude/knowledge/skill/behaviour pattern required by an individual in order to perform adequately a given job'. Skills may also be defined in a variety of ways, to include both knowledge and attitudes, with cognitive and behavioural, as well as practical, dimensions (Knowles, 1973).

The most commonly assumed definition of skill (outside professional skills) is still that of ability to *do* things, rather than of understanding. This can create problems in training for new technology if workers are assumed to be trained once they have adequate keyboard skills, despite their lack of understanding of the system, or of ability to think through it and feel confident with it, which may take much longer to learn.

As Cockburn (1985) has shown, in work in the printing industry, skills may be seen as deriving from (a) the demands of the job, (b) the attributes of the person, or (c) the political system of the organization, whereby management or trade unions may establish that certain activities, or attitudes, or even sex, constitute skilled status, regardless of what the objective observer might assess.

Research has shown that the use of skill may also in practice be interpreted largely in terms of 'attitude and willingness', 'being the right sort of person', so that 'will do' attitudes are as important as 'can do' attributes (Oliver and Turton, 1982; Murray and Wickham, 1983). Elsewhere it may be a synonym for experience, or alternatively it may be largely a description of a pay grade.

Not only do definitions of skill tend to be blurred, but so do usages of and attitudes to the terms education, training, and development. Historically the emphasis in training in Britain has been on 'sitting next to Nellie', on learning by working alongside other skilled operators. The legacy of this imitative training stems from the attitudes and practices of the Industrial Revolution, when labour was regarded as being plentiful, cheap, and adaptable to the new machinery (Downs, 1983).

Modern training techniques probably originate in F. W. Taylor's rules of scientific management, which led to the development of work analysis and in turn to the concept of training needs analysis. Engineers and occupational psychologists have developed more advanced techniques for this, to identify the skills required, and to develop tests of employees' ability. Many aptitude and other diagnostic tests of types of manual dexterity or of spatial intelligence, available for selection purposes, are in this category. Trainability testing has also been developed for a few specific skills to test the likelihood of employees being able to benefit from certain types of training. More work is still needed, however, to develop different types of assessment approaches for information technology.

In practice, greater attention is generally given to the content and methods of training once it is found, or assumed, to be necessary. There is considerable variation between the emphasis given to, and the timing of, the inculcation of theoretical knowledge or the use of demonstration and of practical activity by trainees. Research has shown the importance of training design taking into account characteristics such as age, ethnic group, and educational level of trainees (Downs, 1983) in relation to both the content and methods.

The range of choice available in training techniques includes the media used for communication; the techniques used, such as case studies, role playing or experiential learning; the instructor's style, personality, and status; as well as the type of evaluation and testing techniques.

The internal or external locus and location of training are further critical dimensions which are beginning to change in response to demands for more training in new technology; while the timing and phasing of training is also critical in terms of the working career or the new task. Should training be all in one lump at the beginning, or modular? How long is it before the benefits wear off? More thought also needs to be given to the incentive and motivation to train, and whether there are tangible rewards likely in terms of higher earnings, or less tangible ones such as the higher status attributed to a skilled worker. Or is training seen as a threatening process in which ignorance and weakness are exposed?

The costs of training in terms of work and output forgone, as much as the training process itself, are the major reasons put forward by employers to explain their lack of training; although in practice it is often extremely difficult to find evidence of training costs now that statutory levy-grant or exemption systems have been abolished. The underlying attitude regarding training as a cost rather than an investment probably explains this, and also the approaches taken to it in the implementation of new technology.

THE APPLICATION OF SELECTION AND TRAINING TECHNIQUES TO THE INTRODUCTION OF ADVANCED MANUFACTURING TECHNOLOGIES

A major influence on the priority given to human resources in the implementation of advanced manufacturing technology is the business rationale for its introduction in the first place. Not that it is easy to distinguish between 'real' and 'given' reasons for the investment, or between the priorities of various competing interests. Nevertheless, where the main emphasis is explicitly on cutting costs and undercutting the competition, then there is likely to be greater impact on employee numbers and methods of utilization than one in which the prime aim is to 'meet the needs of the customer', 'extend the product range', and 'enter new markets' or 'improve quality of the product' (Cross, 1985). Whatever the primary aim, however, justification for the capital investment is often expressed in terms of head-count reduction, with payback in terms of lower labour costs and better utilization of resources, as well as higher output.

Even where advanced manufacturing technologies are introduced as part of a radical reorganization and restructuring of the business, our research at Henley found that decisions taken over whether to develop a greenfield site or an existing location, were influenced to some extent by employee relations issues. That is, the desire to leave behind old unco-operative attitudes took precedence over the concern to utilize existing skills.

Secondly, all aspects of the handling of the human side of manufacturing technology relate to the philosophy or culture of the organization; that is, the extent to which there is an explicit concern for employee development and welfare which is seen as integral to, rather than subordinate to, a concern with profit maximization and the bottom line. Otherwise, the search for the technological best within a narrowly defined cost-effective criterion is likely to result in the treatment of personnel as at best a second-order issue or even to overlook it entirely (Rothwell, 1984a).

Research approaches

The literature on the implementation of new technology ranges from the academic, which is largely aimed at testing or developing theoretical propositions relating to labour process (Wood, 1982), organizational decision making and trade union power, to the policy advisory reports often sponsored by governmental organizations (MSC, NEDO, DTI) or professional organizations (IPM, TUC). These are aimed at exploring innovation or analysing its impact, and generalizing from national or industry studies to generate good practice policy advice in areas of found need. In between are studies by academics and consultants drawing on both areas, and written from either a managerialist or a labour viewpoint. Perhaps the only generalization to be drawn from the field is the evidence of the *lack* of serious attention paid to human resources or infrastructure issues (Gerwin, 1984), at least until a very late stage, by most organizations. Evidence on what is happening in practice, therefore, can often only be deduced from certain empirical evidence, if it is not explicitly described.

Operators (semi-skilled)

An increase in automation has meant a sharp reduction in the number of unskilled (and semi-skilled) jobs in manufacturing industry. Nevertheless, many people are still employed in those areas which have not yet been automated or where the jobs are either not readily susceptible to it, or simply too low-paid for it to be worthwhile—for example, in packing, loading, and certain types of assembly. In a time of high unemployment there are few problems of recruitment, and the main selection criterion is the 'right attitude'. Younger and older women, and older men, are largely found in this low-level, routine, and physically demanding type of work.

Semi-skilled work is, however, an extremely broad category which in some cases has decreased and in some increased in status, with the selection of certain operators to work on the new automated lines and to undertake elements of craft work, through added responsibility for certain aspects of machine fault diagnosis and repair.

Our research found that, at a time of recession, recruitment was frozen in most firms, and it was only on green-field sites where external recruitment was necessary, and often deliberately chosen, for example at an automated warehouse for packet foods, and at a photoproducts manufacturer. In both cases, careful attention was said to have been given to planning for selection procedures. In the latter a proportion of existing employees chose to transfer from a sister factory but the majority were recruited locally, from a plentiful supply in an ex-mining area. In the former, recruitment was frozen by the Board, because of fears of trade union unrest over redundancies at another site; progress was also retarded by the fact that key staff of the consultancy agency retained to select and train left, leaving no-one else with an understanding of the new warehouse system. Thus, 6 weeks before commissioning was due, no staff other than four craftsmen had been recruited.

No women were selected in either of the above cases (partly through use of criteria such as shift-working or relevant experience), or in most other organizations, unless existing staff were being redeployed and retrained to do their old jobs in new ways. Even here, when some redundancies were needed, usually on a voluntary basis, it tended to be the women who were encouraged to leave, or were not replaced if they left.

Where existing operators were selected to work on the automated lines at a confectionery manufacturer, selection at first was largely left to the unions who opted for volunteers on a seniority basis. While some preferred to remain in their own jobs, in the (mistaken) belief that there was greater security there, those who transferred were mostly over 50 years of age and often reluctant to accept training. In the second phase of new technology, therefore, management was determined to retain greater control of the process, thus discussions did not take place until a few weeks prior to commissioning. The technical manager would have preferred the formalized establishment of qualification and ability levels, but the personnel director argued that this seemed inappropriate in view of the uncertainty over the precise qualities needed in such a new area, and the lack of any rigorous criteria at higher levels, such as for technicians or management! Good eyesight, the right attitude, and a willingness to accept training and complete it to a satisfactory standard, were chosen as the main criteria. A compromise between management preference for younger people and trade union preference for seniority was achieved in an agreement to accept volunteers who met the above requirements.

Most of the organizations we studied had ambitious intentions of training for information technology, although concepts of training ranged from propaganda, communications, and persuasion at the beginning in order to shape attitudes and encourage employees to look forward to change, to classroom lectures, and on-the-job practice at implementation. In practice, however, because of technical schedule slippages and management pressure to get systems up and running, training was often abandoned or crammed in at the last minute as part of the implementation process, adding to the stress of all involved, and to the delays in debugging. As one manager remarked, 'If you think education is costly, try ignorance!' Most managers, when asked what, with hindsight, they would have done differently or what they would do next time, usually remarked unhesitatingly 'more training, and allow more time for it'.

Other examples can be found in the literature; for example, the selection of operators for the Metro assembly line at the New West works at Longbridge (Winch, 1983), was from volunteers, from whom management selected the most 'suitable' (e.g. non-activists in the union), and from compulsory transfers from the old works (on the basis of seniority), which meant the younger and less experienced workers were transferred. The breakdown of work groups meant that training in new working practices was as significant as new working methods, and reflected management's concern to retain control, partly made feasible through the 'impersonal' technology itself but also through the shift in the balance of power within British Leyland at that time (Scarbrough and Moran, 1985).

This trial-and-error basis of selection procedure is now being superseded in some firms by more formalized testing procedures in abilities required, whilst other firms are using qualifications for screening purposes.

In a high-tech. Irish electronics factory (Murray and Wickham, 1983), selection for semi-skilled jobs was formalized with relatively high levels of school-leaving educational qualifications being demanded, although assembly jobs were designed to require as little skill as possible. The authors illustrate how access to jobs at Hi-tech was connected to the wider social structure through educational training requirements, and how upward mobility was blocked in the same way. Recruitment of assemblers (largely school-leavers, half of whom were female) was either through those who had completed a 6-week ANCO (Irish National Training Authority) course in electronic assembly, or through personal contacts, friends, and relatives already working in the factory. Murray and Wickham therefore illustrate the significance here of training as a mode of access to work, rather than as a provider of minimal skills needed at work.

The type and extent of selection and training, and of skill definition, often depends critically on the nature of the production process, the size of the plant, and the previous organization of work, as Sorge *et al.* (1983) found in their study of NC and CNC operations. In general, in small batch operations and in small plants, operators were able to take on operating, setting, and even programming activities, whereas in larger batch production and in larger plants these occupations remained the work of operators, craftsmen, and programmers respectively. As they show, the patterns chosen (not necessarily as a result of conscious management decision) also reflect national cultural traditions of work organization and assumptions about worker ability. For example, the British preferred occupational differentiation and hierarchy, compared with a more integrative skill approach in Germany.

Wilkinson's case studies (Wilkinson, 1983) similarly show a variety of approaches. At one company, operators were deliberately prevented from acquiring programming skills and discouraged from any 'twiddling' or use of the manual override; whereas at a factory making optical lenses, management saw and disliked the deskilling implications of the new technology and deliberately introduced a programme of job rotation and of training so that everyone could (and did) perform all the tasks in turn. These selection and training decisions tended to evolve *de facto* rather than through any conscious decision-making process, let alone any preliminary analysis of job needs and operators' skills. Even if they had, however, the results might not have been any different. Managerial values of control and efficiency are so intermixed in certain instances that it is likely that operator jobs would have been defined as 'routine operation of pre-programmed equipment' (and separate from programmers' functions) whether or not this was really likely to achieve lower costs or higher output. The lack of prior analysis and the gradual implementation meant that in practice operators often acquired or retained more skill and control than if management had taken a more analytical textbook approach.

Craftsmen

Most of the literature, both academic and policy-oriented, has concentrated on the effects of new manufacturing technology on craft skills (or vice-versa). In some cases it is not always clear whether skilled operator production or maintenance skills are under discussion, or what level of craftsman or technician is included. Another major confusion is that debate over changing the requirements of the traditional British apprenticeship system is taking place simultaneously with major changes in the nature of the work being done (Cross, 1985).

Thus, while the training emphasis has shifted from time served to standards reached, there is still some uncertainty as to the nature of the skills required: broad generalist, or highly task- and company-specific, or both? Consequently there is also uncertainty about the content, method, assessment, duration, and location of training; as well as about the occupational and pay structure required. Age is another controversial subject and despite lip service to, and some practical evidence of, retraining for older workers, entry to craft and technician level training and occupations is still largely restricted to 16-year-old school-leavers, to the exclusion of 18- or 20-year-olds, let alone of other adults.

In view of the great loss of jobs in manufacturing industry, it could be expected that there would not be a shortage of craft skills, but whether these are appropriate to the new technology is often doubted, and shortage of skills at these and higher levels is becoming an increasingly widely heard slogan in British industry. At one of the organizations in the Henley research, ex-RAF service craftsmen were deliberately recruited as being seen to be more likely to have relevant electronic skills than those who had left the engineering industry. They were in fact almost immediately promoted to supervisors at the new automated warehouse and given a large measure of responsibility for both selecting and training new staff.

The most detailed study of maintenance craftsmen in the process industries has been undertaken by Michael Cross (1985). He documents in detail the approaches taken by a large variety of different companies to select and train craftsmen and to reorganize working practices. Much of this was found to be on an ad hoc basis. However, companies also simply gave insufficient time and thought to planning or implementing their requirements; if they did so it was at such a late stage that delays were inevitable, and costs greater than anticipated.

In particular, Cross found among personnel and training functions a serious lack of hard information, or even the use of such information as they did have, to make any direct (and measured) 'assessment of the skill and knowledge needs of a particular job, and hence of the required education and training inputs' (Cross, 1985). Nevertheless, discussions revealed four major requirements which needed to be introduced into existing training arrangements:

1. An increase in the standard/competence of those being trained.
2. A broader base in the training with the aim of producing multi-role/multi-skilled craftsmen.

3. An increase in components aimed at developing an analytical ability and a capability for evaluating and using information.
4. Methods of developing a positive attitude/motivation.

Indeed, Cross states that there is a 'need for a broader based training for engineering craftsmen . . . which does not necessarily mean producing "jacks of all trades", but more people who have a wider appreciation and approach to the application of their skills and knowledge to a particular task' (Cross, 1985).

Changes in recruitment or in training practices were not seen as being necessary by at least half the companies. The other half saw the need for a more planned training structure and better adherence to it, and for the introduction of a broader multi-skilled base (to speed up fault diagnosis in plants and to increase the mobility of the student). 'Parrot-like' repetition of the argument that, to fault-find, craftsmen need to be electromechanically trained, seemed to Cross to be based on little real understanding and often led to neglect of, or obscured the real need for, multi-skilled, multi-role craftsmen in certain specific areas or circumstances.

Although intensive and extensive multi-skilled training might have appeared to meet companies' new needs, there was a fear of trade union problems. However, this was more often assumed than explored by the managers involved in many cases. In practice, a variety of methods of reorganizing work and achieving flexible teams was used, with varying measures of additional training in AMT. One working party in the food industry listed some of the likely pros and cons of the multi-skill approach for them, and concluded that full multi-skilling would be unnecessary, but that an extra skills approach would be more helpful (Cross, 1985). Cross-trading, dual trading, or just extra trading were examples of patterns found.

Until recently, 90 per cent of a craftsman's training has been undertaken during the apprenticeship period. Even if the content of that training is reorganized, it is likely that far more adult craft training will be needed in future. The recommendations of Cross, and others, all emphasize the need to: allow for a lengthy time scale of 3 − 5 years; assess a company's own job and task skill needs carefully; give attention to monetary rewards; assess and monitor craftsmen's current abilities and aptitudes; allow self-selection for, and open entry into, relevant training courses; start a training programme gradually, with pilot and testing exercises to allow adaptation to trainees' own comments; and develop multi-modular programmes of a few days each, which are in turn divisible into part or full shift sessions, to allow training to become a normal part of everyday working.

Decisions about sources of training and of training methods were not always based on adequate preliminary analysis in the companies studied by Cross, or in the Henley research. The gap between off-the-job, college-based courses (usually used at apprentice level) and in-company needs, was seen to be considerable; but little evidence was found of systematic attempts to improve the linkage. Preference was for in-company training, but management expertise was often found to be inadequate. Suppliers' courses were welcomed for adult retraining, but these were usually off-the-job and fairly superficial in the light of subsequent needs. On the other hand, reliance on suppliers to provide maintenance systems instead of acquiring or adapting internal skills, was usually found to be more expensive and time-consuming in the longer run.

Frequently, Henley researchers found that training through on-the-job problem solving was particularly valued, and much greater use than ever before was made of detailed training manuals, owned and updateable by trainees. Occasional use was made of videos, computer technology and interactive programmes and simulations to assist in fault diagnosis and to refresh memories.

Some companies were introducing more sophisticated testing procedures for evaluating achievement after training (especially where new pay and grading systems were involved), but otherwise the only innovation tended to be an improved system of maintaining individual training records and logging of skill acquisitions. At one plant this was kept as an open chart adjacent to the production line, detailing craft and operator training, for the information of supervisors and workers themselves.

Technicians

The dividing line between craft and technician skills has never been defined very precisely (Brady and Liff, 1983; Burgess, 1984) and is becoming increasingly difficult in practice in many industries, as tasks change and boundaries between them become blurred. Sorge, Warner and their colleagues, in their study of applications of CNC control, found that the tendency to use tradesmen or more skilled people as CNC operators is strongly linked with the integration of operating and machine-setting functions. Their study of the background, training, and qualifications of the workers involved, tended in Britain (where it was generally less formalized) to have meant that individuals were trained in either craftsmen or technician skills separately, whereas in Germany technician-level training (including planning, programming, etc.) followed after craft training and built on it.

The lack of career progression (and pay progression) systems for craftsmen, and to some extent for technicians, is one factor in the skills shortages found. The integrating potential of the technology, and the increased breadth and depth of the skills required, simply do not fit neatly into the traditional 'boxes' of most manufacturing companies.

The use of computer-aided design (CAD) methods has also been the subject of some research and policy studies (Arnold, 1983; Carnall and Medland, 1984; Burgess, 1984). There has been considerable comment on the deskilling nature of some of this, in the loss of design creativity (for design engineers as well), and the loss of drawing and detailing skills of draughtsmen and tracers as well as the reduction in numbers involved. In some cases trade union awareness of the implications has shaped management selection and training practices, in ensuring that all drawing office staff are trained in CAD use and that rotation is ensured in practice. Moreover, experience has shown that existing draughting skills remain the most essential requirement for efficient operation (Arnold, 1983; Brady and Liff, 1983). A NEDO report comments on the number of new skills which have to be learned by draughtsmen before CAD can be operated to utilize its full potential (NEDO, 1983).

Research by Carnall and Medland (1984) has shown that it is possible to devise systems and data bases that facilitate and support the creative work of draughtmen. These allow for similar 'controls' to those found in manual methods, but no more, and the roles of the designer/draughtsman and checker are deliberately retained. These systems also facilitate the training and learning process of people rather than deskilling them, even if the achievement of optimal solutions may take a little longer.

The shortage of technicians has been given new emphasis recently by various government reports (DTI, 1984; Burgess, 1984) identifying the usual reasons of cutbacks in training budgets and in recruitment, and the lack of 'update' training. As elsewhere, it is recognized that

> companies are reluctant to release key staff even for short courses because of skill shortages . . . especially for the smaller firms. Employers do not always recognise that better trained personnel are likely soon to repay the investment in their training. Even when they do, the cost pressures against releasing people for training may be difficult to resist (DTI, 1984).

Recommendations include the use of distance learning techniques, improving education/industry links, and in attempts to interest young women in such training. None of the research studies so far mentioned has found women trained or employed at this level in advanced manufacturing technologies, nor were they in a more specialized investigation (Cockburn, 1985) although a few have now been trained on special EITB schemes.

Supervisors

Many supervisors have risen to their present position through possession of craft or technician skills, although in some organizations this is becoming increasingly an entry-level, first-line management, graduate position. The implication of AMT for supervisory jobs is particularly serious since it means that they need either higher-level technological skills, or greater managerial skills, or both. Alternatively, the position may become superfluous and gradually disappear as many of the traditional jobs such as parts ordering, planning, co-ordinating, and general fixing skills are replaced by computer systems and incorporated in operators' tasks. Gerwin (1984) also found a dramatic loss of control by first-line supervisors to electronic maintenance people due to the technical complexity of flexible manufacturing lines.

Examples of all patterns of supervisory working arrangements were found in the Henley and other research studies. Sometimes there was a conscious managerial decision gradually to reduce the number of supervisors (and other indirects) and over time the implications for future selection and for new training programmes were realized and implemented, for example, in interpersonal skills and team-building 'hands-off' style at the photo-products factory. At a heavy engineering company a new training programme for supervisors was devised in advance of restructuring operators' roles (Rothwell, 1984b). In some instances supervisors were the first ones sent on suppliers' courses and played a large part in installation of the new equipment. In many instances foremen were given a computer or VDU in their office and expected to use it to co-ordinate materials management and diagnose inefficiencies. In some cases, however, supervisors were the last group to receive any training—only operators understood the new system. On the other hand, supervisors usually retained responsibility for maintaining output levels, and ensuring that corrective or alternative action was taken to avoid the worst effects of machine or system breakdowns. They thus acquired a measure of knowledge of the new technologies and retained their old fixing skills of making things work and acting as a lubricant between what managers or systems engineers thought would happen and what actually occurred on the shopfloor.

In Warner's CNC study (Sorge *et al.*, 1983) a variety of patterns was found; for example, at Brown's engineering factory the foreman remained largely a facilitator whereas his counterparts at the Braun factory in Germany were under greater pressure to help in technical setting and programme-changing problems. The background, training, and role of the German 'Meister' differs substantially from that of most English foremen in any case.

Wilkinson (1983) found in one case that foremen who had themselves been craft-trained tended to be most supportive of the retention of craft skills among machinists, and of their extension to include programming and editing, although the programmers' section leader naturally took the opposing view. In another case the control position of the foremen over the shopfloor was strengthened through the new shop scheduling system, under which they became responsible for completing variance codings on work tickets (eliminating progress chasers) but were themselves more closely controlled within the management hierarchy.

In many cases supervisors still retain a large measure of responsibility for on-the-job training of apprentices and craftsmen. Several of the criticisms and inadequacies found by Cross (1985) related to the lack of experience or ability of traditionally trained supervisors to provide the new technology skills that were needed. Moreover, where supervisors feel threatened or inadequate in coping with technological change, they are unlikely to perform the communicating and attitude change functions that higher management often expects of them, however much involvement they have in initial decision making about the new technology.

Where supervisors are expected to perform more managerial rather than shopfloor functions, then they need training in handling of data, completion of paperwork, and report writing. If they are given the cost control responsibilities they need training in analysing computer printouts, forward planning, and problem identification, to replace or augment their previous skills.

Computer specialists

The shortage of high-level computer staff is met by companies in much the same way as that of other professional engineers and scientists in short supply, for example, by recruitment or head-hunting practices. More use, however, is likely to be made of contract staff since the work is more likely to be of a project, one-off variety. Such contracts often range from 3 months to 3 years, and may be longer in some instances. Requirements for systems analysts and programmers are often similarly met since these are regarded as mobile, cosmopolitan rather than locally or company-oriented professionals. Yet the need for people with an understanding of the business is also critical, and the loss of key skills through staff leaving at a critical stage in a project is a problem with contractors as well as with in-house employees. The difficulty of paying sufficiently well to attract and retain such staff is largely met by creating separate pay structures and supplements and by increasing fringe benefits; for example, a company car at a job grade below that normally provided. 'Golden hello' techniques are reported as being increasingly common.

The need for frequent training and retraining is often regarded as self-evident at all levels and considerable use is made of suppliers' courses both for in-house and contract staff. Graduate recruitment techniques usually make use of computer aptitude tests, in addition to other procedures, and these are also used for selecting and training programmers at other entry levels. The occupation is often still regarded as requiring high-level educational qualifications despite evidence tending to cast doubt on this (NEDO, 1980).

In our research at Henley, hardly any instances were found of clerks from accounting departments, for example, being retrained as programmers, apart for a few in data preparation, although many of the skills needed can be readily acquired if systematically taught. In many service areas implementing a range of applications of information technology, managers have been surprised by the ease with which people (including older ones) appeared to acquire the new skills, although those unwilling, or unable, were probably self-selected out at an early stage. Skills related to VDU operation and data processing are mainly acquired on short courses of 1 – 6 weeks' duration.

Professional engineers and managers

Most of the studies of the skills needed and the means of recruiting and training professional engineers are of the policy study type in the context of national skill shortage evaluations. National statistics of the supply of professional engineers by specialism, and their inability to meet company demands (DTI, 1984), are often accompanied by details of steps being taken by companies to make good the short-fall, in addition to attempting to influence the government and universities to give higher priority to provision of such graduates. Company methods include: recruit-ment abroad; sponsoring university undergraduates; providing extra in-house training courses for existing engineers and technologists; and using sub-contractors and consultants. Studies by economists, however, query the reality of a shortage in view of the comparatively low rates of pay offered. Other studies suggest that the organiza-tion of work or the lack of a career structure may be more significant.

All the policy reports suggest that demand is likely to increase, and recommend that urgent efforts be made to increase supply through expansion of first degree provision; postgraduate (1 year) conversion courses; in-company training (including schemes in conjunction with educational institutes for both sponsored and unsponsored students); upgrading and updating of existing professionals (through such schemes as TOPS and MAP); and the use of distance or open learning techniques, including tutored video instruction techniques. Constraints are mainly seen to be in the areas of: finance; teaching staff; accommodation and equipment; and negative attitudes to returning to 'school'.

Many studies of skill shortage, both at higher and lower levels, however, have found that experience is often as important a selection requirement as qualification, in all except very large companies with developed internal labour markets. Here, too, those in the hi-tech industries which are particularly vulnerable to poaching and head-hunting by the smaller, rapidly growing companies who expect to buy expertise rather than train it, are also seeking experienced professionals and managers. The problem of poaching is cited by many companies as a reason for lack of training. Some consideration is currently being given to proposals to meet the costs of training by means of loans to the individual (by the company, or government) to counter this argument.

The experience that is valued is partly company-specific, but also includes experience in combining new and old skills. In particular, a new breed of electronic or quasi-systems manager is beginning to develop, and to be highly valued. This person generally has the combination of engineering, computing, and management skills which is critically needed by many companies.

More than any other single factor, lack of innovation, and slow or unsuccessful innovation is largely attributed, by a range of research studies, to management inadequacies in: strategic commitment, design, choice of equipment, training and preparation, implementation, and utilization. These originate from a lack of both technical and managerial expertise. This is compounded by an inability to overcome functional department and occupational differences, and to integrate the organization adequately to realize more of the advantages of the new technology. While engineers and managers cannot be trained for all possible future technologies, they can be trained to be better engineers and managers; to have an appropriate mix of engineering and management skills; and to have an understanding of the interrelationships between these skills. The more skilled they are, the smaller the problems of new technology adaptation. Management skills are needed in combination with engineering skills to assess not merely returns on investment at profit centres, but system costs and benefits (Arnold, 1983). Skills in the management of change, and especially of infrastructure issues, are particularly needed (Gerwin, 1984). This is illustrated by two quotes. First, 'Many companies were overly optimistic of the ease with which the "human" aspects of introducing new plant and equipment could be resolved' (Cross, 1985); and second, 'Planning, production and marketing, technical capability and industrial relations are amongst the managerial skills involved in the introduction of new technology. Planning, particularly manpower and training planning, becomes more important when the dimension of technological change is added to the others that management have to assess' (Brady and Liff, 1983).

ALTERNATIVE APPROACHES

Technology- or people-oriented?

Most of the research into the implementation of advanced manufacturing technology has found too little management awareness of the choices available over its organization and an assumption that technology dominates this process. This is partly explained by the lack of influence and credibility of personnel managers, but a few systems and engineering designers and specialists are also beginning to be aware that systems do not work unless people make them work, and that in the initial design stage it is possible to build in specifications about the degree of simplification or skill use required; the scope for interchangeability or specialization; and the need for a total or segmented system which allows for human adjustment and intervention at different levels.

Going beyond technical aspects to the whole management of change programme, one can see that the selection and training of the people involved is more likely to be effectively handled if it is planned within a comprehensive organizational manpower policy. Otherwise there is only a tinkering with existing numbers, or the skills of a small section, which encourages the 'jam tomorrow' philosophy, in which training is always something that should have been given more attention with hindsight, or would be in the future, but is only hastily touched on at the present time. Within a comprehensive policy: (a) redundancy can be reduced by more creative redeployment and retraining; (b) jobs and departments can be restructured and reintegrated more appropriately, together with pay and career systems; and (c) consultation and negotiation can take place over a longer period and on a broader front, including the exploration of alternatives, for example, by implementing a desirable end such as greater craft flexibility. The whole question of whether selection and training issues are proper subjects for management and union discussion is rarely made explicit in many organizations (Rush and Williams, 1984).

Analysis or assumption?

Even when focusing more narrowly on the selection area, there is theoretically a wide range of choices feasible (which could also meet other policy aims), but these are unlikely to be realized unless there is an objective analysis of job requirements and person specifications. Otherwise, assumptions that young (in their twenties), white, technically qualified males are the only desirable candidates become too readily accepted. Whether CNC programming, setting, and machining should be shared with shopfloor operators, craftsmen, or technicians also needs careful consideration by both management and unions, not only in terms of respective control and industrial relations issues, but also in terms of skill, trainability, costs, and other future implications. If objective aptitude tests can be devised, less reliance needs to be placed on the use of formal educational qualifications for screening purposes. The question can be posed: what elements of experience or attitude are really needed?

Deskilling or reskilling?

The question of whether jobs are being deskilled or reskilled by advanced manufacturing technology cannot be answered across the board; nor can easy decisions be reached within one company, or a particular section of it. In some cases both may be happening—for example, as people lose direct machining skills, but acquire CNC operating and programming skills. In other cases there may be a loss of 'vertical' skill— for example, electrical fault diagnostic skills become less significant, but mechanical fault finding and repair skills are acquired, so that 'horizontal' skills are increased; or electronic as well as electrical skills are acquired, but they are only utilized in one specialist department, instead of across the plant. While there are different implications for training in these different patterns, and whether it is block or modular, it is not clear that deskilling is necessarily involved. Acquisition of keyboard skills may be seen as adding to skills, by an objective measurement; however, it may be seen by workers as an aspect of deskilling if it is regarded as 'women's work'.

Many different patterns of combining the elements of training, skill, technology, and job design can be found according to particular circumstances, and thus the degree of determining influence of any one of them and its direction is also highly variable.

The range of choices available about training has similarly wide implications for the overall employment policy and the use of advanced manufacturing technology in an organization. But again these are rarely perceived if there is no attempt at an initial analysis of training needs, nor an exploration of the traditional assumptions of an older generation, for example, about apprenticeship, or the 'difficulty' of programming, or of conventional wisdom about the new skills required. Training issues also go back to job design and thus to technical design issues—for example, no one is interested in providing or doing high-quality training for low-quality jobs (Tipton, 1979). The whole pattern of the division of labour and whether jobs will be rotated may determine training patterns and vice versa, as was found in research work in an insurance company (Rothwell and Davidson, 1983), and in Wilkinson's study of an optical lenses factory (Wilkinson, 1983). New training may be needed for managers, and other levels, in skills that were previously learned through on-the-job career progression, but are now in the system and leave 'blanks' in understanding unless specifically taught to the new generation.

Discussion of alternatives and choices must necessarily depend in the last resort on whether a managerial or labour viewpoint is taken, and also on one's value system as to what extent these can ever be complementary or are inevitably contradictory.

Pay or promotion?

Value systems are prominent in discussions about pay systems and advanced manufacturing technology. The subject of pay has so far been largely avoided as not strictly speaking included (at least in personnel texts) under selection and training. Yet it may well be one of the most significant factors from the point of view of both managers and workers; particularly in manufacturing industry where definitions of skill and pay grade have become synonymous. Do new skills mean new pay levels?

Managers who are concerned to reduce labour costs, especially in the short run, are reluctant not only to spend time and money on extra job analysis and selection tests or comprehensive new training programmes, but also to specify higher level staff requirements or provide new training qualifications which might require higher pay. What is the point of training fork-lift truck operators or warehousemen to use a VDU if they can then claim the same pay grades as skilled operators, who may in turn claim craft or technician rates? What is the point of restricting CNC programming to technicians or planners if they have to be more highly paid than lower-grade operators? On the other hand, what will be operators' attitudes to training in and utilization of AMT if they see no reward or incentive in it? May there not be even less likelihood of co-operation by skilled workers who then find that their jobs have been deskilled by the new system and downgraded in pay as a result? (Gerwin, 1984, quotes American and British examples of dissatisfaction arising from lower rates paid to operators of the new machines).

Traditional incentive systems were found to inhibit change in some of the maintenance areas studied by Cross (1985); while Wilkinson (1983) found examples of traditional piecework payments resulting in higher earnings for operators than parts-programmers. Elsewhere, incentive systems which rewarded output often needed to be replaced by new ones (such as those based on utilization) appropriate to an automated system, but changes might rationally be resisted by workers on these grounds.

Our research found considerable management ambivalence on this issue. On the one hand there was resistance to payment for change or payment for training; on the other, a belief that it was fair for employees to obtain a share of the benefits of new involvement and higher productivity. Which view predominated related largely to the financial position of the company, and the economy; nevertheless, an increasing number of organizations were developing new lower-level pay grading systems which allowed for a measure of career progression and linked pay grade with skill level and training achievements.

The lack of costing of recruitment, training, and co-operation payments in initial investment proposals for AMT (which were usually justified by predicted savings in labour costs), often led to subsequent industrial relations problems for managers trapped in a 'Catch 22' position of facing demands for extra pay to operate new equipment purchased to reduce labour costs. Moreover, in office information systems (as one suspects in manufacturing), the costs saved by losing, say, 50 low-paid (often part-time) clerks from accounts was often counterbalanced by the cost of recruiting, in management services, ten computer programmers and analysts who were much more highly paid.

Selection decisions, such as the use of contract staff rather than recruiting regular employees, or hiring experience rather than providing training, were usually justified in terms of saving time in the short run and costs in the long run, although short-run costs, particularly rates of pay, were invariably higher, even if the work was of a temporary nature.

Personnel theories or market forces?

The shortage of higher-level (technician and above) skills is leading in practice to the major challenge to personnel theories of selection standards and to 'Seven Point Plan Man' (Brown, 1983), particularly in the petrochemical and engineering construction sectors. This is illustrated in the following quotes: 'Concepts such as the Seven Point Plan for interviewing may work in the static environments in which they were conceived, but they certainly don't in situations where 250 people are wanted next month, but it would be a help if you could get them next Tuesday'; and 'Selection becomes a matter not of careful sifting through the personality traits and home circumstances, but who you worked for last and did they like you, and how much experience of gas turbines you've got. Interviewing has a known conclusion about it a long while before you ever get there because you (more or less) know in advance if the man will *fit*.'

Thus, agents claiming to be able to shift any number of men on to a job at a moment's notice, and at a price, have come into being to service the market, and are booming. The rates paid to contract agency staff, or 'shortage' professionals recruited through them are, however, often more than twice those of similarly graded jobs elsewhere in the organization, which plays havoc with internal pay systems and relativities. Thus the increased 'casualization' of employment may in time decrease as companies find disadvantages in terms of both costs and unpredictability, while skilled workers seek security and career progression as well as high earnings.

CONCLUSIONS

There is considerable evidence of rapid change in labour markets, which is not only external, in the juxtaposition of high unemployment levels with high skill shortages, but also internal to organizations. This results from the interaction between the economy, the technology, and the pattern of decision making in the organization. Thus: (a) certain groups of low-skill workers become increasingly marginalized, either by being depleted in numbers or made readily interchangeable and substitutable through the skills being in the computer system; (b) higher-skill professionals become a mobile craft workforce, of high-fliers who move on where pay or greater interest is on offer, with little expectation or realization of career progression with a particular employer; and (c) a core of line managers, maintenance technicians, and skilled operators become essential to the development, implementation, and operation of the new technology mainstream of the business, but who may be selected, trained and managed in a variety of different ways, determined more by management policies (or their absence) than the technology alone (itself also a result of certain designs and managerial choices).

Moreover, the pattern of managerial decision-making is by no means a homogeneous and unilateral force. The priorities and preferences of the various functional managers in personnel, production, engineering, computing, finance, or marketing all have slightly different implications for selection and training decisions.

The interplay between various management preferences will also be shaped by trade union strengths and policies. These too are rarely homogeneous or unilateral, as evidenced between different unions, or even within the same union (for different groups of workers), or in relation to different issues. Thus, elements of Taylorism and traditional divisions of labour may be as likely to be supported by, as well as opposed by, unions and workers, in certain circumstances. Issues of job design or training may relate differently to pay priorities and to job control aims, and in turn shape responses to redundancy or recruitment. The introduction of advanced manufacturing technologies thus disturbs many traditional policies, and raises more contradictory issues than some have yet realized. Union aims may be positive, negative, or indirectly mediated, but nevertheless they have a significant impact. For example, positive trade union aims seek to increase job control, protect particular craft skills, protect and increase pay for job change, and protect job security. Negative trade union aims provide opposition to inter-craft flexibility or to the development of operator rather than programmer skills, to new pay systems, and to external recruitment or sub-contracting. Finally, indirect aims can be seen in management fears of trade union opposition which remain untested but shape action, and unforeseen or unintended consequences of new practices, combining with the representational or pay practices of different unions.

The outcome of this intra-organizational bargaining or dialectic of management control (Storey, 1985), may also be shaped by the style and philosophy of the organization as formulated by its founder, chairman, or managing director. It is perhaps significant that some of the 'high-tech.' computer companies are also those with the greatest emphasis on people in their company 'credo', even if the style varies considerably between them, and even if elements of Taylorism or Fordism as well as human relations, or human-centred (Smith, 1985) approaches might also be found in some of them.

Concepts of selection, training, skill, technology, and work design are all highly complex and multi-dimensional in themselves. They can be combined together in a variety of different ways, in which concepts of training or skill may have as much determining or driving force as technology. On the other hand, training may be seen only as a short-run intervening lubricant between the driving force of technology and its operation.

The major dynamic, however, is likely to be company philosophy and aims (at a particular point in time). This includes the reasons for the innovation, the critical cost factors, and the attitudes to human resources. Management (and trade union) strategies can shape the direction of change, even by default. If selection and training techniques are to make any positive contribution to the way in which advanced manufacturing technology is introduced and used, then positive strategic action by management and by unions is needed. Perhaps, however, reluctance to innovate or to depart from established procedures at a time of high uncertainty has a certain rationality for both interests. As one manager remarked, 'If I can get away with changing three things, rather than six, I'll do that, because people can't take too much change.'

REFERENCES

Arnold, A. (1983). Information technology as a technological fix: CAD in the UK. In G. Winch (ed.), *Information Technology in Manufacturing Processes*. London: Rossendale.

Brady, M., and Liff, S. (1983). *Monitoring New Technology and Employment*. Sheffield: Manpower Services Commission.

Braun, E., and Senker, P. (1982). *New Technology and Employment*. Sheffield: Manpower Services Commission.

Brown, T. (1983). Recruitment and recession in the process plants industry. *Personnel Executive*, February, pp. 38−41.

Burgess, C. J. (1984). *New Technology and the Demand for Skills*. Sheffield: Manpower Services Commission.

Carnall, C., and Medland, A. J. (1984). Computer-aided design: social and technical choices for development. In M. Warner (ed.), *Microprocessors, Manpower and Society*. Aldershot: Gower.

Cockburn, C. (1985). Women and technology. *W.E.A. Studies for Trade Unionists*, Vol. 11, No. 41, March.

Cross, M. (1985). *Towards the Flexible Craftsman*. London: Technical Change Centre.

Department of Trade and Industry (1984). *IT Skills Shortage Committee—First Report: The Human Factor—The Supply Side Problem; Second Report: Changing Technology— Changing Skills, Shortages at Technician Level*. London: Department of Trade and Industry.

Downs, S. (1983). Industrial training. In A. P. O. Williams (ed.), *Using Personnel Research*. Aldershot: Gower.

Gerwin, D. (1984). Innovation, microelectronics and manufacturing technology. In M. Warner (ed.), *Microprocessors, Manpower and Society*. Aldershot: Gower.

Higham, M. (1983). Choosing the method of recruitment. In B. Ungerson (ed.), *Recruitment Handbook*, 3rd edn. Aldershot: Gower.

Knowles, M. S. (1973). *The Adult Learner: A Neglected Species*. Houston: Gulf Publishing.

Murray, P., and Wickham, J. (1983). Technical training and technical knowledge in an Irish electronics factory. In G. Winch (ed.), *Information Technology in Manufacturing Processes*. London: Rossendale.

National Economic Development Office (1980). *Final Report of Manpower Committee of the Electronic Computers Sectoral Working Party on Computer Manpower in the 1980s. The Supply and Demand for Computer-related Manpower to 1985*. A report carried out by A. Anderson and A. Hersleb of the Institute of Manpower Studies on behalf of the Manpower Sub Committee. London: HMSO.

82   The Human Side of Advanced Manufacturing Technology

National Economic Development Office (1983). *Skills and Technology: The Framework for Change—Heavy Electrical Machinery*. Economic Development Committee. London: HMSO.

Oliver, J. M., and Turton, J. R. (1982). Is there a shortage of skilled labour? *British Journal of Industrial Relations*, **20**, 199−200.

Rodger, A. (1952). *The Seven Point Plan*. Paper No. 1. London: National Institute of Industrial Psychology.

Rothwell, S. G. (1984a). Company employment policies and new technology in manufacturing and service sectors. In M. Warner (ed.), *Microprocessors, Manpower and Society*. Aldershot: Gower.

Rothwell, S. G. (1984b). Supervisors and new technology. *Employment Gazette*. January, pp. 21−5.

Rothwell, S. G., and Davidson, D. (1983). Training and new technology. In G. Winch (ed.), *Information Technology in Manufacturing Processes*. London: Rossendale.

Rothwell, S. G., and Davidson, D. (1984). *Technological Change, Company Personnel Policies and Skill Deployment*, Sheffield: Manpower Services Commission.

Rush, H., and Williams, R. (1984). Consultation and change: new technology and manpower in the electronics industry. In M. Warner (ed.), *Microprocessors, Manpower and Society*. Aldershot: Gower.

Scarbrough, H., and Moran, P. (1985). How new technology won at Longbridge. *New Society*, 7 February, pp. 207−9.

Smith, C. (1985). Work organisation, gender and technical change in banking: the social limits of scientific management. Paper delivered at UMIST−Aston, Organisation and Control of the Labour Process, 3rd Annual Conference, April.

Sorge, A., Hartman, G., Warner, M., and Nicholas, I. (1983). *Microelectronics and Manpower in Manufacturing*. Aldershot: Gower.

Storey, J. (1985). Means of management control. *Sociology*, **19**, 193−208.

Tipton, B. (1979). The quality of training and the design of work. *Industrial Relations Journal*, **13**, 27−42.

Ungerson, B. (ed.) (1983). *Recruitment Handbook*, 3rd edn. Aldershot: Gower.

Warner, M. (ed.) (1984). *Microprocessors, Manpower and Society*. Aldershot: Gower.

Wilkinson, B. (1983). *Shopfloor Politics of New Technology*. London: Heinemann Educational.

Winch, G. (ed.) (1983). *Information Technology in Manufacturing Processes*. London: Rossendale.

Winch, G., Francis, A., Snell, M., and Willman, P. (1984). Industrial relations, new technology and the BL Metro. In M. Warner (ed.), *Microprocessors, Manpower and Society*. Aldershot: Gower.

Wood, S. (ed.) (1982). *The Degradation of Work*. London: Hutchinson.

CHAPTER 5

Control of Advanced Manufacturing Technology: Supervision Without Supervisors?

BERNARD BURNES AND MIKE FITTER

There is a popular view that new technology is creating a revolution in manufacturing organizations (Rumelt, 1981). If this is the case then the speed of changes taking place may prevent any effective planning, evaluation, and control of the change process. Also, if the 'revolution' is seen as essentially technological it is unlikely to be seen in terms of social consequences. Indeed, from the viewpoint of the individual organization, speed of adoption is crucial. Rapid changes may require the organization to 'flow with the tide'. However, if the process is 'evolutionary rather than revolutionary', as has been suggested (Bessant, 1983), and we will argue here, then it becomes possible for organizations to investigate the potential of AMT, and systematically plan and control the development process.

The evidence from manufacturing industries world-wide is that, despite well-publicized instances such as Fiat's 'Robogate system', the adoption of AMT is proceeding at a 'modest' pace (Attenborough, 1984; Beckler, 1982; Northcott and Rogers, 1984; Rempp, 1982). Indeed, even the American car giant, General Motors, which is spending billions of dollars to develop a fully computerized car plant, estimates that this will take another 10 years (Brody, 1985; NEDO, 1984a). This does not mean that where AMT is being introduced now, such as at British Leyland (Scarbrough, 1984), its impact is not dramatic. What it does mean, however, is that these cases are the exception rather than the rule.

It is easier to understand why this should be so if it is recognized that whilst we are dealing with a generic technology, the computer, it has a multitude of manifestations, each of which can have different implications, and throw up different problems, for organizations.

In manufacturing, it has been claimed (Hyer and Wemmerlov, 1984) that the ultimate aim is to computerize the entire manufacturing process from design to delivery. This has been called computer integrated manufacture (CIM), which incorporates many different forms of AMT: computer aided design; robots; automated storage and retrieval systems; flexible manufacturing systems; management information systems; and a host of other developments.

Given this array of different, though in theory compatible, systems it is hardly surprising that most companies choose to introduce one or two of the available technologies rather than contemplate introducing CIM in its entirety. Indeed, this piecemeal approach is perfectly understandable given that to most decision makers, new technology is exactly that—'new'. It is an unknown quantity which not only offers opportunities but also brings uncertainties. AMT is also costly; financing and justifying such changes, at a time when manufacturing industries have been experiencing their worst recession for 50 years, is not easy. Lastly there is the tendency, not just in Britain, for management at all levels to be cautious and conservative.

However, a relatively slower rate of adoption of microelectronics is not necessarily as bad as some people have suggested (Huhne, 1985; NEDO, 1984b), if the result is that organizations fully evaluate their needs and plan accordingly, and are thus able to use the technology in the most effective manner for them.

In this process of evaluating and planning there is a need for companies to take account of the effect of change on job numbers, job content, and organizational structures. They must also recognize that whilst they may be dealing with individual systems, the eventual objective is for these systems to be integrated into a unified whole. Therefore, planning must be long-term rather than short-term, and the implications of change have to be considered across the organization rather than limited to one department (Brady and Liff, 1983; NEDO, 1984a).

A crucial element in this is the future role to be played by line managers and supervisors in the management and control of the new production processes. The experience of job redesign studies has shown that these groups play a crucial role in any change process (Klein, 1984). Yet the tendency, in Britain at least, has been for the shopfloor jobs of operators and supervisors to become narrower, and for more and more of their traditional duties to be taken over by specialist groups (Child and Partridge, 1982).

If this trend were to continue with the introduction of AMT, then it could hinder introduction and reduce its benefits. Therefore the most meticulous planning is needed, and decision makers will have to decide, in most cases even in advance of actual systems design, how the system will be managed and controlled, and what the role of supervisors and line managers will be. This is because, as systems become larger and cover more areas, the technology can be more and more involved in co-ordinating and directing functions which were previously co-ordinated and directed by human beings. Therefore, the result can be that managers, and workers, find themselves 'computer controlled' rather than 'computer aided' (Bjorn-Andersen, 1983).

This may not be the case at the moment with all forms of AMT. Computer numerically controlled machine tools, for example, are primarily used as stand-alone systems. They need not be, and at the moment usually are not, linked to other machines or computers. Therefore, choices as to how the machines are used are not constrained by how such choices would affect other parts of the 'system'. Not only does this allow greater flexibility in the design of shopfloor jobs—including supervisors'—but it also allows modifications of the work organization to take place after the machines have been installed (Burnes, 1984).

However, with a multi-user system such as a computer aided process planning system, the situation is different. Decisions regarding whether or not its production schedules can be overridden manually, and by whom, have to be taken at the design stage. This can result in supervisors relinquishing the control they previously enjoyed with manual scheduling systems, or finding that every time they exercise discretion and alter a schedule, their superiors are automatically informed by the computer and they are called to account for their actions (Wilkinson, 1983). Consequently, whilst the supervisors' primary responsibility remains the achievement of output and quality targets, their discretion to cope with problems which threaten this can be severely constrained. Therefore, as systems get bigger and integrate more functions, so the impact they have on managers and workers at all levels of the organization can become more predetermined. The shape of the organization and individual responsibilities and skills can become pre-programmed and pre-ordained by those who have responsibility for determining the criteria for and design of the new systems. This could mean that it becomes harder for organizations to adapt to changing circumstances and to evolve over time.

Instead, it becomes the responsibility of senior managers to decide in advance whether to increase and centralize control or to decentralize decision-making. The result can be improved control for top managers, and worse jobs, with reduced ability to influence the quality and quantity of work, for line managers and supervisors; or alternatively control can be decentralized, and line managers and supervisors can gain an increased level of discretion over production.

Therefore, the choices that are made at the design stage are crucial as are the (often unquestioned) assumptions upon which they are based. A powerful example is the common belief amongst managers that tight control over workers equates with reduced uncertainty and higher output; yet this is by no means a proven fact (Blumberg and Gerwin, 1981; Child, 1984; Mumford, 1979, 1981; Burnes, 1985).

From this it becomes clear that in order to understand the management and control implications that arise from the introduction of new technology, it is necessary to examine both the management literature and the current experience of technology. This will be done in the next two sections of this chapter, focusing in particular on the impact of AMT on the supervision of the production process.

SUPERVISION OF THE PRODUCTION PROCESS

Supervision is widely regarded as a problem area in British industry, as it is in many other countries. Whilst there is agreement that the supervisor's role has changed over the years, there is less consensus on what it should be. Torrington and Chapman (1979), in a review of the literature on leadership in organizations, defined a supervisor as 'the first level of management, an organizational position involving direct supervision of workers. . . The occupants of these positions are usually expected to exercise leadership of others towards organizational goals.' Thurley and Hamblin (1962) saw the term 'supervisor' as referring to a common status and authority position in the management hierarchy which was separate from any particular work role content. They chose an operational definition as 'managers who spent over 10% of their time on the shopfloor', and who were concerned with shopfloor control within different production systems geared to most aspects of control.

Historically, supervisors played an important part in the control of production systems devised by Taylor (1903) through his principles of scientific management. The worker was assigned a daily quota of work by management, and to ensure it was performed, various 'functional foremen' would attend to aspects of his work.

> The emphasis on the payment system and a time-and-motion study as the fundamental tools of management in the pursuit of higher productivity, had now been thoroughly overhauled, and increased stress placed on the role of supervisor and assignment of work quotas, and organization more generally (Kelly, 1982, p. 11).

Thus the traditional role was one of 'man management' in order to ensure that production went according to plan. It was assumed that this direct control was necessary, and would normally be sufficient, to achieve the plan—provided, of course, that it had been derived from sound scientific principles. A popularly voiced criticism of supervisory styles assumes that the archetypal supervisor operates ineffectively in this tradition. More than 20 years ago, Thurley and Hamblin (1962) commented:

> It is very common to find critics of management organization and performance putting a lot of stress on inadequate supervisory control over shopfloor factors affecting production. Supervisors are said to be hostile to new techniques, new ideas, new specialists in management; to be prone to keep up operative jobs rather than sitting at a desk and planning; to be very unskilled in handling labour and particularly shop stewards; to be ignorant of techniques of programming production systematically, and so on (p. 1).

Perhaps as a result of this commonly held view of supervisory style, researchers have attempted to discover what characteristics, qualities, and skills a good supervisor requires. One particular focus has been on leadership ability, though Torrington and Chapman (1979) have concluded (p. 242) that there are no combinations of personal characteristics which accurately predict effectiveness of any individual in a particular leader role; that there is no general model of behaviour, or ideal style which will be consistently effective in a variety of situations; and that leadership involves a dynamic interaction between characteristics of the leaders, of the followers and of more general situational variables. They argue that leadership training needs to focus on the development of specific skills and abilities, among which the more important are: the ability to exhibit a wide range of behaviour patterns, coupled with the flexibility to deploy these alternatives in practice; an understanding of human behaviour in social context, together with an appreciation of possible consequences of one's own behaviour for others; diagnostic skills to identify the particular needs or demands of different interpersonal, group, or organizational situations in terms of appropriate behaviour; and general development of social skills needed for effective communication, interpersonal interaction, group activity, and social influence.

However, Torrington and Chapman recognize that effectiveness may also be influenced by lack of other skills and abilities in technical and other non-leadership functions of the particular role. Thurley and Hamblin (1962) saw these 'non-human relations' skills as particularly concerned with technological and organizational variables. From the results of five case studies focusing on the supervisor's role in production control they concluded that the main role of 'supervisory systems' is to deal with breakdowns and alterations in production planning rather than, as F. W. Taylor believed, ensuring that the shopfloor operators complied with management's plan. Therefore, Thurley and Hamblin saw supervisors intervening and making decisions only when it was no longer possible for operators to do so. Breakdowns required the calling of maintenance engineers, and if lengthy, the redeployment of labour. Shortages of materials needed chasing, and if possible this was done in anticipation of a shortage to prevent a stoppage. Generally, a major part of the job involved keeping track of everything going on, and to act as part of a trouble-shooting team. Thus supervisors formed the key component in a supervisory control system which smoothed out variations in the production process and attempted to present to higher management the appearance of a trouble-free system.

In a recent major review of supervisors' roles, Child and Partridge (1982) found that whilst supervisors had, in the main, a high degree of responsibility within the confines of their department or section, they had severely limited discretion in carrying out those responsibilities. This resulted both in their being frustrated with their inability to control situations for which they were responsible, and in the workers below them, and managers above them, having an unrealistically high expectation of what supervisors could achieve.

This led Child and Partridge to put forward four alternative models of how supervisors' jobs could develop. The first is that their role could be abolished altogether, and the responsibility for routine supervisory tasks be delegated to semi-autonomous work groups. The second alternative would be to clarify and generally tidy up the existing role of supervisors. This would reduce the extent and scope of supervisors' responsibilities to a level compatible with the discretion they were permitted. The third model for the supervisors' job would, in contrast, adjust their level of discretion upwards so as to be compatible with their level of responsibility. The fourth alternative sees supervisors developing a more specialist role related to the technical problems that arise. Within this narrow field of responsibilities, the supervisor would enjoy considerable discretion.

However, in examining the present and future role of supervisors, Child and Partridge did not, as such, examine how AMT would affect them, though they did acknowledge that technology played an important role in shaping the environment in which supervisors operated. To redress the balance, this will now be examined.

THE EFFECT OF ADVANCED MANUFACTURING TECHNOLOGY ON SUPERVISORS

This section will review the literature on AMT and its effects on organizational structure and individual jobs, especially those of supervisory staff. It will conclude by arguing that senior managers and systems designers can exercise a high degree of choice as to what these effects will be.

It should be pointed out that it is difficult to examine the effects of AMT on line managers and supervisors in isolation from their effects on others in the organization. Indeed, it is important that their roles and the effects of technical change are seen in the context of the whole organization. Only in this way is it possible to show that change which brings benefits for one group of employees, or the achievement of particular organizational objectives, can bring disbenefits for other employees or other objectives (Buchanan and Boddy, 1983; Perrow, 1983; Winch, 1983). In this respect a parallel can be drawn with job redesign, which seeks to increase workers' satisfaction by changing their job content. In such cases it is not unknown for shopfloor workers' jobs to be improved by transferring functions from supervisors or line managers, whose jobs may thereby be made worse, or in some cases disappear altogether (Burnes, 1985; Child, 1984). Thus the benefits of change may not be distributed evenly across the organization.

In examining the literature it becomes clear that technical change can affect groups of workers in three main ways. The first is by changing the structure of the organization: it may become larger or smaller; more centralized or less centralized; flatter or more hierarchical. These changes in turn will affect the power structure of the organization and the amount of autonomy and discretion that individuals and groups of workers can exercise. The second way that change can affect workers is by altering the actual functions they perform: on the one hand, they could acquire new skills or be given additional duties; on the other hand, they could find their existing skills no longer necessary and their functions and responsibilities much reduced. The third way is by reducing or increasing the need for particular types of workers—in this instance, supervisors. Therefore, in looking at the literature on the effects of AMT, special attention will be paid to these areas.

The impact of AMT on organizational structure

There appears to be little disagreement in the literature on new technology that its introduction will lead to organizational change. Rothwell (1984) has argued that it affects the total management system. Ahlin and Svensson (1980) have observed that it will lead to organizational change affecting all workers. The disagreement in the literature is not, then, about whether change will take place, but about the nature of that change.

At the risk of over-simplifying what is a very complex and confused picture, there seem to be two distinct views on what changes will take place. The first is that the introduction of microelectronics will lead to greater centralization of control—that is, more rigid bureaucratic structures with less discretion for those at the lower end of the organization. The second view is the reverse of the first: that computerization will aid decentralization and delegation of authority.

More centralization of control

Bjorn-Andersen (1983) has argued that the introduction of computers leads to substantial power changes within organizations. He believes that computers will come to co-ordinate functions that were previously co-ordinated by supervisory staff, and that this will lead to greater centralization of decision-making by fewer people. This point has also been made by Hennestad (1982), who points out that computers can be used to allow senior managers to centralize and control production to such an extent that the need for supervisory staff and line managers is much reduced. He has also argued that computerization leads to greater formalization of practices and procedures, which results in more rigid and centralized organizations and a reduction in individual autonomy.

Brady and Liff (1983) concluded from an examination of manufacturing companies that the introduction of computerized equipment onto the shopfloor resulted in the transference of decision-making farther up the organizational hierarchy. Blumberg and Gerwin (1981) have made similar comments about the introduction of new technology. Wieser (1981), in a five-plant Austrian study, noted that the introduction of computers leads to a reduction in workers' discretion at the lower levels of the organization. Indeed, Perrow (1983) also noted that there is a tendency for senior managers to use their influence over developments to introduce new technology in such a way that it bolsters and extends their power.

Less centralization of control

Earlier studies (Withington, 1969; Blau *et al.*, 1976), have suggested that computers will lead to the decentralization of decision-making. Klatzky (1970) also noted that computers could allow the delegation of authority to take place. Land, Dettejaruwat, and Smith (1983) believe that up to the 1970s it was the case that computers led to the centralization of control in electronic data processing (EDP) departments. However, they point out that the advent of microcomputers has led to a reversal of this trend. Lucas (1984) denies that there was ever a tendency towards the centralization of control in EDP departments.

Walton (1982) is another who has pointed out that the cheapness and flexibility of microelectronic equipment will lead to the decentralization of power within organizations. Both Sell (1984) and White (1983) believe that new technology will lead to flatter organizational structures which they and others (Child, 1984) equate with more participative types of organization.

The impact of AMT on job content

Writers have used a wide range of terms in describing the effects of microelectronics on jobs: skill, control, variety, boredom, monotony, division of labour, responsibility, etc. However, in the main these terms tend to be subsumed under the general heading of skill. Increased variety, responsibility, and control for the individual are seen as increasing his or her skill and creating a better job. On the other hand, fragmenting the job, increasing boredom, and reducing control are seen as reducing skill and thus creating a worse job for the individual. Using the concept of skill, it is possible to separate the writers on new technology into two groups: those who see new technology as deskilling, and those who see it as enhancing skill.

Deskilling

It should be said that no writer has suggested that everybody will be deskilled by new technology. In the main, proponents of deskilling effects adhere to Braverman's (1974) polarization thesis. He argued that microelectronics would lead to the majority of the workforce being deskilled whilst a few, at the top end of the organizational hierarchy, would be highly skilled and highly rewarded. They would have the responsibility and discretion necessary to control the work of the majority.

In reviewing the literature, there is much evidence to support this view. In Sweden, Ahlin and Svensson (1980) surveyed sixteen engineering companies which had introduced new technology. They found that this led to a worsening of shopfloor jobs including those of supervisory staff; there was an increase in job fragmentation, shift work and the use of unskilled labour. Artandi (1982), in America, found that the introduction of computers onto the shopfloor turned skilled workers into 'button-pushers'. She also found that computers tended to mystify the production process and increase organizations' reliance on technical specialists. Blumberg and Gerwin (1981), using American case studies, came to similar conclusions. In addition, they found not only that the introduction of computers removed shopfloor workers' decision-making skills and put decisions into the hands of a few experts, but that this led to inefficient production methods which would not have been the case if skilled workers had been able to exercise control. Dostal (1982) has observed that new technology is leading to skill polarization in West German manufacturing industry.

Cooley (1983), in Britain, has pointed out that deskilling is not isolated to the shopfloor. Such developments as computer aided design can, he believes, result in the deskilling of draughtsmen and designers. Wynn and Otway (1982) concluded from their research that even middle management were not immune. They found that computer systems that were supposed to aid them actually resulted in their being deskilled and alienated.

Enhancing skills

The viewpoint that new technology will maintain and increase skill is put forward by a wide range of writers from different countries. Aguren *et al.* (1984) examined the Volvo car plant at Kalmar in Sweden and found that new technology had improved shopfloor jobs but reduced the need for supervisors. Forslin, Soderlund and Zackrisson (1979), also in Sweden, came to a similar conclusion when examining another large engineering company. Lay and Rempp (1981) concluded that in West Germany the introduction of computer numerically controlled (CNC) machine tools tended to maintain and upgrade shopfloor skill, including that of supervisory staff.

Hyer and Wemmerlov (1984), surveying the American engineering scene, found that new technology offered opportunities to create better jobs for those at the lower levels of organizations. Cross (1983), in Britain, noted that microelectronics required shopfloor workers to develop new and wider skills. Ouellette *et al.* (1983) have observed that shopfloor automation can cut out boring, monotonous, and dangerous jobs. From a trade union perspective, a Labour Research Department (1982) survey found no evidence for deskilling with new technology; instead, they found it tended to bring increased responsibility for workers.

The effects of AMT on the demand for supervisors

As the above indicates, the evidence currently available regarding the effects of AMT on the demand for supervisors is somewhat contradictory. There are indications that, at least in some situations, the new manufacturing technology leads to a reduction in the need for supervisors. But there is also evidence that increased demands are placed on the supervisor as a result of technological change. These opposing viewpoints will now be examined.

Reducing the need for supervisors

The first, and most obvious, point is that advanced manufacturing technology typically requires less shopfloor operators. For example, the introduction of CNC machine tools can more than halve the number required. Flexible manufacturing systems carry this even further (Shaiken, 1979). Therefore, as the number of shopfloor workers decreases so does the number of supervisors required to oversee them.

Secondly, the past 15 years have seen the development of semi-autonomous work groups (Wall *et al.*, 1984). The principle underlying these groups is similar to Child and Partridge's (1982) first model for supervisors, which is that operators, by forming into a team, take responsibility for the production process they are directly involved in and deal with problems as they arise without need for a supervisor. This would include regulating the pace of production, liaising directly with maintenance engineers over breakdowns, etc., and handling their own material needs. Clegg and Fitter (1978), in a study examining the changing requirements for information systems when semi-autonomous work groups are developed, reported that supervisory posts were eliminated as a direct result of such developments. Such developments have in the past been neither widespread nor without problems. However, Cummings and Blumberg (see Chapter 3) argue that the higher levels of technical interdependence and uncertainty resulting from the development and use of AMT should lead to more semi-autonomous work groups.

The third factor is a direct consequence of the thinking that underlies the design of the new systems. The information and control system is typically as much as possible pre-planned by systems engineering specialists. The design takes place away from the shopfloor and when implemented is intended to operate according to plan with only minimal need for shopfloor decision making. This of course follows directly the tradition of scientific management which, as argued earlier, failed in its original aim to predetermine how all functions would be performed, and therefore necessitated giving supervisors their important 'regulatory' role. The difference now is that AMT, combined with the more sophisticated techniques of systems analysis, allows these long-desired objectives to be actually achieved, or so it is believed. Levie and Williams (1983) see these developments as reducing the opportunities for trade unions to re-establish their labour rights as they have traditionally done following the introduction of new work systems and tooling changes. They see this as a reduced opportunity for 'clawback' because 'both the game and pitch are changing. Components of existing trade union power, such as control over skills, experience, and basic work organization could turn out to be based on quicksand.' For the same reasons there may be less need for the supervisor to intervene in the production process.

The final factor which can lead to a reduced role for supervisors emerges directly from the previous one. The adoption of new technology reinforces the existing trend towards the increased involvement of more specialist management functions which to some extent usurp the traditional supervisory functions (Rothwell, 1984). For example, the introduction of a CNC machine tool can increase the amount of time that a production engineer spends dealing with problems on the shopfloor and can by-pass the role of the supervisor.

> The supervisors' skills of fixing and by-passing the formal system through a mixture of experience, cunning, personal contacts and trading favours or indulgences, could appear to count for nought overnight. Even more straight-forward expertise in planning and scheduling work, acquired through years of experience, could now be available to anyone who could operate the system (Rothwell, 1984, p. 377).

Increasing the need for supervisors

Most of the above outcomes are based on the assumption that the application of the technology is completely successful in achieving the objectives of pre-planned control. However, this objective has rarely been fully achieved in the past, and it may continue to elude systems designers, at least in some situations. There are several reasons why this may be the case.

Firstly, flexibility of production can be an important aim which it is difficult, impossible, or too expensive to build into a predetermined, automated production process. Even with the technical sophistication of a flexible manufacturing system steered by an 'intelligent' control system, it may not be feasible to anticipate all possible contingencies that need to be taken into account when the design parameters are determined.

Secondly, the production process itself can be too complex and costly, and its reliability too critical, to rely on total automation. Blumberg and Gerwin (1981) argue that performance pressures and loss of control will undoubtedly be intensified for the supervisors of computer integrated manufacturing systems. Capital cost considerations are greater, causing utilization to be more critical, and problems with machine reliability hamper the achievement of utilization objectives. These authors conclude:

> Control problems arise out of a CIM's complexity, especially the tight interconnections among sub-systems. Automating one aspect such as material handling leads to difficulties with another aspect such as quality control. To solve these problems it is often necessary to increase the amount of human intervention thus partially reversing the trend towards automation (p. 20).

The complexity appears to arise, in particular, in systems that integrate functions across the manufacturing process. And it is precisely these systems that are difficult to control at operator level. Job redesign initiatives, which have eliminated some supervisory roles, are located *within* the boundaries of the work group's system. Integration of functions requires a perspective and a decision horizon which crosses functional boundaries, but which nevertheless still requires the moment-to-moment interventions usually associated with shopfloor supervision. Thus the third reason is that 'supervisory control' of an integrated manufacturing system can be the most effective way of controlling a complex process. For supervisory control to be effective it must be possible for the supervisor to monitor the automated process and augment or overrule it when necessary. Thus supervisory control is being exercised 'on top of' the automated process, rather than as an alternative to it. However, to be effective the supervisor must be able to understand the mechanisms of the automated process, and thus a high degree of communication between the automated system and the supervisor will be essential. This may also mean the supervisor using information received from operators or by direct observation of the process, rather than relying on information from the console of the computer control system. Frequently, 'informal' sources of information, which are impossible to automate, can be vital for an appropriate intervention (Fitter and Sime, 1980).

It may be that future integrated manufacturing systems will be of such complexity that, for supervisory control to be effective across a network of functions, a *team* of supervisors will need to co-ordinate production.

An example of the importance of supervisory control can be found in a leading British garment manufacturing company which uses some of the most sophisticated production technology in the UK. Their new computerized production control system allows planners at head office to keep track of production at the outlying factories. Supervisors can also monitor the work of individual machinists through terminals on the shopfloor. Although the associated technology is designed to deskill shopfloor operators, the control system is designed to enhance the supervisors' scope for decision making. When production is halted, for example due to a machine breakdown or material shortage, the supervisor can immediately switch the operators affected to another work area where there is a labour shortage. To aid this decision, the computer contains a 'skills inventory' of each individual operator so that the supervisor can maximize the effectiveness of the transfer. The technology, of course, also enables head office to monitor the effectiveness of supervisors in dealing with problems and maximizing machine utilization. Thus this system, although Tayloristic in concept, also depends on the skills of the supervisors to maintain an effective production process.

The case for choice

As can be seen, there is much evidence to show that AMT has a particular impact; however, this evidence is contradictory. It shows that AMT can, and does, lead to more centralization of control and also to less centralization of control; to more skilled jobs and to less skilled jobs; to a greater demand for supervisors and to less demand for them.

A way of resolving these conflicting conclusions has been put forward by Wall *et al.* (1984), who argue that, within limits, there are choices in how technology is used, and also by Rosenbrock (1981), who points out that choices also exist as to how technology is designed. The results of these choices, depending on how choice is exercised, can be to create good, bad, or indifferent jobs.

Other writers have also supported the argument that choice exists in these areas. Mumford (1979) has pointed out that, in practice, new technology is flexible and can be used in a variety of ways. Kemp, Clegg, and Wall (1984) have observed that microelectronics offers a wide range of choice in how it can be used, and that it would be misguided to adopt a deterministic view of its effects. Sorge *et al.* (1983) have reported that a variety of organizational arrangements can and do accompany the introduction of the same technology. Wilkinson (1983) has concluded that there is no general impact of new technology, and that its effects will vary from organization to organization, depending on their particular circumstances.

This argument, particularly as put forward by Perrow (1983) and Noble (1979), is that decisions made by senior managers and systems analysts, when specifying and designing AMT, can substantially determine the shape of the organization, and the form of the individual jobs that result from the change of technology. Therefore, depending on the choices taken, some systems will be designed to produce one effect, for example a greater need for skilled supervisors, and other systems will be designed to have the opposite effect.

In the case of AMT it would appear that organizations, and those within them, can and do, either consciously or unconsciously, exercise some control over how AMT will affect them.

CONCLUSIONS

There is no general agreement on how the supervisor's role will develop in future, or on the impact that AMT will have on supervisory functions. However, it is clear that the traditional leadership role of supervisors as being 'man-managers', overseeing shopfloor performance, has substantially changed and will continue to change. Whereas there can still be an important motivational element in the role—by encouraging better performance or making sanctions against poor behaviour—there is a transition towards dealing with 'system' problems. These are not necessarily a consequence of operator behaviour but can be a result of equipment failure, or the breakdown of a production plan due to lack of suitable raw materials, etc. This shift in emphasis, and increased need for trouble-shooting, is a consequence of the increased complexity of the technology used in the production process and the increased interdependence of component stages. The striving for greater efficiency has led to tighter coupling between stages, and reduced stock levels for raw and intermediate materials. Thus there has been an increased need for 'supervisory control', i.e. the monitoring of activities against a plan and interventions to make the appropriate regulatory actions when necessary.

From the supervisor's point of view, a rather fundamental question is how much of this 'supervisory control', if any, will be carried out by human beings and how much by sophisticated, microelectronics-based systems. To methods and systems engineers, brought up in the tradition of scientific management, the goal is to eliminate the need for human intervention in the production process, but this rarely seems to succeed if the system is complex and operated without slack. In many situations, as has been illustrated, the attempt to eliminate the need for human supervision is dysfunctional to management's objectives. The 'informal' supervisory practices that took place previously are an important part of the process of maintaining an effective production system.

However, the increased ability to monitor performance allows management to assess supervisors' interventions. This can make supervisors wary of taking any 'risks' in the exercising of their discretion, which can lead to cautious and sub-optimal decisions. Because of their relatively low status, supervisors can be reluctant to take responsibility for overriding the system, even when it would be desirable (Fitter and Sime, 1980).

Continuing ambiguity and uncertainty regarding the supervisor's role is obviously dysfunctional. However, it is not clear that organizations which are introducing AMT are either aware of, or prepared to tackle, this problem. Nevertheless, if they don't, the result will be that much of the benefits of AMT, in terms of increased productivity and quality, will be lost. Therefore, in the absence of any concrete proof that the supervisor's job can be automated, the alternative should be promoted. The supervisor's role should be enhanced to encompass the skills needed to use information and control systems as *aids* to human decision making, particularly for co-ordinating production across functional boundaries. Supervisors will also need interpersonal skills, not so much of the traditional 'carrot and stick' motivational character, but for negotiating rapid access to the support services vital to the maintenance of the production process.

One final point which should be made is that there is nothing inherently deterministic in the way that AMT will affect supervisory functions—managers and designers do have choice as to the type of systems which are produced. However, unless these choices are made in the conscious knowledge of what their impact will be, the final outcome will be unlikely to meet either the objectives of the organization or the aspirations of those who work in it.

REFERENCES

ACARD (1980). *Technological Change: Threats and Opportunities for the UK*. London: HMSO.

Aguren, S., Bredbaka, C., Hansson, R., Ihregren, K., and Karlson, K. G. (1984). *Volvo/Kalmar Revisited: Ten Years of Experience*. Sweden: DCS.

Ahlin, J. E., and Svensson, L. J. P. (1980). New technology in mechanical engineering industry: how can workers gain control? *Economic and Industrial Democracy*, 1, 487−521.

Artandi, S. (1982). Computers and the post-industrial society: symbiosis or information tyranny? *Journal of the American Society for Information Science*, 33(5), 302−7.

Attenborough, N. G. (1984). *Employment and Technical Change: The Case of Micro-Electronic Based Production Technologies in UK Manufacturing Industry*. Working Paper 74, Government Economic Service. London: DTI.

Beckler, D. Z. (1982). The electronic revolution in the workplace. *OECD Observer*, March 1985, pp. 16−22.

Bessant, J. (1983). Management and manufacturing innovation: the case of information technology. In G. Winch (ed.), *Information Technology in Manufacturing Processes*. London: Rossendale.

Bjorn-Andersen, N. (1983). Information technology and power change in organizations— prospects of technology agreements and technology assessments. In K. Grewlich and E. H. Pedersen (eds), *Power and Participation in an Information Society*. Brussels: EEC.

Blau, P. M., McHugh, F., McKinley, W., and Phillips, K. T. (1976). Technology and organization in manufacture. *Administrative Science Quarterly*, 21, 21−40.

Blumberg, M., and Gerwin, D. (1981). *Coping with Advanced Manufacturing Technology*. Discussion Paper 81-12. Berlin: International Institute of Management.

Brady, T., and Liff, S. (1983). *Monitoring New Technology and Employment*. Sheffield: MSC.

Braverman, H. (1974). *Labor and Monopoly Capital*. New York: Monthly Review Press.

Brody, M. (1985). Can GM manage it all? *Fortune*, 8 July, pp. 14−20.

Buchanan, D. A., and Boddy, D. (1983). *Organisations in the Computer Age*. Aldershot: Gower.

Burnes, B. (1984). Factors affecting the introduction and use of computer numerically controlled machine tools. In T. Lupton (ed.), *Proceedings of the First International Conference on Human Factors in Manufacturing*. Bedford: IFS.

Burnes, B. (1985). The impact of new technology on job design and work organization. Unpublished PhD thesis, Sheffield University.

Child, J. (1984). *Organisation*. London: Harper & Row.

Child, J., and Partridge, B. (1982). *Lost Managers: Supervisors in Industry and Society*. Cambridge: Cambridge University Press.

Clegg, C. W., and Fitter, M. J. (1978). Information systems: the Achilles heel of job redesign? *Personnel Review*, **7**, 5−11.

Cooley, M. J. (1983). *The New Technology—Social Impacts and Human-Centred Alternatives*. Technology Policy Group, Occasional Paper 4. Milton Keynes: Open University.

Cross, M. (1983). *Changing Requirements for Craftsmen in Process Industries*. Stage 1, Interim Report (April). London: Technical Change Centre.

Dostal, W. C. (1982). *The Introduction of NC/CNC Machine Tools and Employment*. Nuremberg: IAB.

Fitter, M. J., and Sime, M. (1980). Creating responsive computers: responsibility and shared decision-making. In H. Smith and T. R. G. Green (eds), *Human Interaction with Computers*. London: Academic Press.

Forslin, J., Soderlund, J., and Zackrisson, B. (1979). Automation and work organization in a Swedish experience. In J. Forslin, A. Sarapata, and A. M. Whitehill (eds), *Automation and Industrial Workers*, Volume 1, Part 1. Oxford: Pergamon Press.

Hennestad, B. J. (1982). *Computer Technology, Work Organisation and Industrial Democracy*. Working Paper WP82/1. Beddestua, Norway: Norwegian School of Management.

Hyer, N. L. and Wemmerlov, U. (1984). Group Technology and Productivity. *Harvard Business Review*, **62**, 140−149.

Huhne, C. (1985). British investment alarm. *Guardian*, 21 January.

Jenkins, C., and Sherman, B. (1979). *The Collapse of Work*. London: Methuen.

Kelly, J. E. (1982). *Scientific Management, Job Redesign and Work Performance*. London: Academic Press.

Kemp, N. J., Clegg, C. W., and Wall, T. D. (1984). Human Aspects of CAM. Paper presented to IEE International Conference on Computer-Aided Engineering, University of Warwick, 10−12 December.

Klatzky, S. R. (1970). Automation, size and locus of decision-making: the cascade effect. *Journal of Business*, **43**, 141−51.

Klein, J. A. (1984). Why supervisors resist employee involvement. *Harvard Business Review*, **62**, 87−95.

Labour Research Department (1982). *Bargaining Report 22: Survey of New Technology*. London: LRD.

Land, F., Dettejaruwat, N., and Smith, C. (1983). Factors affecting social control: the reasons and values—Part 1. *Systems, Objectives, Solutions*, **3**, 155−64.

Lay, G., and Rempp, H. (1981). CNC-technik verandert NC—organization. *VDI Nachrichten*, **11**, 8−9.

Levie, H., and Williams, R. (1983). User involvement and industrial democracy: problems and strategies in Britain. In IFIP WG91 Conference Proceedings, *Systems Design: For, By and With the Users*. Amsterdam: North Holland.

Lucas, H. C. (1984). Organisational power and the information services department. *Communications of the ACM*, **27**(1), 58−65.

Lynch, B. (1982). *IT: An Introductory Bibliography*. Marketing Communication Group. London: Mullard.

Metalworking Production (1983). *The Fifth Survey of Machine Tools and Production Equipment in Britain*. London: Morgan-Grampian.

Mumford, E. (1979). The design of work: new approaches and new needs. In J. E. Rijnsdorp (ed.), *Case Studies in Automation Related to the Humanisation of Work*. Oxford: Pergamon.

Mumford, E. (1981). *Values, Technology and Work*. London: Martinus Nijhoff.

NEDO (1984a). *New Technology: Manpower Aspects of the Management of Change*. London: NEDO.

NEDO (1984b). *Crises Facing UK Information Technology*. London: NEDO.

Noble, D. F. (1979). Social choice in machine design: the case of automatically controlled machine tools. In Z. Zimbalist (ed.), *Case Studies in the Labor Process*. New York: Monthly Review Press.

Northcott, J., and Rogers, P. (1984). *Microelectronics in British Industry: The Pattern of Change*. London: PSI.

Ouellette, R. P., Mangold, E. C., Thomas, L. W., and Cheremisinoff, P. N. (1983). *Automation Impacts on Industry*. Ann Arbor: Michigan Institute for Social Research.

Perrow, C. (1983). The organizational context of human factors engineering. *Administrative Science Quarterly*, **24**, 570−81.

Rathenau Commission (1980). *Societal Consequences of Microelectronics*. The Hague: State Publishing House.

Rempp, H. (1982). The economic and social effects of the introduction of CNC machine tools and flexible manufacturing systems. In L. Bekemans (ed.), *European Employment and Technical Change*. Maastrict: European Centre for Work and Society.

Rosenbrock, H. H. (1981). *Engineers and the Work People Do*. London: Work Research Unit.

Rothwell, S. (1984). Supervisors and new technology. *Employment Gazette*, January, pp. 21−4.

Rumelt, P. (1981). The Electronic Reorganization of Industry. Paper presented to the Strategic Management Society, London, October.

Scarbrough, H. (1984). Maintenance work and new technology: the case of Longbridge. *Industrial Relations Journal*, **15**(4), 9−16.

Sell, R. (1984). New technology and the effects on jobs. In H. W. Hendrick and O. Brown (eds), *Human Factors in Organisational Design and Management*. London: Elsevier.

Shaiken, H. (1979). *The Impact of New Technology on Employees and Their Organisations*. Berlin: Wissenschaftszentrum.

Sorge, A., Hartmann, G., Warner, M., and Nicholas, I. (1983). *Microelectronics and Manpower in Manufacturing*. Aldershot: Gower.

Taylor, F. W. (1903). Shop management. In F. W. Taylor (ed.), *Scientific Management*. New York (1947 edition): Harper & Row.

Thurley, K. E., and Hamblin, A. C. (1962). The supervisor's role in production control. *International Journal of Production Research*, **1**, 1−12.

Torrington, D., and Chapman, J. (1979). *Personnel Management*. London: Prentice-Hall.

Wall, T. D. (1985). Information technology and shopfloor jobs: opportunities and challenges for psychologists. *Occupational Psychology Section Newsletter*, **19**, 3−10.

Wall, T. D., Burnes, B., Clegg, C. W., and Kemp, N. J. (1984). New technology, old jobs. *Work and People*, **10**(2), 15−21.

Walton, R. E. (1982). New perspectives on the world of work: social choice in the development of advanced information technology. *Human Relations*, **35**(12), 1073−84.

White, G. C. (1983). Technological change and the content of jobs. *Employment Gazette*, August, pp. 329−34.

Wieser, G. (1981). Automation and industrial workers—the Austrian national report. In J. Forslin, A. Sarapata and A. M. Whitehill (eds), *Automation and Industrial Workers*, Volume 1, Part 1. Oxford: Pergamon Press.

Wilkinson, B. (1983). *The Shopfloor Politics of New Technology*. London: Heinemann.

Winch, G. (ed.) (1983). *Information Technology in Manufacturing Processes*. London: Rossendale.

Withington, F. G. (1969). Data processing's evolving place in the organization. *Datamation*, June, pp. 58–69.

Wynn, B., and Otway, H. J. (1982). Information technology, power and managers. In N. Bjorn-Andersen, M. Earl, O. Holst, and E. Mumford (eds), *Information Society: For Richer, For Poorer*. Amsterdam: North Holland.

The Human Side of Advanced Manufacturing Technology
Edited by T. D. Wall, C. W. Clegg, and N. J. Kemp
© 1987 John Wiley & Sons Ltd.

CHAPTER 6

Organizational Design for Advanced Manufacturing Technology

JOHN CHILD

From the late 1970s concern grew that British industry was adopting new technologies at a slower rate than its major competitors. This led to the establishment of various government support schemes, and to the official designation of 1982 as Information Technology Year. British manufacturing industry still lags behind some countries in its use of certain forms of advanced manufacturing technology, such as Japan and Sweden in the number of robots per 10 000 production workers (British Robot Association, 1985). However, its general rate of adoption compares reasonably well with that of, say, France and West Germany (Northcott et al., 1985). The present cause for concern is rather that British industry is failing to make good use of the advanced manufacturing technology it has acquired, whether because companies have not worked out a strategy for innovation (MORI, 1984), lack the relevant technical skills (DTI, 1984, 1985; MSC, 1984) or are reluctant to tackle the required changes in work organization (NEDO, 1985a).

It is now being emphasized that attention has to be given to problems arising in the implementation of advanced manufacturing technology, of which failure to adopt an appropriate organization structure may be one (NEDO, 1985b; Voss, 1985). The significance of organization in this context is enhanced by the changing perspective on advanced technology and the nature of its contribution. This has developed from a limited focus on improving the productivity of specific operations to the concept of a computer integration of production systems as a whole, thus rendering them more responsive to changing competitive requirements. The integrative concept cuts across existing lines of task and functional specialization, and so speaks for corresponding changes in organization. On these grounds, fresh cause for concern is given by evidence that established organizational structures show considerable persistence in the face of changing conditions, and that opportunities to redesign jobs and structures are frequently passed over (Hedberg, 1979; Pettigrew, 1985). Strassman (1985), for instance, concludes that the failure of companies to reorganize their archaic structures when investing in new computer-based systems has been the chief cause of poor returns from that investment.

The relationship between organization structure and operations technology, and whether there are particular matchings of the two which enhance performance, has been the subject of a long-standing debate. Its outcome is unfortunately far from clear, largely due to theoretical and methodological shortcomings which need to be avoided when now considering organization in relation to advanced manufacturing technology. The debate itself began with Joan Woodward's pioneering research.

Woodward (1965) concluded from a comparative investigation of 100 English manufacturing firms that 'there was a particular form of organization most appropriate to each technical situation' and 'a link between technology, organization and success' (p. 72). She drew attention to the practical significance of this finding which would 'make it possible to plan organizational change simultaneously with technical change' (*ibid.*). The relationships mapped out by her comparative research, and by the further investigations it would stimulate, promised to furnish guidelines from which it would be possible to specify the appropriate organizational design for a new manufacturing technology.

This promise was not fulfilled. Although Woodward's work did stimulate a number of subsequent studies into organization and technology, with one exception consistent reliable findings did not emerge. The exception concerned the relation between level of automation or capital intensity and certain employment ratios. Donaldson (1976) reviewed studies which had addressed Woodward's main concern, the relation between manufacturing technology and management organization, and he had to conclude that 'the plainest way of interpreting the current evidence is that it disconfirms core aspects of the original Woodward thesis' (p. 273). At the same time, various sociotechnical system studies (e.g. Trist *et al.*, 1963), and initiatives inspired by quality of working life considerations (e.g. Davis and Cherns, 1975), had suggested that more than one form of work organization could be an economically viable accompaniment to a given technology. It therefore appeared that the significance of matching a particular form of organization to the technical situation had been considerably overstated.

It remains evident, nonetheless, that there must be a degree of interdependence between the technology applied to a work process and the way that same process is organized in terms of manning, operating procedures, and information processing. It is therefore difficult to accept that the mutual arrangement of organizational and technological design will be of little or no consequence for performance, although this does not rule out the possibility that there may be a range of different viable configurations. Moreover, some critics of previous research into organization and technology have ascribed its lack of conclusive findings more to methodological shortcomings than to any intrinsic qualities of the relationship.

Rousseau (1979), for example, criticized the way that the concept of technology had been inconsistently operationalized. Davis and Taylor (1976) were equally critical of the loose use of terms such as 'automation' and 'mechanization'. Reimann and Inzerilli (1979) ascribed the lack of consistent findings on the organization – technology relationship to a diversity of conceptual and operational definition, including a confusion between the 'macro' view of technology as pertaining to the total production system of a plant or firm and the 'micro' view referring to specific equipment or processes. These authors concluded that:

> upon closer examination of the various studies, it becomes readily apparent that the lack of consistent findings is not so much an indictment against technological determinism [of organization] per se as against the profusion of theoretical models and methodologies employed by researchers in this field (pp. 187 – 8).

The absence of a well-developed theory of organizational design and technology remains a problem, although some foundations have been laid. What these indicate is that the issue must be placed within the context of the strategic contingencies to which *both* organization and technology have ultimately to be addressed for survival under competitive conditions, and that this focus is theoretically more adequate than one that bears narrowly on organization and technology in isolation. It has also become clear that the structuring of organization is liable to be conditioned by the specific contingencies, traditions and internal political forces pertaining to individual firms. Moreover, the technology has to be defined precisely. Just as 'automation' has been used in an indiscriminate manner to cover a range of quite disparate technologies and production systems, so there is an equal danger of this happening with the blanket term 'advanced manufacturing technology'. The problem is increased by the incorporation in new computer-based technologies of software which permits a range of equipment uses. The identification of technologies has therefore to be made with even more careful reference to their applications than to their intrinsic physical hardware characteristics.

With these points in mind, this chapter begins by summarizing the distinctive characteristics of the technologies normally included under the generic heading of 'advanced manufacturing technology' (AMT). This leads to the question of their significance for strategic manufacturing objectives, and hence to the related strategic contribution of organizational design. Specific organizational design possibilities are then discussed in relation to AMT within this perspective, and note taken finally of major problems. Since this subject has not yet been well informed by research, there will necessarily be a speculative character about most of the conclusions drawn. They amount to possibilities as much as probabilities.

ADVANCED MANUFACTURING TECHNOLOGY

A number of specific technologies are usually included within the definition of advanced manufacturing technology (AMT). These are:

1. Robotics and programmed manipulation.
2. Numerically controlled (NC) machines which can be controlled by tape, or in more modern installations controlled and reprogrammed via a built-in computer (CNC), or via the linkage of several machines to a central mini-computer (direct numerical control: DNC).
3. Computer-aided design (CAD) linked increasingly to computer-aided manufacture (CAM) of which NC machine tools are a major constituent. The term CAM is sometimes extended to cover other computer assistance in manufacturing in a way that approaches the concept of CIM (see 5 below).
4. Flexible manufacturing systems (FMS).
5. Computer-integrated manufacture (CIM), which denotes an overall and systematic computer control and integration of the manufacturing process.

In addition, automated handling, storage, and warehousing, together with automatic in-process guaging, inspection, and quality assurance procedures, are often associated with the above technologies and generally form part of the concept of advanced manufacturing technology. The rapid growth expected in investment in all these technologies is indicated by a recent estimate that world-wide sales of AMT could reach an annual rate of £25 billion by 1990 (Townsend, 1985).

The intrinsic features of these advanced manufacturing technologies were described in Chapter 1, and there is no need to retread the same ground here. It is, however, important to note the general thrust of their development and likely speed of their dissemination. In a nutshell, their development is moving towards the incorporation of greater power and intelligence into computer control, towards increases in the programmable flexibility of the equipment, and towards its integration with technologies supporting other activities within the overall production system. Speed of dissemination is expected to be rapid, despite attendant problems.

For example, in the area of robotics a considerable amount of research is being undertaken into the development of robot sensors and 'intelligence' in the form of rudimentary reasoning powers. Some machines already have the capacity to 'recognize' different items and can therefore offer a degree of flexible response. Other robots can now be reprogrammed rapidly to permit the manufacture or handling of different batches of items (Wild, 1985). These developments in robotics hold out the prospect of removing the need for manual assistance to CNC machines working on non-standard workpieces. Up to now, workpieces of widely differing sizes and shapes have had to be changed and clamped manually, particularly for turning operations. Equipment manufacturers are now working on methods of automating this process, including the use of robots.

The present frontier in computer machining control is represented by attempts to link CNC machining centres in two ways. First, to bring together a number of such machines under the combined control of one central computer (DNC) which would permit the more ready reprogramming of work. The second is to build physical links between the machining centres by means of a pallet transporter or other suitable devices. This combination of greater flexibility of programming with integration of workflow constitutes the move towards the FMS concept. According to Voss (1984, p. 3):

> A flexible manufacturing system can be defined as a computer-controlled configuration of semi-independent work stations connected by automated material handling and machine loading. They are designed to efficiently manufacture more than one kind of part at low to medium volumes. A true FMS is considered to have the ability to schedule parts in random order.

In CAD/CAM technology, the specification of engineering details for products and components via CAD forms the basis for the direct link to computer-aided manufacture (CAM). A number of possible developments follow from the fact that the item of work or part is now completely defined geometrically, and each of these offers the potential for integration. For instance, when data on materials density are added and more software provided, volumes and weights become available for bill of materials purposes. The same data can be used to generate specifications for moulds, dies, tools, and cutting instructions for CNC machines. Similarly, the computer can devise programmes for controlling robots. While in theory each of these tasks once integrated informationally through precise product specifications could be undertaken in separate locations with co-ordination no longer dependent on close organizational linkages, the weight of informed opinion stresses that in practice considerable additional benefits of mutual learning, time-saving, and economy arise when organizational roles are integrated in a complementary manner.

The combination of CAD/CAM, generating precise specifications and programmes, with factory automation based on robotics, automated materials handling, transfer equipment, and so on, under the umbrella of computer-integrated information and control systems, provides the model for the 'factory of the future' (Voss, 1984). This is the computer-integrated manufacturing (CIM) system envisaged by Diebold (1952) in his pioneering book, *Automation*. In CIM,

> the database is available to all the computer-assisted manufacturing 'islands' that are emerging in design, engineering, robotic and other handling systems, flexible machining, flexible assembly and product test. They will all 'talk' to each other to make products in a harmonized and integrated fashion (Charlish, 1985, p. 18).

CIM remains a futuristic concept and companies are still in the learning stages with the more advanced uses of CAD and with FMS. Wild (1985) found in his study of European manufacturing plants that few claimed to use CAM, and fewer still had integrated CAD/CAM systems even in limited areas of application. Although their numbers are now growing rapidly, Bessant (1985) reports that the present level of FMS systems worldwide is perhaps only 150−200.

The direction of development in advanced manufacturing technology is nevertheless clearly discernible even though many of its facets remain experimental and carry a significant risk of failure (Cane, 1985). Computer-based technological advance in this area is seen to meet a number of strategic business requirements, and for this reason its dissemination is expected to be rapid. For example, worldwide sales of robotic equipment have been predicted to grow at around 30 per cent each year (subject to some fluctuation with business conditions) between 1984 and 1990 (Marsh, 1984). It has also been calculated that the CAD/CAM market is growing at over 40 per cent a year with the mechanical engineering industry being the largest purchaser of CAD, followed by aerospace, defence, and vehicle design (Charlish, 1985).

The development of AMT is therefore proceeding towards the integrated manufacturing system. The main vehicle of this development is computer integration, complemented by the continued extension of automation. The concept of an integrated manufacturing system is not a new one, and recent technological advances have been along a path clearly envisaged by John Diebold over 30 years ago. It is worth reminding ourselves of Diebold's concept because it amounted more to a model of organization for the manufacturing system than to the representation of a technology.

The sub-title of Diebold's book (1952) on *Automation* was 'the Advent of the Automatic Factory'. In looking forward to that prospect, Diebold emphasized that he did not have primarily in mind the capabilities of automatic machines, nor their computer processors, but something much more systemic. The significance of automation for Diebold lay in a reconceptualization of the organization of production as a whole. This included the design of products to suit the new manufacturing technologies with advantage to cost and quality, and it extended to the management process as well. His concept of automation was that of the integrated system which drew together (1) the design of products and processes, (2) the physical production process and its control, and (3) the automatic gathering of management information directly from the production process. Diebold identified as objectives for this philosophy of automation both the *integration* of complementary functions and the development of *flexible* handling and control processes (1952, pp. 66−7). He thus foreshadowed the two key attributes of modern AMT which render it such a powerful facilitator of the innovatory manufacturing strategies described in the next section.

There are several necessary philosophical and organizational conditions for the reconceptualization of production along these lines. First, it requires analysis of the entire production processes so that each operation can contribute more effectively to the goals of the whole system. This was recognized by Buckingham (1961) in another influential text on automation, and it is reflected today in the advice given in a recent report by Ingersoll Engineers (1985), who are leading consultants on AMT:

> This report advocates that integrated manufacturing is approached, not as a combination of existing or known technologies and equipment that must be linked together, but rather from first principles, by examining all aspects of a total business—its future, markets, people, manufacturing and products—and combining them in a new way to meet long-term business objectives (p. 121).

Second, this approach requires the acquisition by management of control over the production process in order to achieve the integration and flexibility required.

Apart from the industrial relations issues that may arise in the achievement of this control, it presents a challenge to organizational design as well. The need to bring the whole manufacturing process under control was stressed as a precondition for success in introducing FMS by Peter Dempsey of Ingersoll Engineers in a 1983 paper (Charlish, 1983). A third condition, also expressed in the quotation above, is that AMT should be envisaged not merely as integrated within itself but with other business processes such as marketing, design engineering, accounting, and finance. The argument is that advanced technology and organizational structure should both be constituted so as to facilitate the co-ordinated and controlled pursuit of strategic objectives. This returns us to the point that the system-building potential of AMT is considerably more significant than are the qualities of its physical hardware. It is at this level that organizational and technological design can combine to meet the requirements presented by a firm's strategic contingencies.

STRATEGIC CONTINGENCIES FOR ADVANCED MANUFACTURING TECHNOLOGY AND ORGANIZATIONAL DESIGN

There are two levels of strategic contingency relevant to the choice of AMT and the design of manufacturing organization. The first is macroeconomic and affects most industries in common; the second is specific to particular enterprises. The common contingencies arise from the slowing of economic growth, the intensification of international competition, and the rapidity of technical and other change. The specific contingencies relate to the particular positioning of an enterprise in the market, as well as its configuration of inherited characteristics including its scale, available competences and skills, traditional modes of operating and organizing, and internal power structure.

General strategic contingencies

The general macroeconomic trend generates pressures on enterprises to safeguard their competitive positions and to seek new avenues for growth. Some may decide to stay within mass markets and to compete on the basis of their experience with relatively dedicated mass production technology, but now seeking to improve design-for-manufacture through CAD and also to reduce production, inventory, and other costs with computer control. It is argued, however, that homogeneous mass markets are receding for firms in the older industrial economies because of competition from newly industrialized countries combined with demands for product differentiation and for the incorporation into products of the latest technical advances (Sabel, 1982; Piore and Sabel, 1984). An alternative strategic response, Piore and Sabel suggest, is that of 'flexible specialization', which is based on flexible multi-use equipment, skilled adaptable workers, and competition through innovation. This strategy offers the prospect of being able to absorb market uncertainties through a flexible response and of specializing in high added-value products. Piore and Sabel take the view that networks of small firms and community co-operatives are better adapted than large corporations to pursue this strategy. Judkins and West (1984) of Rank Xerox have accounted for that large corporation's development of flexible 'networking' sub-contractual arrangements in terms of 'the new form of competition that we are facing'. They continue: 'The essence of modern business is change and speed of change and the flexibility to handle that change. The product life cycle, certainly in our business, and no doubt in many other company's businesses, is shortening with every product we launch' (p. 13). Judkins and West draw the conclusion that these changed competitive conditions render obsolete the familiar rigid organization based on hierarchy, a marked division of labour and stable employment. In regard to the latter, Atkinson (1984) associates the emergent 'flexible firm' with new 'manpower strategies which are predicated on the achievement of flexibility both in the level of employment and the deployment of the workforce' (p. 1).

The significant point is that the new strategic competitive contingencies are encouraging adaptive developments not just in manufacturing technology but also in the other components to the production system including its organization and the deployment of manpower. It would therefore be misleading to adopt a narrow view of 'organizational design for advanced manufacturing technology' if this were taken to imply that AMT was the sole point of reference for such design. In fact, the guiding principle lies in the integration of both technological and organizational design to suit strategic requirements, and in so doing to organize in a way that helps to break down barriers of perspective and discourse between those responsible for strategic, technological, and work organizational policies within the enterprise, as well as between the people who contribute to different stages of the production cycle itself.

AMT plays a key role in the new manufacturing strategies both in improved computer integration and control for dedicated production systems, and in supporting the more flexible systems which are growing in importance (and on which we shall therefore concentrate). Sorge *et al.* (1983) note that the 'logic of CNC application . . . extends from macro-economic factors, marketing strategies, through equipment choice and justification, to production engineering and organization, training and personnel policy' (p. 153). The flexible manufacturing strategy includes a capacity to innovate to meet new demands and raise product sophistication, the consequent offering of more product variants, and an ability to produce economically in smaller batches. In regard to innovation and sophistication, CNC machines can readily accept new designs and can perform a level of complex and precise machining not possible with conventional equipment. This facility was an important motivation for the original US military sponsorship of NC development (Noble, 1984). The program-mability and potential for computer integration of CNC machines can also cope better with throughput variety, and helps to reduce the cost of batch changes.

Apart from any productivity benefits which AMT can offer through substitution for direct labour, the non-labour productivity benefits claimed for it are generally consistent with the strategy of flexible response. These include (Voss, 1984):

1. reduced design to production lead times, especially via CAD and CAD/CAM;
2. reduced manufacturing lead times, especially via CAM, FMS, and computer process control;
3. reduction in inventory and work-in-progress, through CAM, FMS, and robotics;
4. better design and engineering analysis, through CAD and CAD/CAM;
5. assurance of quality and consistency, which is assisted by all types of AMT;
6. increased responsiveness and flexibility of production, via the reprogrammability of AMT and the possibility of an integrated data base which it offers.

The ability of computer-controlled AMT systems to process complex data rapidly, and to adjust equipment settings accordingly, gives rise to the so-called economies of scope, whereby a greater variety of specifications can now be produced at the same cost or a given variety produced at lower cost. AMT also has the potential to support a 'just-in-time' (JIT) production system, manufacturing items when required rather than for stock. JIT relies upon precise system integration to reduce inventory towards zero. In producing only what is immediately required, batches tend to become smaller, set-up times have to be reduced, and the need to carry surplus stocks in order to cover for quality defects has to be avoided.

The potential of AMT for assisting the adjustment of manufacturing companies to new market conditions is usually discussed with reference to the engineering industries. Comparable developments can, however, be found in other manufacturing sectors. For example, British companies in chemicals and paper-making which had been characterized by the continuous processing of single products, or of a limited range, have been turning to markets for speciality products which can offer them niches segmented from the mass markets in which cost-effective international competition is based on now unattainable economies of scale and vertical integration (Williams, 1983; Jackson, 1985). This strategic adjustment means that it is important for manufacturers to be able to make several products or versions of the same product on a batch basis using the same process plant. The need is therefore for versatile plant and for computer control equipment and software which can cope with complex mixes of product.

The case of regional newspaper production provides another example of this general strategic shift. Here the need to maintain advertising revenue under recently adverse market conditions (including competition from 'free sheets') has encouraged companies to 'editionize' their daily and weekly papers. This means producing separate editions for local areas as well as increasing the time availability of the daily paper through more editions. This permits advertisers to display selectively in different geographical segments of the regional market, increases the local appeal of the paper, and expands its coverage over the day. In many cases, production has also been rationalized in pursuit of cost-effectiveness through concentrating the previously separate production of weekly titles onto the daily paper plant, and sometimes by taking in contract printing as well. Editorial teams for morning and evening dailies have also been merged. The computerization of editorial and advertising input is regarded by the management of these companies as essential to providing the flexibility required to cope with a more varied and intrinsically interdependent set of papers and their component sections without incurring unacceptable time delays. In its fully developed stage, with full-page make-up being designed on-screen and transmitted direct to printing plates, this approximates to a newspaper CAD/CAM system. The direct entry of input via computer terminals is also seen by management as providing the means of escaping from its historically long dependence on composing room workers who have been strategically placed to exploit a major production bottleneck.

The advantages which AMT in general promises to offer for the pursuit of the new manufacturing strategy centre on integration, control, and flexibility. The drive towards 'integrated manufacture' carries clear implications for organizational design, encouraging a corresponding level of integration between what are likely to have been hitherto separate departments and roles. The search for enhanced system control and flexibility, however, might be assisted organizationally in a number of quite different ways—some, for example, involving centralization and others decentralization. Apart from the political and cultural factors that are likely to influence this choice, note has to be taken of other contingencies which are operative in a given situation. These draw attention to the more specific circumstances which will influence both the choice between types of AMT and the details of organizational design.

Specific strategic contingencies

It is a truism that a viable enterprise can only produce what it can sell, and that production parameters are therefore highly dependent upon the selection of markets to supply and the positioning of the enterprise within these. Two such parameters have been most frequently singled out as of relevance to the specific choice of AMT: the quantity of items produced; and the variety of types of items produced. Organizational theorists have also given prominence to these parameters, but have in addition also stressed the importance of 'variability' in operating conditions because of the uncertainty and planning difficulties which high variability generates (Child, 1972).

Woodward's (1965) scheme of technological classification was based upon the quantity or volume of items produced, distinguishing, in its simpler and better-known format, between the three main categories of: continuous-flow (process); large-batch and mass production; and small-batch and unit production. Bessant (1985) has employed a similar scheme in order to locate within a continuum of item quantities the small-to-medium batch-size production for which FMS is favoured on economic grounds. Woodward did not define her small and large-batch categories by reference to any specific ranges of item quantities; Bessant appears to regard the small-to-medium category as ranging between about 25 and 1,000 items or parts per batch. Although Woodward actually placed most emphasis on the more narrowly focused notion of matching organization to whichever category of technology dominated, she also presented an analysis of 'manufacturing cycles' characterizing her three main categories. By widening the perspective in this way to take in the manufacturing cycle as a whole, attention was drawn not only to the problem of co-ordination between production, design ('development') and marketing functions, but also to the way that each type of cycle was attuned to a different market situation. The emphasis Woodward placed on achieving a matching of organizational design to technology in terms of item volume, could be modified, therefore, in favour of the thesis that markets are the strategic contingency to which both the design of organization and choice of technology need to be sensitive.

Over a sample of companies one would expect to find a negative relationship between the quantity of items and the variety of item types produced. High quantity implies larger average batch size, while a production schedule containing greater variety of items will entail more frequent changes of batches, which, other things being equal, will be of smaller average size. The combination of item quantity and item variety is again dependent on the strategy adopted in particular market conditions. The high quantity, low variety production which was made possible at a time of buoyant demand and less intense international competition in markets such as that for the popular car, encouraged investment in highly capitalized dedicated plant and transfer lines. Even when robots were introduced, to perform functions such as body welding, automobile manufacturing technology remained relatively inflexible (Abernathy, Clark and Kantrow, 1983). Some commentators such as D. T. Jones (1985) now argue that plants with high levels of dedicated automation such as Volkswagen's Hall 54 are counterproductive for a number of reasons. They cannot cater flexibly for product design changes, and so compromise the freedom to design cars in response to market trends and/or in search of market niches. They are costly in their indirect labour requirements and vulnerable to stoppage in the case of failure in the automated equipment.

Jelinek and Golhar (1983) place manufacturing technologies which are dedicated to a single product, such as transfer lines and some chemical plants, at one end of a range of AMT possibilities, being suited to the production of large item or part quantities (from several thousand upwards) and low variety (one, two, or three different types). For the range between about 500 and 10,000 items and two to eight item types, they cite the suitability of flexible production technologies which can accommodate a range of product designs within a single configuration. Examples would include papermaking machines and automobile lines that can manufacture different models. Suited to small—medium batch sizes, (between about 25 and 1,000 items and 6 to 200 types) is the category of 'programmable systems'. These include FMS and FMC (flexible machining centres), with Bessant (1985) regarding FMS as better suited to the higher volume, lower variety end of this category. As one moves towards the combination of small batch quantities (no more than about 40 items) and high variety of types, so it becomes appropriate to use non-integrated systems of stand-alone CNC and manually controlled tools. CNC machines offer the benefits of flexibility, but in an independent mode they cannot cope efficiently with high quantities of production.

Significant implications for organizational design stem from the parameters of production quantity and variety. There is a wide measure of agreement among authorities on organization that the high volume, standardized production situation can be managed adequately through a relatively mechanistic model. The situation here is one in which there is relatively infrequent change in the requirements placed upon the producing system, and where rapid unanticipated shifts in contingencies are not expected. The level of uncertainty with which management has to deal is therefore low. The conditions of decision making and information processing are of a correspondingly routine nature. This is the kind of situation to be expected when a company has a dominant position in a market not subject to rapid technological change or serious threat of new entry. It is no longer a typical situation, and not one to which the general thrust of AMT development is directed.

An enterprise in this situation would probably find it sufficient to integrate manufacturing programmes with marketing requirements and design/development programmes on the basis of a long-term forward plan. The plan would be drawn up and updated according to a timetabled cycle, probably involving inputs from separate functions and units, which are then centrally consolidated and approved. The more day-to-day operations within the planning parameters would be laid down by rules and procedures. The high volume producing company or plant will generally be a larger one, and a strong tendency has emerged, particularly in western enterprises, for larger ones to adopt more formalized and impersonal modes of integration, administered by large staff components (Child, 1973; Donaldson, 1985a). In short, based on the findings of Anglo-American research and argument (e.g. Woodward, 1965; Thompson, 1967; Perrow, 1970; Van de Ven and Ferry, 1980), the following organizational design characteristics could be regarded as fairly typical of the high volume, low variety company:

1. a low percentage of direct workers, particularly where dedicated automation has been introduced;
2. a high percentage of managerial, administrative, and staff employees;
3. a highly departmentalized structure of a functional kind;
4. a heavy reliance on formal procedure for planning and operational control;
5. integration through an impersonal mode—setting programmes of work and establishing procedures;
6. a heavy emphasis in information and control systems on reporting variance from 'standards'—standard costs, capacity utilization, and other productivity indicators;
7. centralized policy initiatives, with any delegation being intended to relieve higher-level overload rather than to encourage local initiative—hence heavily constrained by procedure and exception-reporting rules.

The implications for organizational design of producing a greater variety of items or parts depends on how predictable are the forward requirements for the different products. The difference here between variety and variability is organizationally a

very significant one. A diverse production programme, the changing content of which
can be forecast well in advance, merely presents problems of processing a more complex set of data than the high volume, low variety situation, and it places a premium
on devising plant and methods which permit speedy and economical changeover from
one batch or run to another. This case exemplifies high variety but low variability,
where the latter is defined as 'the degree of irregularity in the overall pattern of change'
(Child, 1972, p. 3). If the changes associated with product variety are sufficiently
regular or negotiable as to be predictable, then it may well be possible to cope with
them on the basis of forward planning. There would no doubt need to be provision
for securing good warning of any need to deviate from plan which arose from either
external or internal disturbances. However, a short-term continually adjusting response
to uncertainty comparable to Williamson's (1975) notion of 'spot' adjustment, and
involving a high degree of interpersonal discussion and problem solving within the
organization, should not be necessary. The organization can, in other words, still
function along relatively mechanistic lines, though the need to carry out quite frequent
changes of product will speak in favour of decentralizing that activity.

It is in the situation where variety in product specification is required in a competitive context which is itself changing and placing a premium on innovation that
the greatest challenge arises both in the use of AMT and in organizational design.
Here the pattern of orders that can be secured is either not predictable, and thus
requires unanticipated adjustments within the production system, and/or the products
required may be continually advancing in technical specification, so that their design
and method of manufacture itself requires a considerable amount of new problem
solving to be undertaken. Perrow (1970) characterized this situation as one in which
there was both: considerable variety in the work to be performed by an organization;
and a need to investigate new problems and devise appropriate methods and programmes without necessarily being able to derive much help from manuals, personal
experience, or other repositories of existing know-how. He labelled this 'nonroutine
manufacturing', which is an apt term by which to characterize the direction of general
movement in manufacturing strategy noted earlier (*ibid.*, p. 83).

Perrow considered these two dimensions of input variety and need to cope with
unfamiliar product requirements to be technological in nature, which they are so
long as the definition of technology is stretched to extend beyond hardware to
encompass the mode of productive activity in general (cf. Macdonald and Mandeville,
1981). However, their orientation towards the product market strategy pursued by
an enterprise is evident, and they could advantageously be considered as market-
related contingencies. Perrow's analysis of the organizational design implications
of location in the high variety/new intrinsic specifications category sets out the
essentials of a model which a number of others have since taken up and developed.
These essentials are the devolution of initiative, rapid mutual adjustment to new
circumstances, and a high level of integration between groups and levels in the
organization. The emphasis on decentralization, flexibility, and integration is evident
in Perrow's own description:

> In the nonroutine type of firm . . . discretion and power are high in both groups [supervisors of production and technical support specialists]; in both, coordination is through feedback (mutual adjustment) rather than through advance planning (programmed), and finally the interdependence of the groups is high. . . . Both groups are free to define situations as best they can (1970, pp. 80−1).

Later writers have suggested that this flexible, 'loose-coupled', yet integrated mode of organization is suited to coping with conditions of increasing uncertainty (e.g. Hedberg, Nystrom and Starbuck, 1976; Weick, 1976). It approximates to what Mintzberg (1979) calls the 'Adhocary', somewhat misleadingly because this mode of organization can be just as intentionally designed as any other. Indeed, it has been adopted as a design model by consultants such as Peters and Waterman (1982), who summarize its combination of devolved flexible initiative with integrated control in the phrase 'simultaneous loose − tight properties'.

Figure 6.1 draws together in a summary representation the types of AMT and approaches to organizational design which are argued to suit different combinations of production quantity and variability. Although the general shift in competitive manufacturing strategies is from quadrant A towards quadrants B and D, the figure serves to recall that the differences in the strategic positioning of any one enterprise at a particular time render it invalid to recommend as a generalization the use of any one AMT or organizational design. In making strategically informed choices on AMT and organizational design, managers need both to assess the extent to which the general trend is manifest within their own sector, and to consider what their own company's strategic position is within that sector and its markets.

A company will also have a particular configuration of inherited characteristics which bear upon its ability to adjust its organization so as to adapt strategically and employ AMT to that end. These characteristics include: the size of the company and its plants; the stock of competences and skills it has available; its traditional modes of operating; and its internal power structure. These factors will have contributed to a distinctive culture within the company, and will relate to a particular policy towards employment and organization. Their significance has already been indicated by case studies on the introduction of AMT, and they constitute yet a further qualification as to the form of organization which it is realistic to design as a complement. In other words, they serve to recall that any organizational design has to be translated into practical operation and that a number of hurdles or constraints can present themselves in this process (Whipp and Clark, 1986).

Many studies have concluded that larger company and plant size tends to be associated with a more internally differentiated and formalized organization structure (Child, 1984a; Donaldson, 1985b). As Sorge *et al.* (1983) found, one manifestation of this trend is that larger companies tended to separate the programming of CNC machines from their operation, reserving the former to separate white-collar departments. This was particularly marked in the UK, where it has been argued that a stronger tradition of functional specialization is present than in West Germany, the other country studied by Sorge and his colleagues (cf. Child *et al.*, 1983). In view

Level of product variability

	Low	High
Large	A Dedicated production plant and systems	B Use of CAD with computer-controlled machines: possibly linked into FMC/FMS. Equipment able to manufacture 'families' of similar items or products
	Mechanistic organization, with high level of functional differentiation. Centralized formal planning and co-ordination of production	Range of central functional departments, but product design, production planning and control decentralized to cross-functional teams or product groups
Quantity of total products (items) produced	C Conventional machines possibly specially adapted	D Flexible manufacturing centres and CNC machines
Small	Probably a small plant with largely semi-skilled labour. Simple structure with centralized planning by plant manager or small management group. Detailed shopfloor control, machine adjustment and handling of operational contingencies by first-line supervisors	Flexible non-formalized organization with close integration between marketing, design, machine programming and operating activities: trend towards role integration. Decentralized production planning and operational decisions

Examples of the above quadrants:
A: mass production white goods; oil refineries;
B: clothing manufacturer supplying one or more large monopsonistic retailers;
C: small specialist parts makers—e.g. brass fittings;
D: jobbing engineering firm.

Figure 6.1   The implications of production contingencies for appropriate new manufacturing technology and organizational design.

of the tendency for larger scale to be associated with greater specialization and formalization, it is to be expected that bigger organizations will experience a greater challenge in adjusting their modes of organization to suit strategic requirements for a more flexible and integrated mode of production.

The Sorge *et al.* Anglo-German comparison also pointed to the stock of available competence and skills as a contingency for the use of AMT and for the organization of jobs and work around the technology. It is easier to build the programming of CNC machines into the operator's role if the person concerned is more highly trained (including training relevant to programming) and has therefore had his or her competences developed to a higher level. A decentralized operator-programming approach ought to facilitate the objectives of speedy transfer from one batch to another and an immediate correction of settings where necessary due to variation in materials, for which CNC and other computer-controlled equipment has been purchased. The concern over the shortage of skilled technical staff and instrument engineers to develop and service AMT equipment is another pointer to skill as a relevant contingency (DTI, 1984, 1985).

A company's operating tradition will be associated, *inter alia*, with its policies relating to the use of skill: whether it has favoured what Friedman (1977) called a 'direct control' mode with its thrust towards deskilling, or a 'responsible autonomy' mode which is compatible with a greater reliance on the informed discretion of workers whose roles are accordingly enlarged in scope. As Friedman (1984) points out, a shift between these modes is not cost-free and cannot necessarily be accomplished in a short time. The tradition of the plant in terms of operating in a direct control or responsible autonomy mode could therefore affect the decision whether to run AMT facilities through central control and programming departments leaving shopfloor operators as machine minders, or whether to operate in a more decentralized and integrated fashion with activities being centred on the operator or work group and line supervisor.

Particular geographies of job and functional territories grow to be associated with established modes of operating and structures of organization. These entrenched positions of power and adherence to precedent can become crystallized in, and reinforced by, structures of meaning, in the form of group, departmental, occupational, and corporate cultures. Studies of organizational change both at shopfloor level (e.g. Wilkinson, 1983) and managerial level (e.g. Warwick, 1975; Pettigrew, 1985) indicate how resistant to change an established cultural and political situation can be in organizations. Wilkinson's case studies, and those of Jones and Rose (1985, 1986), illustrate how organizational changes intended by senior management to accompany the use of NC machines could be modified during their translation into practical arrangements by traditionally minded middle-level production and personnel managers, and sometimes successfully contested by workers and their representatives. The political process of introducing new organizational arrangements in conjunction with AMT therefore constitutes a source of uncertainty, especially in conditions where effective resistance may be mounted. Among these conditions are: dependence by management on the 'tacit knowledge' of workers (Jones and Wood, 1984); the occupancy by workers of key roles for keeping the production system going and for coping with unexpected contingencies such as breakdown (Sayles, 1958; Crozier, 1964); and difficulties in the way of management replacing such workers, either by recourse to the labour market or to substitution through automation or deskilling. Another condition, the achievement of cohesive workplace group organization (Seashore, 1954), will be assisted by the presence of these favourable structural features, but is also likely to depend on the will to act of the workers themselves and their avoidance of mutual divisions due to multi-unionism.

ORGANIZATIONAL DESIGN AND
ADVANCED MANUFACTURING TECHNOLOGY

The preceding discussion has injected elements of uncertainty and indetermination into the analysis. Uncertainty arises because of the dependence of technological and organizational policies upon corporate strategies which have to address external complexities, and the imperfectly predictable actions of competitors. Indeterminacy arises because the design and implementation of technological and organizational policies is a social process whose outcome depends partly on the interpretation of change in the light of precedents and existing structure, on the political skill and will to overcome established interests, and on available competences. It is therefore not realistic to set out any firm guidelines on organizational design for AMT since each company will have to arrive at its own particular solution. It is, however, valid and useful to return to the common elements in the new manufacturing strategies associated with AMT and to examine which organizational arrangements are consistent with these—bearing in mind that in practice specific solutions will have to be worked through for each company. These new manufacturing strategies stress system integration and precise operational control in order to achieve benefits such as flexible throughput, low inventory, and manufactured quality. This directs the discussion of organizational design to integration and control, and to related changes in managerial roles and organization.

Computer-based integration

It will be recalled that the systems being developed around AMT aspire to achieve integration along two dimensions. First, the physical dimension such that the transformation and transfer of material and parts can approximate to the concept of continuous flow. Second, the informational or managerial dimension, such that marketing, design, engineering, production, and accounting activities achieve a high level of co-ordination in the interests of achieving a flexible and economic response to market opportunities.

Bhattacharyya (1985) has concluded from his studies of discrete part manufacturing companies in the medium-to-high volume sector of British engineering that many of them have been prevented from securing sufficient benefit from AMT because of incompatible interfacing between the new technology and existing organization. He estimates, moreover, that total costs are about 15—40 per cent higher in the UK, largely due to high overheads occurring in management and specialist functional areas. The general difference between British companies and their major competitors such as Japan and Germany lies in the predominance of the functional type of organization in Britain. This is expensive because of its proliferation of white-collar and managerial manpower, and is incompatible with the logic of an integrated manufacturing system. Functional structures in Bhattacharyya's assessment create 'enormous problems of information flow' because of poorly defined interfaces between functions which result in long lead times and the corruption of data. Managerial time is taken up in attempting to correct these problems by collating, analysing, and interpreting information, and co-ordinating the activities of different departments which tend to diverge in pursuit of their own sub-unit goals. Jelinek and Golhar (1983) also make the point that the new integration sought between marketing and design, design and manufacture, and manufacture and strategic positioning, 'suggest the pending demise of older, functionally specialized structures—or, perhaps, their radical revision' (p. 35).

The challenge of achieving cross-functional integration has already become widely recognized in the literature on organizing, and a number of comprehensive analyses of structural design solutions have been developed (e.g. Galbraith, 1977; Knight, 1977). These offer a range of integrative mechanisms, from the simple and inexpensive designation of cross-functional liaison roles to the complex and costly overlay of additional integrative hierarchies as in matrix organization. Organizational designers, broadly speaking, can endeavour to enhance integration in two ways'; through convergence within the same role of tasks previously performed within separate roles, and through a closer coupling or overlapping of different roles.

Voss (1984) discusses these two forms of integration with reference to the use of CAD/CAM technology. CAD/CAM provides the opportunity to link the functions involved in moving a product from design into manufacturing, because it furnishes a common and readily accessible data base. In the past each stage in the process—design, draughting, toolmaking and production engineering, and machine programming—has been performed by a separate group of people with well-defined distinct roles. Voss's studies of successful CAD/CAM users indicate that they tended to remove the distinctiveness between these roles and to integrate them, and that without this organizational adjustment many of the benefits of CAD/CAM will not be realized. In other words, role convergence assists the use of CAD/CAM as a means of improving the design-to-manufacture process as a whole—speeding it up, improving the quality of design and simulated testing, providing a better design for manufacture in terms of production cost—rather than simply using the technology as a device to increase the labour productivity of particular stages such as producing drawings. As a participant from the car industry put it to a recent workshop on new technology, the purpose of his company's investment in CAD systems was not primarily to improve the productivity of producing drawings but to improve the quality of design (Wyman, 1985). A combination of organizational and technological integration within the marketing, design, and manufacturing process is expected to improve design by providing for a more marketable product and by producing a better design to manufacture.

In some cases role convergence has been achieved through combining hitherto separate roles. The scope of the new role is expanded to cover a wider range of tasks, though the burden of some of these tasks may now be substantially lightened by computerization. Voss (1984) cites the case at the beginning of the CAD/CAM process where one can find the designer now doing his or her draughting on CAD rather than using a draughtsman, and this could extend to preparing NC tapes for shopfloor operation. At the other end, machine operators may extend their role to programming their own tapes or machine controllers. Sorge *et al.* (1983) found that this latter example of role convergence was most common in smaller firms which had not developed functionally separate programming sections, and that it also appeared to be facilitated by the generally more comprehensive skill base among German as opposed to British machine operators.

The introduction of computer process control with visual feedback to central display areas replaces the need for visual supervision and manual adjustment of plant. In a food factory, where management had adopted headcount reduction as a major criterion for evaluating new process investment, some operator roles have been extended to cover whole manufacturing lines and have had added to them additional tasks such as cleaning and minor maintenance (Smith, Child, and Rowlinson, 1987). Similarly, the introduction of computer production control and monitoring systems has in certain paper mills been used to facilitate the merging of hitherto separate supervisory roles, again because the technology saves considerable time in direct visual supervision of the plant and in making adjustments from one batch to another. It was reported to the writer on site visits that this integration has reduced delays and wastage of paper previously due to poor communication between different stages of the process when these were supervised separately.

Studies undertaken by the Technical Change Centre (Mitchell and Cross, 1984; Cross, 1985) examine the integration of traditionally separate craft maintenance roles within the general context of AMT. Cross concludes that 'the single disciplined craftsman has no foreseeable future in most frontline maintenance situations' (1985, p. 203). The combination of new manufacturing strategies and use of AMT is seen to generate three significant developments: first, the need for multi-disciplinary understanding of mixed technology (electronic – microelectronic – mechanical) machines, which calls the division between specialist crafts into question; second, the elimination of traditional distinctions between skilled and unskilled, production and maintenance tasks; and finally, the combining of decision making, technical knowledge, and action which calls into question the traditional works/staff distinction. Cross identifies as a requirement associated with these pressures towards role convergence 'a mental ability to cope with manufacturing systems rather than just isolated components which make up those systems' (Cross, 1985, p. 206). As well as the possibility of eliminating distinctions between production and maintenance tasks, another instance of integration which is encouraged by the in-built quality assurance offered by AMT is the incorporation of quality responsibilities into the production operative role.

The combination of hitherto separate roles offers the advantages of integration and flexibility that have been mentioned; it is consistent with the integrative properties of AMT and is facilitated by these. Even though some commentators on AMT play down its productivity potentiality, this form of role convergence involves an intensification of labour. Labour productivity is raised because employees now perform more tasks, though the new technology relieves the burden of some. Apart from physical constraints, the main limit on this development is likely to lie in the capabilities of the individuals concerned to cope with enlarged jobs, which has obvious implications for policy on selection and training.

The second approach within organizational design towards enhancing multi-functional integration does not necessarily involve an intensification of labour. It consists of various devices to couple different roles or groups more closely together. Where the need for close integration is only periodic, or can be foreseen well in advance, it may be sufficient merely to ensure that the staff concerned are in regular contact and that responsibility for that contact is clearly understood. Where the need for integration is more intense, with time pressures to achieve solutions for novel problems such as new product design and manufacturing specifications, a correspondingly closer, more intense, and flexible form of integration between the roles involved is required. This level and mode of multi-functional integration is more appropriate for the newer adaptive manufacturing strategies and matches the integrative potential of AMT. It will typically be attempted through the establishment of teams or project groups, of varying life-spans.

Voss (1984) cites the example of a small die manufacturing company which organizes its users of CAD/CAM into a permanent team of four, consisting of two designers, a toolmaker, and a draughtsman. Bringing these roles into a closely coupled working relationship has reduced design-to-manufacturing lead times and improved the ease of manufacture of new work. In cases where an integrated effort is required to carry through new projects or to solve particular problems, temporary teams of the kind recommended by Peters and Waterman (1982) will normally be more appropriate. The occupants of functionally defined roles would in that case typically move from one team to another over time, and may belong to more than one team at a given point in time. Voss's research uncovered examples of this more temporary form of team organization, as when teams using CAD/CAM are reformed for each new development project.

Löwstedt's (1985) studies of the use of CAD in ten Swedish engineering companies led him to suggest three models for further organizational integration. This was in response to finding that Swedish engineering design organization tends to be highly specialized in terms of horizontal role divisions, and has on the whole not adapted to the new strategic requirements which justify investment in the improved technology. The first model is that of the 'integrated design organization', which would mean incorporating different design roles into teams (including support functions such as calculation or CAD development and operation), and perhaps aligning the scope of team responsibilities to that of product families. The second, and not mutually exclusive, model is the 'customer-oriented design organization' where marketing and design functions are closely coupled. One of the companies in Löwstedt's study had, for example, moved salesmen into design teams with the intention of reaching design solutions that better satisfied perceived customer requirements. Under this model the development of computer aids is likely to be oriented towards increased flexibility and manageability of information so as to rapidly generate sketches and other information to provide the basis for discussion with customers, in addition to the precise and perfect specifications required for manufacturing. The third organizational design model is that most frequently identified in connection with CAD/CAM and already illustrated, namely the 'production oriented design organization', in which the roles spanning the range from concept to machine programming and tool making are brought together in teams.

The value of Löwstedt's identification of these organizational possibilities lies in its indication of the alternative approaches that can be pursued around the same technological capabilities, and of the point that the choice between them should be made with reference to the strategic advantage each promises to offer. For example, if there is a logistical or managerial limit to the number of specialists who could be allocated to CAD/CAM teams, it would be necessary to consider whether the priority is to improve the responsiveness of design to customer enquiries by coupling the sales−design interface, or whether it is to reduce design-to-manufacture lead times by coupling design−manufacture−materials procurement interfaces.

Willman and Winch (1985) describe the product teams which were intended to constitute the mode of shopfloor organization in the new and relatively automated BL Cars Metro plant. They summarize the principles of integration and flexible task performance behind this design: 'operations should be organized into a team under a supervisor: within this team there would be little demarcation between the jobs of particular members, and some rotation of tasks, including some routine maintenance. The teams would be responsible for all aspects of production within a defined area' (p. 99). Each team would consist of materials handlers, operators, quality controller and on-line maintenance. The four traditional maintenance trades—machine tool fitters, millwrights, pipefitters, and electricians—were to be combined into two groups, mechanical and electrical/electronics. BL management did not succeed in negotiating this increase of role integration and flexibility within maintenance, though it has imposed some other aspects of the scheme.

A number of factors will bear on the decision whether to attempt cross-functional integration through convergence within roles or between roles. First, it may be thought necessary to retain some specialist roles intact. Where a specialist formal qualification is legally required, as with electrical maintenance, this only permits role convergence through extensions of electrician roles rather than the other way round. If certain categories of specialist staff are in short supply, this may oblige an employer to retain a distinctive role in order to attract suitable recruits. The level of knowledge and ability required in certain specialist areas, combined perhaps with their relatively specific application, may decide management to retain these as distinct roles and groups. Voss (1984) points out that in these circumstances a mixed organizational arrangement may be preferred in which, within the CAD/CAM context, specialist groups support design-to-production teams. The matrix form of organization is another mixed design solution which attempts to provide integrating roles and hierarchies while retaining functional specialization. It has not, however, proved to be a universally satisfactory solution (Child, 1984a).

The size of the firm and the range of products it manufactures will also be relevant. A larger firm is likely to exhibit greater internal resistance to role convergence because it will normally have a well-established and rigid departmental structure. If it concentrates its manufacturing onto a single product range which changes only infrequently, and employs a dedicated form of manufacturing automation, then it may be able to perform satisfactorily with the lower degree of inter-functional integration which Woodward (1965) tended to find among mass-production firms. If, on the other hand, the large firm diversifies, then the pressures which encourage divisionalization will operate and speak for the integration of specialist contributions into product group teams. The small firm is less likely to have the staff available to form permanent product teams, and will therefore be more attracted to either a flexible allocation of people between teams having a temporary life-span, or the development of substitutability through a convergence of multiple competences within individual roles. Here again the ability of the people concerned will be a condition of how far their role enlargement can be taken without undue strain on them and risk of inadequacy in their performance.

The degree of internal political resistance which may arise against attempts at organizational integration can constitute a major constraint, especially on the convergence of hitherto distinct roles and groups into single entities. Restructuring away from established departmental or occupational positions suggests potential major shifts in intro-organizational power, even to the extent of threatening livelihoods through the devaluation and obscuration of traditional job identities and skills. Internally territorial preserves are likely to appear threatened, while, externally, the standing of specialists in the labour market and their ability to command mobility and good rewards as members of an identifiable occupation becomes less certain. The present drive by British provincial newspaper 'manufacturers' to achieve a greater level of computer-based integration in their production process, via single key-stroking direct entry of copy, provides a sharply defined illustration of this point. For it is being strenuously, though not very successfully, resisted by the National Graphical Association, which sees the traditional skill and role of compositing being eliminated and its strategic negotiating position in the production process eroded.

Control

The process of operational control involves a two-way flow of information, with instructions passing to the locus of production and feedback on performance achieved returning to the control point. AMT applications such as stand-alone CNC machines use computers only to ensure a very precise transfer of instructions through programmes to the machine operations. However, the paradigm of computer-integrated manufacture which guides virtually all developments in AMT envisages a full development of information technology for control purposes, providing computer-based direct feedback of results as well. When this is achieved, the design of a control system becomes an entirely organizational choice in so far as information can in principle be directed to and from any terminal in the network. The scope of choice for control-related organizational design decisions, such as centralization versus decentralization, becomes technologically unconstrained. In principle, the traditional zero-sum view of control information as a scarce power resource could become redundant.

In practice, traditional political perspectives and stances appear likely to persist. Decisions on new technological investment are taken within guiding parameters laid down by senior managers who in the main seek to preserve hierarchical differences in access to decision making and the vertical distribution of formally acknowledged competence. As a result the predominant interest in new technologies from the perspective of control concentrates on the possibilities these offer for improving managerial control at a centralized level. The concept of integrated manufacture as advanced by Ingersoll Engineers (1985) stresses the need for management to bring the whole manufacturing process under its control in order that effective integration can be achieved and the system run adaptively with the facility for rapid co-ordinated switching between products, yet at the same time tightly in regard to levels of inventory and wastage. In pursuit of this philosophy, and with CAD permitting the more precise definition of specifications, this concept of integration is being extended to suppliers along lines familiar in Japan in regard to their responsibility for meeting these specifications and delivering exactly when required. The whole emphasis is on centralized integrated system control, or as Kaplinsky (1984) has expressed it, on 'systemofacture'.

Information technology (IT) extends the possibilities for managerial control in three main ways discussed in greater detail elsewhere (Child, 1984b). First, it provides faster, more comprehensive, and more accurate knowledge of operations, particularly when relevant data are captured directly from sensors and monitoring devices. Second, the capture of data combined with the application of decision support and other analytical systems reduces the scope for idiosyncratic judgement and mystique in the work of employees on whom management may have previously been dependent for evaluative feedback. Third, IT offers the prospect of unifying previously segmented control systems, and thereby increases the potential for a comprehensive and balanced assessment of performance. The point has already been made that the prospect of integration which AMT is now offering to batch producers is comparable to that of process production; it also offers the opportunity for developing comparably integrated control systems (see Chapter 3, p. 56). The prospect is one of combining control in regard to physical movements, condition of plant, stocks, wastage, energy consumption, unit costs, and manpower.

Computer-integrated manufacturing systems lend themselves to a centralization of managerial control by reducing dependence on the monitoring role of middle-level functional departments and junior line management. Programmed, computer-controlled machining builds a high level of quality assurance into the manufacturing process, and as a result the scope of a separate quality control function can be reduced and its work redirected to less routine and more developmental testing. Once machines are both computer-programmed and integrated, as with DNC and eventually CIM, production scheduling can be performed centrally and concentrate on immediate requirements, rather than weeks ahead, in accordance with the 'just-in-time' principle. When production control data can be secured directly from the plant, and in with superior equipment reliability and consistency, the need for progress chasing and local rescheduling on the shopfloor may disappear. Reliance on junior production managers for this activity, or for collecting control data, should diminish accordingly.

In the thirteen companies he studied, Wild (1985) found an increasing centralization of decisions on production scheduling and control combined with a greater dependency upon computer-based control procedures. These companies were mostly in batch production and had adopted various elements of the new manufacturing strategy and examples of AMT. The greater integration of production activities, and the reliance on consistent and accurate scheduling, made manufacturing systems intolerant of breakdown, parts shortages, or other reasons for stoppage, so that when this occurred rapid rescheduling had to be undertaken at the higher level at which control over the whole system was now located. Similarly the move towards linking computer-based production planning, schedule, and control systems to overall business control systems appeared to reduce the need for production managers to take decisions on workflow control.

Evidence such as this seems to bear out the expectation that organizational design for AMT will shift towards the centralization of control and decision making. Such a conclusion would, however, be premature. The centralization of planning and control with computer assistance is not equally suited to the three types of system interdependence which Thompson (1967) labelled as 'reciprocal', 'pooled', and 'sequential'. It is not well suited to reciprocal interdependence, where the outputs of units become the inputs for each other. Each unit is thus penetrated by the other, and Thompson argues that co-ordination through mutual adjustment is the suitable mode for this situation. Research by Van de Ven and colleagues (1976) tended to support this argument, especially for conditions of uncertainty. Co-ordination through mutual adjustment requires a high degree of organized integration, but at a decentralized level close to the workflow itself. This leads to the proposition that the appropriate locus of control for activities which are developmental or subject to high uncertainty, necessarily handled through the intensive interaction of different contributors, is one decentralized down to their level.

Pooled interdependence refers to the situation where different work units, such as plants or branches, perform a set of often standardized operations relatively independently of one another. Each contributes to the common 'pool', namely the economic well-being of the whole organization, and may draw certain central services from it. In this situation the activities of each unit can normally be co-ordinated on the basis of standard procedures and controlled by periodic examination of results. More detailed central control of each unit's operations is feasible but unnecessary, and would probably be demotivating. In manufacturing terms we might be talking here of a set of independent plants or relatively independent product lines within a plant. In both cases production control can be delegated down to the producing unit. The further development of information technology networks between centres and branches should permit such delegation to co-exist with central monitoring, as is already evident within an industry such as branch banking.

The case typically addressed in discussions of AMT is one of sequential inter-dependence characterized by a serial form of workflow: particular stages need to follow in sequence. With sophisticated products such as motor cars, the pattern of sequential interdependence can become highly complex, but since the sequence is known it is amenable to centralized planning with computers handling the complexity. Once new technologies provide an adequate feedback of operational data, centralized control can advantageously complement this centralized planning. The fact, however, that this is only one category among others makes it impossible to posit any general conclusion to the effect that the organizational design option for AMT is one of centralization. Even in the case of sequential interdependence, one should not overlook the practical problems which still attend the effective centralization of computer data deriving from different local control systems and processors, or the difficulties that can be presented by unreliable sensors.

Management organization

This section considers the design of management organization which would be consistent with the new manufacturing strategy and the use of AMT. A complication arises because the capabilities of IT in its widest sense as a combined computing and communications technology are particularly relevant for managerial and administrative work, and the data systems used in AMT are likely to form only part of a larger IT system involving features such as electronic mail. To some extent, then, a discussion related to AMT must refer also to the possibilities which are offered by IT in general.

The general context of present thinking about management organization is one of consciousness of the inconsistencies which have arisen between the way manage-ment structures have developed and the changing conditions for competitive success reviewed earlier. A trend towards diversification and the growing employment of specialists, particularly in British and American companies, has created difficulties for internal communication and integration. The problem posed by a highly depart-mentalized functional structure for the full realization of AMT potential has been noted. The continued growth in managerial, administrative, and staff employment has led to the elongation of managerial hierarchies and the accumulation of managerial overheads. Even in the recent period of industrial recession, a survey of 180 UK companies found that on average their administrative and managerial costs had risen by 4 per cent in real terms during the 5 years to 1981 (Kransdorff, 1983).

The search is therefore on for ways of restructuring management so as to: direct the focus of its energies more specifically to business needs; develop a decision-making and response capacity that meets the pressures of present competitive conditions; and reduce the burden of overhead costs. The costs of management, in other words, have to be justified by their contribution to performance. This message has been expressed in the widely disseminated *In Search of Excellence* by Peters and Waterman (1982), which identified among the attributes of managerial 'excellence' an action orientation, closeness to the market, scope for initiative, a concentration on the company's distinctive product competence, and a simple, lean management structure. This is a prescription for organization on the basis of cross-functional teams with clear objectives and targets, which are re-formed once a particular project is accomplished. As such it is consistent with the integrative capabilities offered by technologies such as CAD/CAM. The matrix approach to cross-functional integration is viewed with suspicion because it imposes the burden of a further managerial panoply of a permanent nature, one which is in any case likely to be less effective than a team-based organization in securing the commitment of different managers and specialists to a specific common objective.

The concept of integrated manufacture, which looks to CIM as its main enabling technology, encompasses the whole cycle of business. As discussed earlier, its logical organizational counterpart in conditions where product demands are variable and rapidly changing, lies in the integration of relevant cross-functional contributions by means of a convergence onto enlarged roles and/or multi-functional teams. A concept which encompasses the whole cycle of business raises the question of where the boundaries of such teams should be drawn. Löwstedt (1985), for example, has outlined the models of the customer-oriented and production-oriented design organization; each making somewhat different use of CAD facilities. As CAD/CAM is developed and moves towards CIM, it is possible to conceive of a merging of these two models, so that in circumstances where the value of production justified it, there could be a team consisting of sales, design, toolmaking/production engineering, and operations people who together take responsibility for a particular category or family of products. The full potential of CAD/CAM also extends into combining geometrically defined parts data with data on materials and densities, so that precise specifications become available for ordering materials or bought-in parts. This development would assist the closer working with suppliers in order to secure fewer defects and the move towards 'just-in-time' systems exemplified by Japanese companies and now being introduced by companies such as Austin-Rover, Ford, Rolls Royce, and IBM. Supplying companies, it is reported, are themselves pushing for this hardening of the specificity of data given to them by the purchasing company on its requirements, since it eases their own planning and so lowers their overheads (Bhattacharyya, 1985). In terms of organizational design, this points towards a relationship with suppliers being maintained by multi-functional product or management teams, in contrast to traditionally fragmented relationships conducted via separate functional departments such as purchasing, engineering, and quality control.

The attempt to achieve greater integration within management organization is consistent with the concept of a relatively small cross-functionally flexible core group which makes fewer expensive administrative demands because of its organic nature. It is cohesive because of the absence of strong departmental boundaries and as a result of the sharing of a common identity by people who contribute directly to the production cycle. For the core team of managers and other 'primary' employees would be determined by their direct contribution to the product: its marketing, design, production, and so on. The concept forms part of a philosophy of justifying overheads in terms of a direct product contribution, and of securing any other services from the marketplace. The rational decision criteria for whether to retain managerial and specialist services as part of a semi-permanent hierarchy or to secure them from the market (cf. Williamson, 1975) include: whether such services are required only periodically or on a continuing basis; whether they are relatively self-contained in nature and therefore measurable or alternatively require close integration with the contributions of others thus not readily permitting separate measurement; whether the required services can be contributed on the basis of skill or expertise available in the external market or whether such requisites are specific to the company; and whether the cost and availability of services from the market are favourable or not.

The more the first of these alternatives applies, the more attracted are firms likely to be towards contracting-out and so reducing the core oganization. In addition, certain of the organizational adjustments facilitated by AMT, such as the reduction in departments ancillary to production and the automation of middle-management information processing tasks, can themselves be expected to reduce managerial overhead and the number of hierarchical levels. This is a prospect eagerly desired and anticipated by top management, at least in the USA (*Business Week*, 1984).

The movement of senior staff out of the physical organization to working in their own homes is a counterpart to the restructing of employment at a lower level towards more sub-contracting and a greater use of part-time and temporary (short contract) labour. The ability to apply performance 'metering' to discrete tasks or projects, in other words to apply control by measuring outputs (Ouchi, 1978), is a key condition for the contracting-out of managerial and other services. For this reason developments in networking, such as the Rank Xerox scheme, involve self-contained or ancillary specialist activities such as pension management, market intelligence and taxation law (Judkins and West, 1983, 1984). Considerable interest is being expressed in 'executive' homeworking. A survey of 255 of the largest 1,000 UK companies reported that almost two-thirds believed that by 1988 they will be employing executives working from home, and by 1983 over 20 per cent of companies with an annual turnover exceeding £500 million reported having some executives working from home using personal computers (Cane, 1983). However, numbers may remain relatively small; Rank Xerox anticipate an eventual total in their company of around 150. One of the organizational adjustments required for the operation of such a system will be the designation of certain staff as co-ordinators or contact points for services provided from outside, just as it was suggested that relations with suppliers would be better conducted by integrated teams rather than via a fragmented array of separate functional departments.

Networking over data lines may share computer facilities which support AMT. The more significant connection lies in the concept of integrated manufacturing which distinguishes the activities involved in the basic production cycle from the others, and is thus wholly consistant with the distinction between core and periphery. We have noted how in this concept an increase in system integration and managerial control go together. The use of contracting-out and networking reinforces the control dimension because it involves payment only for work actually done or hours spent on a job—both being measured—and so reduces the 'porosity' between productive and unproductive paid-for labour (Massey and Meegan, 1982). The general intention behind the whole gamut of new thinking is to reduce both the vertical and horizontal organizational barriers to management control because this is seen as necessary to render the system more responsive to strategic requirements. This does not necessarily mean greater control over the actual *conduct* of tasks, or indeed any deskilling; the former in fact reduces with networking and contracting-out. It does, however, mean greater control over the *delivery* of work and activity to fit the timing and quality requirements of a finely tuned adaptive production system.

CONCLUSION

Powerful forces of economic change create a need to adopt new manufacturing policies in terms of competitive strategy, organization, and use of technology. The re-design of organization is a key element in this transformation. There can be no certainty, however, that this will be accomplished, because of the degree of organizational conservatism that is inherent in most enterprises and institutions. The UK in particular, during its long period of relatively uninterrupted industrial and political development, has built up through progressive sedimentation a solid structure of statuses, rules and practices, which now present a formidable barrier against organizational change.

Evidence of organizational conservatism appears at all levels and in many forms. It is rife within management itself. Surveys, for example, point to a high level of ignorance in British manufacturing industry about technological change and its possible implications (*Financial Times*, 23 March 1985, p. 8). Forty per cent of UK companies in a MORI survey admitted having no strategy for innovation and the application of new technology, a higher proportion than in four other industrial countries also surveyed (MORI, 1984). Another survey on the use of personal computers in the office found that many managers with exclusive use of one did not continue to use it once the novelty had worn off (*The Times*, 16 July 1985, p. 15). At the junior management level, to the writer's own knowledge, some supervisors recruited from the shopfloor in industries with traditional skills such as paper making have experienced difficulty in using the information now provided by computer production control, and in substituting a more conscious level of diagnosis for reliance on tacit skills. Existing organizational forms are liable to be maintained, even when conditions call for change and new technology can facilitate it, in areas where work roles and demarcations are defined by formalized occupational training and membership. A non-manufacturing example of this is found in hospital laboratories (MESS, 1987). Other conditions under which groups of workers are likely to resist reorganization around new technologies were noted earlier. Where such resistance can be organized, as in the newspaper industry, the drive for change is likely to generate considerable conflict. Similarly, the functional mode of organization so characteristic of the UK embodies established career and power structures from which resistance to cross-functional integration may also be launched.

Although it may be particularly marked in the UK, reluctance to undertake organizational innovation is a widely manifest phenomenon. A number of reasons have been suggested for it (Child, Ganter, and Kieser, 1985). First, there is organizational inertia whereby it is natural to regard existing departments as resources already in place to which technology should be adopted. Second, the labour market provides a stock of skills and a division of labour leading to rigidity in existing job boundaries. A shortage of appropriate skills and training can also constrain organizational innovations such as the combination of hitherto separate roles. Third, there is the cultural factor identified by Meyer and Rowan (1977), in the form of influential established social norms about how organizations should be designed. Fourth, powerful social actors within organizations will defend their established positions. Fifth, this defence of the status quo, in countries such as West Germany, may be supported by legislated rights accorded to works councils and similar bodies. Sixth, the difficulties of evaluating the costs and benefits of new technology in the short term, and the degree of learning required, may appear to speak for the wisdom of leaving organization well alone in the meantime. Finally, the producers of new technologies and systems have themselves become mindful of organizational conservatism and now tend to market their products on the basis of the ease to which they can be adapted to existing structures and systems.

There are many reasons, then, for anticipating organizational conservatism in response to changing conditions. Total obduracy might lead to the conclusion that a destruction of existing structures, including the removal of key actors, is a prerequisite for the implementation of a new organizational design (cf. Biggart, 1977). Even if the necessity for change is accepted in principle, as is generally the case with technological innovation, the political issue of how to distribute its costs and benefits remains. And those groups fearing to bear the brunt of its costs will naturally oppose specific applications which affect them.

Where the situation is not zero-sum with regard to costs, benefits, and attitudes, an organizational learning approach may offer a constructive path towards achieving change. AMT tends to increase the degrees of freedom available for organizational design, and thus the opportunity for finding a solution acceptable to the parties concerned. The technologies themselves can usually be programmed to provide a range of functions and feedback data, and possibilities exist for incorporating manual access and overrides. This gives some flexibility in the design of human roles relating to them (Rosenbrock, 1985). The information network of computer-integrated systems allows for choice in the siting of input and output terminals, and therefore for flexibility in regard to centralization/decentralization as well as to the configuration and spatial location of individuals and groups. As investment in AMT reduces staff costs relative to those of capital (including its maintenance), so the degree of economic freedom for experiment in the organization of people and their work also increases.

Within the general move towards integration, flexibility and cost effectiveness which is obliged by changing competitive conditions, scope therefore exists for working out organizational solutions that suit the needs of the people within particular enterprises. Constructing these solutions requires a process of organizational learning and political accommodation. This takes time, and is itself one reason why organizational design does not usually adapt rapidly to new contexts. Key features of the process are: the creation of a wide understanding of the nature of changing strategic contingencies and the possibilities for responding to these; the participation of members in discussions on appropriate organizational changes and their relation to the use of AMT; and, where practical, the adoption of an incremental approach which permits pilot or pioneer projects (e.g. FMS islands) to have a demonstration effect intended not only to gain acceptance but also to draw forth contributions to the learning process from people's accumulated experience and skills. Questions of the training and competences required for new technologies and modes or organization also have to be resolved.

In short, it is not easy to achieve new forms of organization to accompany AMT. Organizational design is not simply a technical matter; in order to work as intended it requires acceptance and commitment. These qualities depend at least as much on people's perceptions of management's intentions, in the light of past and present experience, as they do on intrinsic qualities of the organizational design itself. Identification of the possibilities reviewed in this chapter is only the starting point for the difficult process of their refinement and implementation within a particular enterprise.

REFERENCES

Abernathy, W. J., Clark, K. B., and Kantrow, A. M. (1983). *Industrial Renaissance*. New York: Basic Books.

Atkinson, J. (1984). Emerging UK work patterns. In: *Flexible Planning: The Way Ahead*. Report no. 88, Institute of Manpower Studies, University of Sussex.

Bessant, J. (1985). Flexible manufacturing systems: an overview. Unpublished paper, Innovation Research Group, Brighton Polytechnic.

Bhattacharyya, S. K. (1985). State-of-the-art and future directions. Presentation to the TCC Workshop on Advanced Manufacturing Technology in the UK Mechanical Engineering Industries, London: Technical Change Centre, June.

Biggart, N. W. (1977). The creative – destructive process of organizational change: the case of the Post Office. *Administrative Science Quarterly*, **22**, 410–26.

British Robot Association (1985). *The Industrial Robot*. March.

Buckingham, W. (1961). *Automation: Its Impact on Business and People*. Westport, Conn: Greenwood Press.

Business Week (1984). Office automation restructures business, 8 October, pp. 42 – 64.

Cane, A. (1983). More expected to work from home. *Financial Times*, 1 September, p. 6.

Cane, A. (1985). False dawn in the new world of manufacturing. *Financial Times*, 14 May, p. 24.

Charlish, G. (1983). FMS—A way of thinking. *Financial Times*, 3 November, p. 9.

Charlish, G. (1985). Competitiveness with computers: computer-aided design. *Financial Times*, 27 February, p. 18.

Child, J. (1972). Organizational structure, environment and performance: the role of strategic choice. *Sociology*, **6**, 1 – 22.

Child, J. (1973). Parkinson's progress: accounting for the number of specialists in organizations. *Administrative Science Quarterly*, **19**, 328 – 48.

Child, J. (1984a). *Organization: A Guide to Problems and Practice*, 2nd edn. London: Harper & Row.

Child, J. (1984b). New technology and developments in management organization. *Omega*, **12**, 211 – 23.

Child, J., Fores, M., Glover, I., and Lawrence, P. (1983). A price to pay? Professionalism and work organization in Britain and West Germany. *Sociology*, **17**, 63 – 78.

Child, J., Ganter, H. D., and Keiser, A. (1985). Technological innovation and organizational conservatism. Paper presented to the Symposium on 'New Technology as Organizational Innovation', Wassenaar, Holland, May.

Cross, M. (1985). *Towards the Flexible Craftsman*. London: Technical Change Centre.

Crozier, M. (1964). *The Bureaucratic Phenomenon*. London: Tavistock.

Davis, L. E., and Cherns, A. B. (eds) (1975). *The Quality of Working Life*. New York: Free Press (2 volumes).

Davis, L. E., and Taylor, J. C. (1976). Technology, organization and job structure. Chapter 9 in R. Dubin (ed.), *Handbook of Work, Organization and Society*. Chicago: Rand McNally.

Diebold, J. (1952). *Automation: The Advent of the Automatic Factory*. New York: Van Nostrand.

Donaldson, L. (1976). Woodward, technology, organizational structure and performance—a critique of the universal generalization. *Journal of Management Studies*, 13, pp. 255 – 73.

Donaldson, L. (1985a). Size and bureaucracy in East and West: a preliminary meta-analysis. Paper given to Conference on 'The Enterprise and Management in East Asia', University of Hong Kong, January.

Donaldson, L. (1985b). *In Defence of Organizational Sociology*. Cambridge: Cambridge University Press.

DTI (1984). *The Human Factor—The Supply Side Problem*. First Report of the IT Skill Shortages Committee. London: Department of Trade and Industry.

DTI (1985). *Changing Technology—Changing Skills: Shortages at Technician Level*. Second Report of the IT Skills Shortages Committee. London: Department of Trade and Industry.

Friedman, A. L. (1977). *Industry and Labour*. London: Macmillan.

Friedman, A. L. (1984). Management strategies, market conditions and the labour process. In F. H. Stephen (ed.), *Firms, Organization and Labour*. London: Macmillan.

Galbraith, J. R. (1977). *Organization Design*. Reading, Mass: Addison-Wesley.

Hedberg, B. L. T. (1979). Design process in the Five Banks. Chapter 9 in N. Bjorn-Andersen *et al.* (eds), *The Impact of Systems Change in Organizations*. Alphen: Sijthoff & Noordhoff.

Hedberg, B. L. T., Nystom, P. C., and Starbuck, W. H. (1976). Camping on seesaws: prescriptions for a self-designing organization. *Administrative Science Quarterly*, **21**, 41 – 65.

Ingersoll Engineers (1985). *Integrated Manufacture*. London: IFS Publications.

Jackson, T. (1985). The old image heads for the shredder. *Financial Times*, 17 May, p. 24.

Jelinek, M., and Golhar, J. D. (1983). The interface between strategy and manufacturing technology. *Columbia Journal of World Business*, Spring, pp. 26–36.

Jones, B., and Rose, M. (1985). Managerial strategy and trade union responses in work reorganization schemes at establishment level. Chapter 6 in D. Knights *et al.* (eds), *Job Redesign*. Aldershot: Gower.

Jones, B., and Rose, M. (1986). Re-dividing labour: factory politics and work reorganization in the current industrial transition. Chapter 3 in K. Purcell *et al.* (eds), *The Changing Experience of Employment*. London: Macmillan.

Jones, B., and Wood, S. (1984). Qualifications tacites, division du travail et nouvelles technologies. *Sociologie du Travail*, **4**, 407–21.

Jones, D. T. (1985). Quoted in J. Griffiths, Warning on dangers of automation. *Financial Times*, 4 March, p. 16.

Judkins, P. E., and West, D. (1983). *Networking: The Distributed Office*. London: Rank Xerox.

Judkins, P. E., and West, D. (1984). A case history: Rank Xerox. In *Flexible Manning: the Way Ahead*. Report No. 88, Institute of Manpower Studies, University of Sussex.

Kaplinsky, R. (1984). Electronics-based automation technologies and the onset of systemofacture. Seminar given to the Work Organization Research Centre and Technology Policy Unit, Aston University, 28 November.

Knight, K. (ed.) (1977). *Matrix Management: A Cross-Functional Approach to Organization*. Farnborough: Gower.

Kransdorff, A. (1983). Now for the white collar shake out. *Financial Times*, 18 April, p. 10.

Löwstedt, J. (1985). Automation or cognition in the design office? Paper given at the 7th EGOS Colloquium on 'Challenges for Organizational Authority', Saltsjobaden, Sweden, June.

Macdonald, S., and Mandeville, T. (1981). The employment impact of technological change. Paper given to the 11th International Conference of the Australasian Commercial and Economics Teachers Association.

Marsh, P. (1984). The dawning of the day of the robot. *Financial Times*, 19 December, p. 20.

Massey, D., and Meegan, R. (1982). *The Anatomy of Job Loss*. London: Methuen.

MESS Project Team (1987). *Microelectronics in the Service Sector* (forthcoming).

Meyer, J. W., and Rowan, B. (1977). Institutionalized organizations: formal structures as myth and ceremony. *American Journal of Sociology*, **83**, 340–63.

Mintzberg, H. (1979). *The Structuring of Organizations*. Englewood Cliffs, NJ: Prentice-Hall.

Mitchell, P., and Cross, M. (1984). *Applying Process Control to Food Processing and its Impact on Maintenance Manpower*. London: Technical Change Centre, December.

MORI (1984). Survey conducted for PA Technology.

MSC (1984). *Skill Shortage Report*. Sheffield: Manpower Services Commission, September.

NEDO (1985a). *New Technology: Manpower Aspects of the Management of Change*. London: National Economic Development Office.

NEDO (1985b). *Advanced Manufacturing Technology: The Impact of New Technology on Engineering Batch Production*. London: National Economic Development Office.

Noble, D. F. (1984). *Forces of Production*. New York: Knopf.

Northcott, J. (with Rogers, P.), Knetsch, W., and De Lestapis, B. (1985). *Micro-electronics in Industry: an International Comparison: Berlin, Germany, France*. London: Policy Studies Unit.

Ouchi, W. G. (1978). The transmission of control through organizational hierarchy. *Academy of Management Journal*, **21**, 173–92.

Perrow, C. (1970). *Organizational Analysis: a Sociological View*. London: Tavistock.

Peters, T. J., and Waterman, R. H. (1982). *In Search of Excellence*. New York: Harper & Row.

Pettigrew, A. M. (1985). *The Awakening Giant*. Oxford: Blackwell.

Piore, M. J., and Sabel, C. F. (1984). *The Second Industrial Divide*. New York: Basic Books.

Reimann, B. C., and Inzerilli, G. (1979). A comparative analysis of empirical research on technology and structure. *Journal of Management,* **5**, 167–92.

Rosenbrock, H. H. (1985). Engineering design and social science. Discussion paper for ESRC/SPRU Workshop on New Technology in Manufacturing Industry, Cumberland Lodge, Windsor, May.

Rousseau, D. M. (1979). Assessment of technology in organizations: closed versus open system approaches. *Academy of Management Review,* **4**, 531–42.

Sabel, C. F. (1982). *Work and Politics.* Cambridge: Cambridge University Press.

Sayles, L. R. (1958). *Behavior of Industrial Work Groups.* New York: Wiley.

Seashore, S. E. (1954). *Group Cohesiveness in the Industrial Work Group.* Ann Arbor, Mich: Institute for Social Research.

Smith, C., Child, J., and Rowlinson, M. (1987). *Innovations in Work Organization.* Cambridge: Cambridge University Press (forthcoming).

Sorge, A., Hartmann, G., Warner, M., and Nicholas, I. (1983). *Microelectronics and Manpower in Manufacturing.* Aldershot: Gower.

Strassman, P. (1985). *Information Payoff.* London: Collier-Macmillan.

Thompson, J. D. (1967). *Organizations in Action.* New York: McGraw-Hill.

Townsend, E. (1985). Factory automation. Special report. *The Times,* 13 May, p. 20.

Trist, E. L. *et al.* (1963). *Organisational Choice.* London: Tavistock.

Van de Ven, A. H., and Ferry, D. L. (1980). *Measuring and Assessing Organizations.* New York: Wiley.

Van de Ven, A. H., Delbecq, A. L., and Koenig, R. Jr. (1976). Determinants of co-ordination modes within organizations. *American Sociological Review,* **41**, 322–38.

Voss, C. A. (1984). Management and the new manufacturing technologies. Unpublished paper, Australian Graduate School of Management, Kensington, New South Wales.

Voss, C. A. (1985). Implementation: a key issue in manufacturing technology: the need for a field of study. Paper presented at ESRC/SPRU Workshop on New Technology in Manufacturing Industry, Cumberland Lodge, Windsor, May.

Warwick, D. P. (1975). *A Theory of Public Bureaucracy.* Cambridge, Mass: Harvard University Press.

Weick, K. E. (1976). Educational organizations as loosely coupled systems. *Administrative Science Quarterly,* **21**, 1–19.

Whipp, R., and Clark, P. A. (1986). *Innovation and the Auto Industry.* London: Frances Pinter.

Wild, R. (1985). The impact of changing manufacturing technology on the production manager. Unpublished report, Brunel University, London.

Wilkinson, B. (1983). *The Shopfloor Politics of New Technology.* London: Heinemann.

Williams, E. (1983). Process control boom near. *Financial Times,* 16 May, p. 9.

Williamson, O. E. (1975). *Markets and Hierarchies.* New York: Free Press.

Willman, P., and Winch, G. (1985). *Innovation and Management Control.* Cambridge: Cambridge University Press.

Woodward, J. (1965). *Industrial Organization: Theory and Practice.* London: Oxford University Press.

Wyman, H. (1985). Contribution to discussion, ESRC/SPRU Workshop on New Technology in Manufacturing Industry, Cumberland Lodge, Windsor, May.

CHAPTER 7

Industrial Relations Issues in Advanced Manufacturing Technology

PAUL WILLMAN

Trade unions have always been concerned by the prospect of technical change. Threats to job security, earnings, skill demarcations and union membership itself have, during the post-war period, prompted the development of policies and bargaining strategies designed to exert some control over changes to industrial processes or products, or to exact a price for change. For this reason alone, employers in unionized firms have frequently needed to take industrial relations issues into account in innovation decisions. However, the frequency with which unions seek to impose adjustment costs does not imply that opposition to technical change is the only response one might expect. The other 'face' of trade union policy is concerned to encourage the sort of technical change which improves job security and offers financial benefits by improving competitiveness. So, throughout the post-war period, union movements in several countries have sought both to promote investment in new processes and products *and* to bargain over implementation (Corina, 1983).

A second feature of union concern with new technology has been a focus on its consequences rather than the technology itself. Despite recent initiatives in this area, the typical union focus has been on the employment levels and terms and conditions of employment attendant on new technology rather than any intrinsic features of the change itself. The explanation of union responses in particular circumstances thus needs to have reference to a range of issues other than the technical properties of advanced manufacturing equipment. Empirically, it appears to be the case that similar 'types' of new equipment, such as CNC or robotic assembly, may be associated with different patterns of work organization and bargaining behaviour (Jones, 1982; Wilkinson, 1983). Important questions surround the managerial intentions behind change, the characteristics of industrial relations institutions prior to change, and the nature and extent of bargaining and consultation.

This chapter will focus on such questions, looking first at the nature of innovation in UK manufacturing, and then at the institutional background of industrial relations. The chapter focuses on observable consequences of the introduction of advanced manufacturing technology to date, rather than on speculation about the future, and looks in particular at events within the car industry and at the impact of new technology on the organization of craftsmen. The final section seeks to explain why, despite their intention to do so, trade unions in the UK have failed to exert any substantial influence over the rate and direction of change. Overall, the conclusion is that both current economic circumstances *and* the structure of trade union organization are obstacles to it.

TYPES OF INNOVATION

It is customary to distinguish between innovations in manufacturing processes and changes to products. The division is not absolute, since changes to products may require new processes and vice versa. For example, in the car industry new product development appears to depend not only on market changes but also on the availability of new processes (Abernathy, 1978). Nevertheless, it is of use here. *Ceteris paribus*, trade unions are unlikely to object to pure product innovation unless it is itself associated with volume changes or process adaptations which could lead to job loss or earnings reduction. Nor are they likely to resist process changes which enhance employment or earnings, although in both cases they may seek to exact some payment for change. However, process changes which are simply labour-displacing or cost-reducing may well face resistance. Historical examples of such changes include the introduction of photocomposition in newspapers, and of containerization in dockwork (Wilson, 1972; Martin, 1981).

Furthermore, there may be differences between industrial sectors in the balance between the generally beneficial employment effects of product innovation and the often negative consequences of process innovation; the former tends to predominate in expanding industries, and the latter in mature or contracting ones (Townsend *et al.*, 1981; Pavitt, 1984). In the case of microelectronics, this distinguishes different parts of the manufacturing sector. On the one hand there are those industries, such as the electronics industry itself and certain parts of the machine tool industry, which incorporate microelectronics into products which become the process innovations of sectors such as printing and motor vehicles. In turn, these latter industries which 'receive' change may be divided between those such as vehicles which are severely affected, and industries such as food and chemicals where new electronic technology improves instrumentation and production control, but is unlikely to have severe employment consequences. The balance between product-innovating and process-innovating sectors within a given economy is likely to influence the overall employment impact, although the application of new office technology throughout manufacturing may reduce demand for clerical work (Wilson, 1984). The recent evidence for the UK is that, within manufacturing industry, microprocessor-based process innovation is much more common than product change, the latter being concentrated in vehicles, electrical engineering, and parts of mechanical engineering (Northcott and Rogers, 1984).

On the macro-level, union policies are concerned to secure investment in expanding sectors and to impose controls over new processes in mature industries. In turn, policies at industry and firm level reflect this. The unions' concern in the UK electronics industry is with recruitment, for which several 'concessions' by trade unions in the form of no-strike guarantees are on offer; while in general printing the main issue is to control the rate of process change and preserve existing demarcations. This largely reflects the pattern of managerial intentions behind the decision to innovate. Labour-saving changes to industrial processes are most likely where labour costs are an important factor in competition, a particular issue in mature industries. These industries may also be among those which seek to reduce inventory and administrative costs through better production control, or to reduce lead times on production or design.

The adoption of innovations may thus take place under very different competitive conditions. De Bresson and Townsend (1978) distinguish between those sectors in which competition occurs on the basis of product quality and performance, those in which economies of scale are important and competitive success is achieved by maximizing sales, and those in which cost minimization is most important. They also provide a classification of industries on this basis. If one applies this distinction to UK manufacturing, then it discriminates between a 'performance maximizing' sector characterized by high rates of product innovation, high rates of growth of output per head, low rates of unit wage growth and positive employment trends, and a 'cost minimizing' one characterized by low per capita growth, employment contraction and high rates of unit wage growth (Table 7.1).

Table 7.1 Employment, output, and productivity in three sectors

Compound rate of growth of	Performance maximizing ($n=23$)	Sales maximizing ($n=34$)	Cost minimizing ($n=23$)
Output	4.28	1.85	1.55
Output per head	4.43	3.18	3.22
Employment	0.07	−1.49	−1.48

Source: Willman (1986).
Note: data are annual average compound rates of growth (unweighted) for industries in each sector for the period 1954−73. From Wragg and Robertson, 1977.

In summary then, there are sectoral differences within manufacturing in the patterns of innovation and the economic background and thus, one might expect, in the industrial relations issues which may arise. However, there are also differences in institutional arrangements and, on the hypothesis that they are differentially receptive of change, one might expect a patterning of differences in this respect also.

INSTITUTIONAL BACKGROUND

In UK manufacturing, according to recent survey evidence, 68 per cent of plants, and a somewhat higher proportion of employees, were covered by collective bargaining in 1980. Such negotiations are likely to involve more than one trade union. Most plants employing more than 100 employees recognize more than one manual trade union, and a quarter recognize more than three (Daniel and Millward, 1983). The characteristic features of collective bargaining in UK manufacturing are its decentralization, its informality, and its reliance on shop stewards rather than full-time officials (Brown and Sisson, 1983).

Moreover, this bargaining extended beyond issues of pay and hours of work. In 88 per cent of establishments manual groups negotiated over redundancy, in 65 per cent they negotiated over major changes in production methods, and in 39 per cent they negotiated over capital investment (Daniel and Millward, 1983). Other surveys support the general conclusion that bargaining over changes to working methods in manufacturing frequently involves negotiations with trade unions of one form or another (Batstone, 1984; Edwards, 1984). Thus, despite the fact that the trade union initiative to sign 'new technology agreements' has met with no widespread success, and despite the existence of recessionary conditions which may have reduced union bargaining leverage, many companies operate new technology under some form of union−management agreement.

However, such agreements may not initially have focused on technology as such; nor may they indeed be explicitly acknowledged as written agreements. For example, the forms of bargaining under piecework described by Brown (1973) allowed employees to secure a financial benefit from changes to materials or products without explicit agreements. Such bargaining may be rarer in the 1980s, but is unlikely to be extinct. Similarly, in general printing, agreements about manning changes or production reorganization extended to technical change automatically. In all such cases the union agreed to work according to managerially determined new arrangements for a trial period, and then to negotiate a price for change (Willman, 1982). Such arrangements are likely to suit the piecemeal adoption of microelectronics by mature industries as much as they apparently suited the automation of transfer and materials handling operations in the 1960s (Turner, Clack, and Roberts, 1967). Both sets of arrangements are essentially forms of 'productivity bargain' in which technical change is a contingent rather than necessary feature. The issue is rather to ensure a share in the benefits of *any* form of change.

Where such arrangements exist, there is likely to be less pressure to move to a comprehensive new technology agreement in the face of change, since recognized mechanisms exist for accommodating it. Manual unions organizing manufacturing firms were not in the forefront of the development of such policy initiatives. There was less emphasis on the development of new bargaining machinery than on ensuring that technical change featured in standard negotiating agendas (Manwaring, 1981; Robins and Webster, 1982). However, such a reliance encouraged a pragmatic rather than strategic response by unions to advanced manufacturing technology. In the manufacturing sector in the UK bargaining (particularly for manual workers) tends to be decentralized, much taking place at plant level, and the capacity of trade unions to exact a price for change has tended to lie with the power of local union representatives to enforce their demands. If this power is attenuated by labour market trends, or if local representatives find themselves competing with each other, then the productivity bargaining model may be unsuitable.

It is reasonable to suggest that recession has caused both conditions to operate. Between December 1979 and the end of 1984 manufacturing employment contracted by 23.6 per cent. The worst falls occurred in traditionally well-organized areas such as metal manufacture (34.8 per cent) and motor vehicles (38.5 per cent). Such innovation as occurred thus tended to happen against a background of voluntary or compulsory redundancy and plant closure, and much of it was likely to be cost-minimizing in nature. While it would be mistaken to suggest that recession has caused the shop-steward system to atrophy or disappear (Batstone, 1984), nevertheless it is likely to have had an effect on bargaining over technical change, particularly process innovation. It is extremely difficult for trade unions to hold up change by negotiation where plant closure is presented by management as the alternative. In such circumstances technical change can be presented as a guarantee of job security rather than as a bargaining item, since it may represent evidence of the company's commitment to operation on the site. In Edwards' (1984) sample, 76 per cent of respondents mentioned technical innovation as part of their changed working arrangements; 73 per cent of respondents said that there had been no resistance to change by the workforce; and overall only 9 per cent mentioned any form of resistance other than bargaining.

Recessionary conditions highlight the ambivalent nature of trade union resistance to change, particularly cost-minimizing process change. The adjustment costs imposed by unions may have very different effects depending on their form. Wage increases may actually accelerate the rate at which capital is substituted for labour by changing relative factor prices. However, the inefficient retention of surplus labour may discourage investment. In extreme cases such costs may encourage disinvestment, or force closure (Prais, 1981). Where multi-plant firms are considering capacity reductions, plants may be in direct competition for new investment with other UK operations or with overseas plants. In such cases, companies may be in a position to extract concessions in return for 'granting' change rather than to pay a price for it, and may even regard the costs of negotiating and operating a technology agreement as excessive.

CHANGE IN THE MOTOR INDUSTRY

Recent events in the motor vehicle industry illustrate these issues in some detail. The industry has traditionally been associated with strong union organization, and particularly with powerful organizations of shop stewards which sought to bargain over pay and workloads. Throughout the 1960s and 1970s a relatively low rate of process innovation had been accommodated through the collective bargaining channels which dealt with other terms and conditions in the context of relatively buoyant product and tight labour markets (Turner *et al.*, 1967; Jones, 1983). However, between 1979 and 1984 the major car plants in the UK were completely retooled in order to produce a new, more competitive range of models. The context of this retooling was critical. The industry faced severe problems of overcapacity within Europe in the period, which highlighted the severe productivity problem experienced by British producers, particularly British Leyland (BL). Along with the need to improve this productivity performance, a rapid launch of new models and a reduction in productive capacity was seen as necessary (Williams, Williams, and Thomas, 1983; Marsden *et al.*, 1985).

The principal innovations involved the use of robotics and automated welding to produce the car body. Later, computer aided design and manufacture were used as well as sophisticated production control devices, and greater automation of press lines (Willman and Winch, 1985). The car industry is one in which process and product innovations have tended to be linked, given the dedication of assembly lines to particular models, and the changes also involved product innovation using microprocessors, for example in the dashboard and in engine management systems (Marsden *et al.*, 1985). However, the *climate* of innovation was also important. The principal car firms were seeking to improve process efficiency without expanding output, hence the innovative period was also one of employment contraction.

After 1979, employment fell in all of the major car firms. Several plants were closed, particularly in BL which contracted most rapidly. The car industry shrank and coalesced around four major assembly plants which were to be retooled, and those plants which were to supply them with components. The four main plants were Halewood and Dagenham (both Ford), and Cowley and Longbridge (both BL). During this period, managers of car firms made it clear that the industrial relations records of plants could figure in the plans made for their future. For example, investment in a new engine plant by General Motors did not come to its UK subsidiary (Vauxhall) in part because the plant concerned was on strike while the decision was being made. In consequence, Vauxhall ceased to be a full-scale car engine producer and employment contracted over the following 5 years. Investment at Halewood was continually discussed in terms of the prospect of getting high capacity utilization on new automated equipment at a plant with a poor strike record, and shop stewards at the plant were briefed on the link between 'good behaviour', new investment and job security (Marsden *et al.*, 1985).

Both Ford and BL sought improved efficiency through the assertion of the right to manage. In this climate negotiation of the terms of introduction of new equipment was seen as inappropriate and, even though new technology had been the subject of an earlier exercise in participation at BL, neither company introduced change by agreement; rather, innovation was seen as a management right, and the unions failed to exact a price for change. The important point to stress is that, in both cases, new technology was introduced into manufacturing processes as part of a general strategy for improving competitiveness in an extremely difficult product market environment, and poor industrial relations were seen as part of the problem to be solved. Because of this, advanced manufacturing technology was withdrawn from the bargaining arena altogether.

The central difficulty this posed for the unions was that although the technology was clearly labour-displacing, the job loss which would result from it appeared to be far less than that following from closure and rationalization. To the extent that this job loss followed from a lack of competitiveness, for which new investment was seen as the cure, technical change could not be opposed. In effect the two forms of job loss were alternatives. The unions themselves had argued in the 1970s that under-capitalization was a source of competitive disadvantage, and certainly the capital intensity of UK car operations increased over the period (Willman, 1986). However, shop stewards in those plants which would *not* receive new investment did not accept the consequences of this view, while those in plants where investment *was* planned were secure in the knowledge that they would regain some power to bargain. The problem which emerged with some severity in BL was that of an increasing divergence of interests between national union leaders concerned (albeit under pressure from employers) with the future of the industry, and shop stewards concerned with terms and conditions of employment and job security in particular plants. In that company it was solved by an employer particularly concerned to communicate directly with employees as a way of circumventing the process of negotiating change (Willman and Winch, 1985).

Once new processes were introduced at the major plants, strike rates tended to rise as employees protested against certain of the consequences of new technology *after* its introduction had guaranteed continued production (Marsden *et al.*, 1985). These strikes tended to be about non-pay items such as rest allowances and working pace. Moreover, although they affected the entire production process, they originated in final assembly areas where the technology itself had had little direct effect. The issues were the speeding up of lines and reductions in manning (Willman, 1984). For example, in one notable strike in 1983 at Cowley assembly plant, the major issue concerned the removal by managers of a traditional 3-minute time allowance at the start and end of each shift. The plant itself was much less affected by advanced manufacturing technology than the 'upstream' body plant, but the company argued that full utilization of assembly facilities was necessary for the economic justification of the new body-making facilities (Marsden *et al.*, 1985).

Despite these disputes, the balance of influence in the industry has shifted away from the shopfloor. By 1984, unions were concerned to deal with issues such as the location of production and the sourcing of components rather than with issues of job control. The central strategy of unions in the industry also came to rely heavily on the willingness of a future government to support a series of planning agreements for the industry under which, with protection by import controls, output would be expanded. Managers concerned with industrial relations tended to deal with full-time officials and to separate consultation within plants from collective bargaining at company level.

The industry has come to be something of a talisman for the changes to shopfloor industrial relations in the 1980s, and indeed the pressures which prompted change—for improved productivity and rapid product innovation—may have affected a range of industries at that time. Moreover, the shift on the part of the unions, from reliance on local bargaining to a concern with political activity to guarantee job security, reflected the path chosen by the TUC as a whole. Because of this, it is worth emphasizing the idiosyncrasies of the industry in terms of the severity of economic crisis, the extent of shopfloor power in the 1970s and the rapidity and scale of the process change. Nevertheless, the example does reinforce the points made above. It is almost impossible for unions to negotiate over process change under the threat of closure or disinvestment. Secondly, plant-level bargaining is highly inappropriate to deal with changes which are company-wide or industry-wide; and thirdly, the climate of change is almost as important for trade unions as the change itself.

A specific example may be useful here. Automation of body assembly has led to an increase in the proportion of skilled workers and to a reduction of overall demand of labour. However, the fact that the workforce in the industry is currently smaller and more highly skilled than 5 years ago has as much to do with the removal of unskilled direct labour simply through process-efficiency improvements. The use of advanced manufacturing technology is best seen as part of a cost-minimizing strategy.

In fact, reform of the organization of skilled work has raised several difficulties in the car firms, as the demands of highly automated lines, as well as cost pressures, encourage moves towards increased flexibility. The organization of maintenance in particular has historically relied on relatively rigid demarcations not only between the tasks covered by the two principal unions, the EETPU and the AUEW (now AEU), but also *within* the territory of the latter between machine tool fitters, pipefitters and millwrights. With an increasing demand for electronics skills, and the need to avoid expensive downtime on high-volume equipment, the retraining of craftsmen and the reorganization of maintenance work became a much higher priority. In BL, the objective was to move towards 'two-trades maintenance', that is the abolition of all demarcations between trades except that between two broadly defined electrical and mechanical trade groups. Moreover, craft workers were to be redeployed away from a central maintenance 'pen' into two-man teams patrolling the lines and responsible to line supervision. Once more the concern was to reduce avoidable machine downtime. In addition, routine maintenance tasks such as oiling, greasing, and tool changing were to be performed by semi-skilled operatives (Willman and Winch, 1985).

Collective agreements were required to cover these changes. For example, those at Vauxhall in 1984 reduced the twelve different 'fitter' classifications while committing the unions to the acceptance of new technology. At Leyland vehicles, agreements identified three 'core' skills—fitter, turner, and electrician—around which 'flexibility and overlap' could occur. As in Vauxhall, 'There will be no restriction on training, commissioning and operation of all new plant and equipment, technology and computerised systems' (Incomes Data Services, 1984). Similar arrangements have been put into effect at Ford (Marsden *et al.*, 1985).

UNION ORGANIZATION AND BARGAINING STRUCTURE

Change to craft organization, however, appears to have gone further in some other industries, particularly process industries. Cross (1985) notes that 'cross-trading', involving an amalgamation of mechanical and electrical skills, is common in industries such as brewing and food processing. In part this is because single pieces of new equipment require a wider skill base for maintenance. This can have severe consequences for collective bargaining. For example at the Mobil Coryton refinery the position of 'refinery craftsman' has been established. Such craftsmen will 'undertake refinery maintenance work in a fully flexible manner without any demarcations and restrictions, subject only to limitations imposed by individual skill levels'. As a consequence the trade basis of union representation has been altered. Whereas in the past stewards were elected by constituencies of their own trade to the Joint Shop Stewards Committee, the new basis was to be election by multi-skilled work groups, with the proviso that any unrepresented signatory union could have a member co-opted (Incomes Data Services, 1984).

In general, technology encourages three distinct types of change within the maintenance function. The first has simply to do with the enhancement of individual skills through retraining, for example, grafting electronics skills onto those of electrical craftsmen. The second has to do with the removal of distinctions *between* different crafts, as in the Coryton example. The third is concerned with the removal of distinctions between craftsmen and other groups such as production or the drawing office.

Craft unions affected by advanced manufacturing technology naturally have reacted differently to such changes depending on the direction of flow of work and thus membership. The EETPU has developed a policy which resists the transfer of work from its members to those of other unions, while emphasizing its right to represent technician and 'super-craft' grades. The AUEW (now AEU) has similarly sought to retain control over work affected by advanced manufacturing technology by stressing the right of its members to programme CNC machine tools. This has led to conflict with TASS, representing draughtsmen and white-collar grades. However, the most severe inter-union conflicts over the right to operate new technology have occurred in the printing industry and have involved the NGA. Despite its ability to hold up the introduction of direct text input by journalists in the national newspapers, the union has had to seek accommodations with the journalists union, the NUJ, and the major production union, SOGAT 82, in the provincial press where its control over labour supply is less secure. In essence, this accommodation involved sharing control over text inputting. The NGA proposal was that there be no demarcation between the three unions in the area of text origination (i.e. the task of setting type by computer), but that within this area a closed shop and guarantee of no redundancy should operate. However, this policy foundered, and several conflicts arose about the unwillingness of the journalists to accept that NGA members could do what had previously been journalistic work. As previous experience in the United States has shown, it is difficult for unions to develop policies which acceptably share a diminishing pool of jobs. Even where the unions agree on a policy, the membership in affected organizations frequently put personal job security above inter-union harmony. In this industry the US experience of a move from outright opposition to change to acceptance of a 'buy-out' price for change is likely to be repeated in the UK.

Such differences between and within unions, and the ways in which employers deal with them, may be crucial for the acceptance of advanced manufacturing technology. Martin (1981) argues that the failure to establish an agreement on new technology covering all of the national newspapers was a major factor in the failure of proprietors to introduce photocomposition. The interests of national unions and the various 'chapels' on Fleet Street could not be reconciled. He draws explicitly on comparison with the USA, where employer co-operation led to more rapid change. Goodman *et al.*'s (1977) well-documented study of change in the footwear industry also associates industry-wide bargaining with the successful adoption of new technology. However, centralization of bargaining may not always assist change. In the process industries those companies which conduct bargaining at plant level apparently have experienced an advantage in implementing change (Cross, 1985). For the reasons outlined above, it is often easier to negotiate change with representatives of employees who are benefiting from it than with national officials seeking to reconcile conflicting plant claims or looking simply to implement union policy.

In some cases technical change itself may encourage change to bargaining structures throughout a company. One of the most striking recent examples of such a strategic change occurred at Pilkingtons, the dominant producer of flat, safety, and optical glass in the UK. In 1980, two-thirds of the company's employees were based in St Helens, producing flat glass and related products. By 1984 this had shrunk dramatically as the company diversified into the manufacture of new products such as fibre optic cable on new or acquired sites elsewhere. A sustained programme of product and process innovation involved an increase in capital intensity and large-scale redundancies. The company sought to treat each plant as a profit centre based around a particular production technology, and to allow site management to negotiate suitable terms and conditions. Central direction consisted of an emphasis on multi-union bargaining and harmonization of manual and non-manual terms and conditions. The changes were implemented despite the opposition of the principal production union, the GMBATU. A proposal to strike against the implementation of plant bargaining was rejected (Industrial Relations Review and Report, 1985).

Such strategic changes may be rare, but the influence of bargaining structure may be important for successful implementation even where change is relatively small-scale. For example, the ability to offer improved terms and conditions to those with enhanced craft skills may require plant bargaining. It may also depend on the existence of separate bargaining rights for craftsmen. If one manual bargaining unit exists, the fact that skilled workers are likely to be the minority may limit the employer's ability to negotiate changes in return for better conditions. Non-craft workers are unlikely to favour proposals which widen differentials. Faced with this problem, and the fear that retrained craftsmen may leave if no improvements in pay are forthcoming, the employer may either include non-craft workers by bargaining working practice changes or not innovate at all.

In the latter case it is at least likely that the firm will seek to establish the preferred production technology or working arrangements on a green-field site. The new sites need not contain radically new processes, it may simply embody 'best practice' in the firm or industry. Nor need it be concerned with new products. It may simply be a branch plant meeting the needs of a mature market. However, several new plants which do involve process innovations or new products are associated with innovative labour relations, in the form of single status agreements, and pendulum arbitration (Incomes Data Services, 1984; Industrial Relations Review and Report, 1984). Two rather different processes may be involved here. In the first, established unionized firms install new or replacement capacity on a green-field site and take a 'clean sheet' approach to work organization and industrial relations, for example, at Whitbread in Wales and Trebor in Colchester. In the second, high technology firms who are inward investors into the UK sign single-union deals involving no-strike clauses or arbitration arrangements in order to secure continuity of production, as for example, at Sanyo, Toshiba, and Control Data.

For the reasons mentioned above, these two situations are very different from the trade union point of view. In the first, the interests of those employed on green-field sites need to be set off against, on the one hand, the interests of those in plants which will not receive new investment and, on the other, the prospect that investment will not occur if hard bargaining does. In the second, the concern is primarily with recruitment. The issue here is to secure sole negotiating rights, in return for which a number of concessions about shopfloor representation and the right to strike may be made.

IMPLEMENTATION

The final set of industrial relations issues concern the way in which technical change is implemented. The style and pattern of implementation is likely to influence the trade union response to change, irrespective of the properties of the technology itself. Indeed, trade union views on the handling of change rely on the proposition that there is nothing immutable or given about the industrial relations consequences of change, and that a range of issues including the selection, design, and programming of advanced manufacturing technology are in principle negotiable.

This view itself is relatively recent. In previous automation debates the TUC has concerned itself solely with the impact of change rather than seeking to influence its rate and direction (Willman, 1986). It reflects a concern, particularly among white-collar unions worried about the impact of office technology, with the severity of the consequences of this particular generation of changes, as well as the recognition that software design has considerable implications for job design and skill levels. Its consequences can be seen in the design of the 'Checklist for Negotiators' produced in 1979 which, from one point of view, can be seen as a statement of the preferred implementation procedure (Table 7.2). The TUC wishes affected unions to be involved at the earliest stages, to be granted access to all relevant information, to have the right of veto over change, and to share in its benefits. It also wants to see inter-union collaboration.

Table 7.2   TUC Checklist for Negotiators: main items

1.	Change must be by agreement: consultation with trade unions should begin prior to the decision to purchase, and status quo provisions should operate until agreement is reached.
2.	Machinery must be developed to cope with technical change which emphasizes the central importance of collective bargaining.
3.	Information relevant to decision making should be made available to union representatives or nominees prior to any decision being taken.
4.	There must be agreement both on employment and output levels within the company. Guarantees of job security, redeployment, and relocation agreements must be achieved. In addition, enterprises should be committed to an expansion of output after technical change.
5.	Company retraining commitments must be stepped up, with priority for those affected by new technology. Earnings levels must be secured.
6.	The working week should be reduced to 35 hours, systematic overtime should be eliminated and shift patterns altered.
7.	The benefits of new technology must be distributed. Innovation must occasion improvements in terms and conditions of service.
8.	Negotiators should seek influence over the design of equipment, and in particular should seek to control work or performance measurement through the new technology.
9.	Stringent health and safety standards must be observed.
10.	Procedures for reviewing progress, and study teams on the new technology, should be established.

Source: Employment and Technology (TUC, 1979).

There is some evidence to suggest that unions have on occasion succeeded in encouraging employers to sign new technology agreements, particularly in the public sector (Williams and Moseley, 1985). There is also evidence from the electronics sector that the signing of new technology agreements led to earlier involvement of white-collar trade unions in innovation decisions and so to an improved flow of information (NEDO, 1983). But the majority of union members in manufacturing industry are not covered by such comprehensive arrangements. Apart from the preference for the tried and tested productivity bargaining model, there appear to be several reasons for this. They have to do with supplier relations, the technical expertise of managers, the nature of union involvement, the absence of statutory support for bargaining of this kind, and the problems of inter-union conflict.

Microprocessor-based process innovations have diffused across manufacturing industry at a rate partly determined by the familiarity of managers with the potential benefits of such change. At later stages in the diffusion process, innovation decisions are likely to be made by managers of firms in mature industries in negotiation with equipment suppliers (Freeman, 1976). For trade unions seeking to become involved in the decision to innovate, or the design of equipment, this can present problems. The first of these is simply that their managers may not be *au fait* with the properties of the new equipment or with design alternatives. They may be reluctant to expose this ignorance by agreeing to negotiate, or they may be simply unaware that there are design options. The second is that the supplier may, on grounds of confidentiality, be unwilling to disclose all relevant information to the purchaser's trade unions in advance of purchase. The third is that, whatever the commitments of the purchasing employer, the supplier may be unwilling to accommodate trade union suggestions. Such a situation might arise where the purchase was a small proportion of the supplier's market, or where because of previous purchases the firm can only rely on one supplier for compatible or replacement equipment. It is unlikely that suppliers would agree to the costs of design modifications without guarantee of purchase and of trade union acceptance, hence the market research conducted by a purchaser might be extremely difficult.

A second set of problems concerns the ability of trade unions in UK manufacturing to become involved in innovation decisions. In many cases the responsibility for involvement in such an exercise falls on shopfloor representatives rather than full-time officials, the latter having typically to cover a large number of workplaces. The central problem here is the capacity of shopfloor representatives seriously to question managerial proposals for the installation of new processes with which the representatives may be unfamiliar. It is highly unlikely that the union will be able to provide expert advice on equipment characteristics, and the stewards may come to rely on managerial expertise and sources of information.

Such was the case during the participative exercise surrounding the purchase of automated equipment for production of the BL Metro in the late 1970s. Representatives of BL unions were involved in a participative structure expressly designed to consider process changes over a period of years. However, they exercised little influence over equipment design despite visiting a number of competitors' plants to see different design configurations in action. There were several reasons for this, including the pace of change, and the turnover of union representatives. However, the principal cause was the development of an imbalance of expertise between a full-time managerial project team concerned to get its definition of equipment requirements across, and union representatives without outside support fitting participation into their normal workload. A standard set of questions concerning the extent of retraining, the manning requirements of new capital equipment, and the possibility of finding British suppliers tended to emerge from the union side (Willman and Winch, 1985).

Once more, experience in one car manufacturer is not necessarily representative, but it does need to be said that the circumstances at BL were reasonably auspicious. The participation scheme was elaborate and endorsed by government, and the shopfloor organizations involved were among the strongest in the manufacturing industry. The problems experienced by representatives at BL are likely to be *more* severe elsewhere.

A third set of obstacles to widespread adoption of new technology agreements concerns the absence of any legal support for this form of bargaining. One could of course argue that such legal support is relatively unimportant in the UK. Unions in the private sector have for the most part operated without any statutory support for collective bargaining (Gospel, 1983), and one ought not to expect, therefore, that it would assume importance in the extension of bargaining to innovation decisions. However, during the 1970s, unions used newly available legislation to establish bargaining rights and to assist the bargaining process. Two legislative items are of particular relevance here. First, the disclosure of information provisions of the Employment Protection Act; and second, the Safety Representatives and Safe Committee Regulations of the Health and Safety at Work Act.

Under S17(1) of the Employment Protection Act the employer must disclose information without which the union would be to a material extent impeded in collective bargaining, and which it would be in accordance with good industrial relations practice to disclose. Disclosure must be about matters for which the union is recognized. Further restrictions on the duty to disclose are contained in S18. Among other exemptions, employers need not disclose any information communicated in confidence, or which involves contravention of any enactment; nor need they allow inspection of any documents. Successful use of the provisions has indicated the very restricted nature of the disclosure on offer. As Gospel and Willman (1981) note, they have tended to be used by relatively weak unions seeking information which more generally tends to be disclosed (for example, about the basis of a job evaluation scheme) and they are unlikely to have extended the scope of bargaining primarily because of the power of the restrictive provisions of S18.

Two particular features of the provisions hamper their use in cases of technical change. The first is that employers cannot be compelled to disclose information to trade unions over which another party holds copyright; thus software which originates with suppliers need not be discussed. The second, based on a decision about the TGWU's rights to information about plant closure, is that there need be no disclosure where the employer refuses to bargain, since the union cannot be said to have suffered a material impediment (Gospel and Willman, 1981). If the employer cannot be compelled to bargain, the provisions cannot operate. The particular importance of this arises from the fact that the employer cannot be compelled to bargain over technical change. Recent case law implies that such change, and the right of the employer to decide about it, is part of a normal employment contract:

An employee is expected to adapt himself to new methods and techniques introduced in the course of his employment. On his side, the employer must provide any necessary training or retraining. It is a question of pure fact in each particular case whether the retraining involved the acquisition of such esoteric skills that it would not be reasonable to expect the employee to acquire them. Nowadays, however, it cannot be considered esoteric or unusual to ask an employee to acquire basic skills as to retrieving information from a computer or feeding information into one (Industrial Relations Law Report, 1985).

In effect, advanced manufacturing technology is covered by the same sorts of management rights clauses as operate in the US (McLaughlin, 1979).

In summary, then, the disclosure provisions are unlikely to secure access to information about advanced manufacturing technology. In fact, the ACAS code of practice specifically mentions 'detailed analysis of proposed investment' as the sort of disclosure which might cause substantial injury to the employer (ACAS, 1977). However, the contents of the Safety Representatives and Safety Committee Regulations (SRSCR) may, despite the similar wording of the exemption provisions on disclosure, offer more information.

These Regulations grant statutory rights to safety representatives appointed by recognized trade unions. These include those more widely granted to union representatives, such as time off, as well as more specific provisions relating to rights of inspection and to information. The latter are more powerful than those of the Employment Protection Act in that no material impediment need be proved, and the representative secures rights to inspect and copy documents. In particular, the accompanying Code of Practice lists as accessible: 'any relevant information provided by consultants or by designers or by the manufacturer, importer or supplier of any article or substance used, or proposed to be used, at work by their employees'.

The Regulations thus imply certain rights to information about equipment. But their importance for unions, particularly white-collar unions, goes beyond this in that it allows the establishment and training of a network of representatives which did not previously exist. Many unions have not been slow to realize the potential of such a network, and it is significant that the TUC checklist for negotiators, and the similar framework agreements proposed by white-collar unions such as TASS and APEX, all lay heavy emphasis on the need to monitor the health hazards of visual display terminals, perhaps the most characteristic feature of any form of new office technology.

However, useful though the safety provisions may be in certain circumstances, the disclosed information will not feature in bargaining over change if the employer does not wish. The central feature of the TUC checklist, that all change must be by agreement, depends on the willingness of employers to subject innovation decisions to union influence. One could argue that they are much more likely to refuse this than to refuse disclosure of information which might be a prelude to retraining in any event. Indeed, the refusal of the CBI to accept even the principle of consultation over change does not indicate a disposition on their part to involve unions.

The fourth set of problems has already been touched upon. The checklist proposes joint union machinery and action to deal with advanced manufacturing and other technology, but it is not at all clear that existing joint machinery will survive the tensions imposed upon it by the requirement to deal with job-displacing technical change, particularly where there are clear winners and losers. It is argued that new technology may accelerate a process of union merger, thus removing problems of inter-union competition. Such a process may be already occurring in the printing industry. However, it is equally likely that the 'beneficiaries' of new technology may prefer to deal separately with employers in order to exploit market scarcity. Currently, salaries for engineering staff with expertise in new technology in the car industry are rising far more quickly than rates for manual grades, and there are shortages within the industry, and more generally of craftsmen with knowledge of information technology (Incomes Data Services, 1985). Such workers may be unwilling to be involved in joint negotiating arrangements.

CONCLUSION

Overall, trade unions in the UK face severe problems in securing influence over the ways in which advanced manufacturing technology is being introduced, and in gaining some tangible benefits from its introduction in the form of improvements to terms and conditions of employment. The technology itself appears to have more effect on the composition of employment than on its level, leading in general to a proportionately greater number of skilled operatives, particularly concerned with maintenance. Of much greater importance for the employment level over the past 5 years has been the experience of severe recession in UK manufacturing, which has defined the purpose for which new investment has been considered as well as the circumstances of its use. Many trade unionists have come to see investment proposals as a guarantee of at least some jobs, and the absence of innovation as a threat to all.

However, the manufacturing sector contains firms which are sellers of new technology products as well as those which are purchasers of new technology processes. It might be expected that differences would occur between firms, but overall it seems fair to say that there has been little resistance to microprocessor-based innovations in manufacturing, even though there may have been problems in specific sectors such as printing. This is despite the widespread indifference by employers to the policy statements and framework agreements suggested by many unions. Over the past 5 years the ambitions of unions in this area have become more modest, and the concern to secure change has taken precedence over the concern to secure negotiated adjustment to it. In part this is because of a lack of bargaining power, but it also follows from a concern to move away from the recent trend of raising the price of redundancy to one of securing the future membership base. In the absence of tight labour markets, or of government support for trade union involvement in change, it is likely that the emphasis in the near future will be on consultation and communication of managerial intentions, rather than negotiations over change in which unions retain the right of veto.

REFERENCES

Abernathy, W. J. (1978). *The Productivity Dilemma*. Baltimore: Johns Hopkins.

Advisory Conciliation and Arbitration Service (1977). *Disclosure of Information to Trade Unions for Collective Bargaining Purposes*. London: HMSO.

Batstone, E. (1984). *Working Order*. Oxford: Blackwell.

Brown, W. (1973). *Piecework Bargaining*. London: Heinemann.Brown, W. (1983). Industrial relations in the private sector: Donovan revisited. In G. Bain (ed.), *Industrial Relations in Britain*. Oxford: Blackwell.

Brown, W., and Sisson, K. (1983). Industrial relations in the next decade: current issues and future possibilities. *Industrial Relations Journal*, **14**(1), 9–22.

Corina, J. (1983). Trade unions and technological change. In S. McDonald *et al.* (eds), *The Trouble with Technology*. London: Frances Pinter.

Cross, M. (1985). *Towards the Flexible Craftsman*. London: Technical Change Centre.

Daniel, W. W., and Millward, N. (1983). *Workplace Industrial Relations in Britain*. London: Heinemann.

De Bresson, C., and Townsend, J. (1978). Notes on the inter-industry flow of technology in post-war Britain. *Research Policy*, **7**, 48–60.

Edwards, P. (1984). *The Management of Productivity*. Warwick University IRRU Discussion Paper.

Freeman, C. (1976). *The Economics of Industrial Innovation*. Harmondsworth: Penguin.

Goodman, J. F. B., Armstrong, E., Davies, J., and Wagner, A. (1977). *Rule Making and Industrial Peace*. London: Croom Helm.

Gospel, H. (1983). Trade unions and the legal obligation to bargain: an American, Swedish and British comparison. *British Journal of Industrial Relations*, **21**, 343–58.

Gospel, H., and Willman, P. (1981). Disclosure of information: the CAC approach. *Industrial Law Journal*, March, pp. 10–22.

Incomes Data Services (1984). Group working and greenfield sites. *Study No. 314*, May.

Incomes Data Services (1984). Craft flexibility. *Study No. 322*, September.

Incomes Data Services (1985). *Report No. 445*, March.

Industrial Relations Law Report (1985). *Cresswell & Others vs Board of Inland Revenue*, pp. 190–200.

Industrial Relations Review and Report (1984). No strike deals in perspective. *No. 324*, July.

Industrial Relations Review and Report (1985). Decentralisation of collective bargaining. *No. 341*, April.

Jones, B. (1982). Destruction or redistribution of engineering skills: the case of numerical control. In S. Wood (ed.), *The Degradation of Work*. London: Hutchinson.

Jones, D. T. (1983). Technology and the U.K. automobile industry. *Lloyds Bank Review*, p. 148.

McLaughlin, D. B. (1979). *The Impact of Labour Unions on the Rate and Direction of Technical Change*. ILIR, Ann Arbor: University of Michigan.

Manwaring, A. (1981). The trade union response to new technology. *Industrial Relations Journal*, **12**(4), 7–26.

Marsden, D., Morris, T., Willman, P., and Wood, S. (1985). *The Car Industry: Labour Relations and Industrial Adjustment*. London: Tavistock.

Martin, R. (1981). *New Technology and Industrial Relations in Fleet St*. Oxford: Oxford University Press.

National Economic Development Office (1983). *The Introduction of New Technology*. London: NEDO.

Northcott, J., and Rogers, P. (1984). *Microelectronics in British Industry: Patterns of Change*. London: Policy Studies Institute.

Pavitt, K. (1984). Sectoral patterns of technical change: towards a taxonomy and a theory. *Research Policy*, **13**, 343–73.

Prais, S. J. (1981). *Productivity and Industrial Structure*. Cambridge: Cambridge University Press.

Robins, K., and Webster, F. (1982). New technology: a survey of trade union responses in Britain. *Industrial Relations Journal*, **13**, 1–12.

Townsend, J., Henwood, F., Thomas, G., Pavitt, K., and Wyatt, S. (1981). Science and technology indicators for the UK: innovations in Britain since 1945. Sussex, SPRU (mimeo).

Trades Union Congress (1979). *Employment and Technology*. London: TUC.

Turner, H. A., Clack, G., and Roberts, G. (1967). *Labour Relations in the Motor Industry*. London: Allen & Unwin.

Wilkinson, B. (1983). *The Shopfloor Politics of New Technology*. London: Heinemann.

Williams, K., Williams, J., and Thomas, D. (1983). *Why are the British Bad at Manufacturing?* London: Routledge.

Williams, R., and Moseley, R. (1985). Technology agreements in Great Britain: a survey 1977–1983. *Industrial Relations Journal*, **16**(3), 58–73.

Willman, P. (1982). *Fairness, Collective Bargaining and Incomes Policy*. Oxford: Oxford University Press.

Willman, P. (1984). The reform of collective bargaining and strike activity at BL Cars. *Industrial Relations Journal*, **15**(2), 1–12.

Willman, P. (1986). *Innovation and Industrial Relations*. Oxford: Oxford University Press.

Willman, P., and Winch, G. (1985). *Innovation and Management Control: Labour Relations at BL Cars*. Cambridge: Cambridge University Press.

Wilson, D. F. (1972). *Dockers: The Impact of Industrial Changes*. London: Fontana.

Wilson, R. A. (1984). *The Impact of Information Technology on the Engineering Industry*. Warwick: University of Warwick Institute of Employment Research.

Wragg, D., and Robertson, J. (1977). *Post War Trends in Employment Productivity Output, Labour Costs and Prices by Industry in the UK*. Department of Employment, Research Paper No. 3. London: HMSO.

CHAPTER 8

Societal Implications of Advanced Manufacturing Technology

JOHN BESSANT AND PETER SENKER

The contribution which advanced manufacturing technology (AMT) can make to economic growth has become an article of faith in most developed countries. In particular, considerable interest has been shown in information technology as a means of providing an urgently needed transfusion of new capabilities in the planning, management, and control of manufacturing.

It is, of course, difficult to separate out the background 'bread and butter' improvements which go on all the time from those innovations which have a major impact. But, as Freeman, Clark, and Soete (1982) point out, there does seem to be evidence for the existence of a cycle with a period of 45−50 years associated with major technological shifts—the so-called Kondratiev 'long waves'. These authors identify four characteristics of such major technologies:

1. They introduce major cost reductions for more than a few products or sectors. Thus railways or electricity qualify whereas float glass, although a radical innovation of considerable importance in the glass industry, does not, because of its limited application.
2. They contribute major technical advantages; for example, reliability, quality, and accuracy, across a wide range of industrial sectors and applications.
3. They have pervasive effects throughout the economic system.
4. They are socially and environmentally acceptable.

It is becoming clear that information technology (IT) meets these criteria and can be rightly considered to be such a major force. With its potential for making significant improvements in the productivity of both labour and capital it is a strong candidate to act as an engine of economic growth, just as steam power or electricity did in earlier cycles. One of IT's most important manifestations occurs in its contribution to the automation of manufacturing processes.

Getting the best out of a major new technology depends on learning how to use it to its full potential; and this may involve totally new ways of working, not just doing what was always done a little better. A good historical example of this can be seen in the early development of electrical power. In factories the first approach to its use was to replace the steam engines driving the central belt drives which served an entire floor of machines. Only later was the full potential of independent engines for each machine realized, with dramatic improvements in overall performance. The same pattern can be seen in the case of new manufacturing and service sector technology, where the general view is that we are still in the early phase of using it as a direct substitute for existing equipment: word processors for typewriters, robots for human handlers, and so on. Most commentators expect the major benefits to come when we move from this discrete automation into a more integrated form in which the full potential of the technology can be exploited in the office and factory of the future (see Bessant *et al.*, 1985, for examples).

Such a move is likely to pose a number of significant challenges, not only to management within manufacturing industry, but to society as a whole. Implicit in the technological trends are major structural and social shifts associated with industrial organization and location, skills and employment distribution, education, leisure, and the overall distribution of wealth. Whilst the future pattern is still evolving, and to some extent fluid, it is already clear that to make the most of the opportunities afforded by advanced technologies (and to minimize the problems posed) will require considerable skill in managing the change.

Central to this theme of adapting to new technology is the question of skill, and in particular of ensuring a balance between the demands posed by the new technology and the education and training system which is intended to meet these needs. On the one hand there is typically an urgent need as the pace of change accelerates for new and different skills and combinations of skills, whilst on the other there may be a decline in the need for other, more traditional skills. The problem posed is how to balance the two, how to match the training and retraining system outputs to the requirements of changing skill structure and composition demand. There is, we believe, strong evidence that some countries manage this process far more efficiently than others.

Even in times of rationalization, where the emphasis is on slower growth and more 'bread and butter' improvement innovation—the 'downswing' of the Kondratiev—the matching of skills to the changing needs of production is critical. For example, the 1950s and 1960s were periods of high investment in manufacturing industry. But in several advanced industrial countries an acceleration in the growth rate of investment in the period 1965−70 was accompanied by a reduction in the growth rate of employment compared with the previous 5-year period. Freeman *et al.* (1982) go on to argue that in the late 1960s, well before the 1973 energy crisis and the 1974/5 recession, factors such as intensifying competition in more slowly growing markets led to the onset of rationalization. This trend involved greater emphasis on more economical production as opposed to increasing production.

Japanese industry, with its greater endowment of relevant skills, was better able to rationalize its production than British or even American industry. By means of competition largely based on success in rationalizing production, Japanese firms were able to increase their shares of relatively stagnant world markets.

A more recent comparison can be seen in the work of Prais at NIESR (1981), where research has shown that although Britain has a relatively good record in the adoption of CNC machine tool technology, the actual performance obtained from this investment is much lower than that of West Germany. The point made by the authors is that most of this difference appears to be explained by differences in the skills, and particularly the educational background, of the operators involved.

In similar vein, Schonberger (1982) points out that although much of the success of Japanese manufacturing industry is ascribed to extensive use of advanced technology, in practice the real differences accounting for productivity improvements are in the area of production organization and management, particularly in the quality and use made of human resources.

So it is clear that for AMT to make its undoubtedly key contribution to economic growth there is a need for skills. It is not just a question of adopting new technology, but of how that technology is used once in place, a factor to which attention is being increasingly drawn. For example, in work on the adoption of computer aided design (CAD) systems, Arnold and Senker (1983) found that in a sample of 34 firms even the adoption of an off-the-shelf, turnkey installation posed important learning difficulties. Best practice productivity levels took an average of 2 years from installation to achieve.

In another case, in his work on industrial robots, Fleck (1982) found that nearly half the firms which he examined had experienced initial problems, and of these around half had subsequently abandoned their projects involving robots.

Finally, in the case of computer-based production management aids (such as materials requirements planning (MRP)), Voss (1985) reports on a number of problems which still prevent many firms from exploiting such systems to their full advantage. In some cases, notably the recently reported case of TI-Raleigh, adoption has actually reduced efficiency: 'the changes in computer control systems have not only failed to produce improvements but caused a serious loss of production efficiency' (*Engineering Computers*, November 1984).

From these and other examples (see Bessant, 1985) it is clear that there can be problems in securing the full potential benefits of AMT. Of these it seems likely that the provision of suitable skills to develop, operate, and maintain the technology is the most difficult problem to be resolved. This requires us to take a closer look at what skills are likely to be in demand and where they will be needed.

WHAT SKILLS AND WHERE?

It is axiomatic to say that using new production processes requires a ready supply of new skills. Because they are usually less labour-intensive, the number of skilled people required is lower. For example, the manufacture of complex plastic injection-moulded components is generally less labour-intensive than the making and subsequent assembly of several relatively simple components. One-piece plastic radiator grilles for cars have widely replaced metal assemblies, whilst one-piece plastic outer tubs for washing machines are continuing to replace vitreous enamel metal tubs onto which several brackets and other attachments have to be fixed.

Successful and economic manufacture of high-quality plastic components demands a wide range of new skills. To ensure that plastics raw materials are of the necessary consistent high quality, technicians are required to test incoming batches of materials. Plastics technologists are needed to measure and study the behaviour of plastic materials during the moulding process to try and prevent quality problems. 'Troubleshooters' may be needed to deal with the problems when, despite precautions, these arise.

One of the significant features of this changing pattern is the move away from direct intervention in plant operation and towards a more indirect, supervisory role. New control systems are no longer simply tools for the operator alone, but part of a complex and flexible system in which the main role is more one of policeman, intervening only when something goes wrong. Whilst it is unlikely that factories will ever become totally automatic, that is run without any human intervention whatsoever, the trend is clearly towards low levels of employment, mostly concentrated in indirect support activities.

In turn this has implications for the way in which support activities are structured. Whereas before these might have been largely reactive systems, they will increasingly need to be planned activities. The traditional picture of production management with its constant atmosphere of crisis and its predominantly 'fire-fighting' style, is incompatible with the way in which advanced manufacturing systems operate. Attempts to 'force-fit' new technology into old production management systems are likely to result in sub-optimal use of that technology, often at considerable cost.

A further complicating feature is the trend towards integration of production activities. As Kaplinsky (1984) points out, the pattern of development in industry has been one of convergence, both within and between what he calls 'spheres' of production activity—that is in design, production, and co-ordination. For example, in machine tools the early pattern was for each operation to be performed on a single-function machine under manual control. Next came multi-function machines, followed by early forms of automatic control based on mechanical principles which began to embody the operator skill in the machine itself. A further breakthrough came with the development of numerical control (NC) and this, coupled with increasing sophistication, now makes it possible for one machining centre to carry out many different functions without any operator intervention. Integration does not stop here, however. The next phase is the linking together of different machines under hierarchical control, in direct numerical control (DNC) networks, for example. Current interest is high in the field of flexible manufacturing systems (FMSs), which takes this integration a stage further, bringing in both machining and handling operations under computer control, and using links with the co-ordination sphere to schedule the routing of batches in optimal fashion to ensure rapid throughput and high utilization of the plant. Such integration, what Halevi (1980) terms 'HAL-automation', from the Hebrew word meaning 'all-embracing', eventually leads to a pattern which has been termed 'computer-integrated manufacturing' (CIM), in which all activities in manufacturing are linked via electronic means. These systems will bring together design and manufacturing via CAD/CAM linkages and underpin them with computer-based stock control, materials management, production scheduling and control, purchasing, quality control, and so on. Many commentators do not expect the process of convergence to stop at the boundaries of the firm. With the possibilities of electronic networks, the links between suppliers on the one hand and customers on the other can also be integrated so that information on components to be purchased, for example, will be passed between CAD installations in the supplier and customer companies. For our purposes the key point about such convergence is that it is creating major new problems for the skills system to resolve.

Similar patterns can be found in any industry as investment in advanced manufacturing technology takes place. Total employment per unit of output declines, but some of the remaining employees need to have broader skills and to be able to deploy them much more flexibly. In another case, that of CNC-based machine shops in engineering, the number of operators and setters goes down, often by 30−50 per cent in overall terms. But there are needs for people with new skills, for example in the maintenance area and particularly in diagnostics. It is likely that future flexible manufacturing system installations will incorporate as much in the way of automatic diagnosis as is feasible but, even allowing for this, it is unlikely that automatic diagnostics will be adequate to diagnose all the fault conditions which might occur.

Maintenance skills

In general, the more production is automated, the more important it becomes to prevent machines breaking down; or, if they do break down, the more vital it is to repair them and get them back into production as quickly as possible. Most of the time taken in this is spent on finding the fault—partly because there are now many potential sites in complex systems—in the machine tools, the software, the raw materials being used, and so on. The contribution which skilled maintenance personnel can make to this is clear. A recent report from West Germany on the large flexible manufacturing system in use at the Augsburg plant of Messerschmidt-Bolkow-Blum, the aerospace firm, highlights this point.

In this plant, making airframe assemblies for Tornado fighter aircraft, 28 machining centres of various kinds are linked in a flexible manufacturing system whose total cost was in excess of 50 million pounds. Such capital investment requires a very high degree of utilization, and maintenance has a key role to play in ensuring that stoppages are kept to an absolute minimum. Analysis of downtime over a period of 6,000 operating hours for 24 of the machines which had run on a three-shift continuous basis revealed stoppages for the following reasons: 56 per cent were for maintenance and repair; 13 per cent for routine maintenance and inspection; and 17 per cent for facility improvement. Only 14 per cent of stoppages were attributed to non-technical causes.

Of the stoppages for maintenance and repair the distribution was: 22 per cent for reaction time; 20 per cent for diagnosis; 9 per cent for the supply of replacement parts; 40 per cent for repair and overhaul; and 9 per cent for resumption of operations.

This places the burden of downtime very squarely on the shoulders of maintenance personnel. The conclusions from the study were that the length of breakdown time in the plant depended on three factors. First, the intensity of machine utilization; second, the degree of monitoring and facility improvement; and finally, the skill levels and qualifications of the maintenance personnel involved. Their overall conclusion was that

> the more complex and automated the systems were, the higher the skills levels
> of maintenance specialists had to be to achieve reasonable failure rates and im-
> plement facility improvements; . . . and . . . the lower the personnel levels were
> (production with automated facilities), the broader the educational background
> of these workers (operators and maintenance) had to be (Handky, 1983).

The case of maintenance is only one out of many which we could highlight. In general, the pattern of skills change with AMT is clear. Overall levels of employment are falling but the requirements of those remaining in work are rising. Data from the EITB on skill structure changes in the engineering industries clearly shows a rise in the proportion of scientist/technologist grades, and a decline in craftsmen and operators. In general, 'the less skilled an occupation is, the more quickly employment in that occupation has declined' (Fidgett, 1983). Figure 8.1 (drawn from Khamis, Lawson, and McGuire (1986) and based on EITB statutory returns), shows that this trend has continued throughout the period 1978 – 84.

Management skills

Although discussion of skills often focuses on specific technical inputs to the design, operation, and maintenance of advanced manufacturing technology, it is important to recognize that in many cases the most serious problem is the need for new management skills.

For example, there have been few serious problems in Britain in retraining draughtsmen in-house to operate computer aided design (CAD) interactive graphics terminals. The principal problems have been in retraining higher level people, for example, design office managers. Arnold and Senker (1982) found that managerial inefficiency was significant in delaying effective use of CAD, particularly in the mechanical engineering industries. In the motor and aircraft industries, delays in effective use were found to result more often from difficulties with industrial relations. They attributed some of these problems partly to design office managers' lack of industrial relations experience and training.

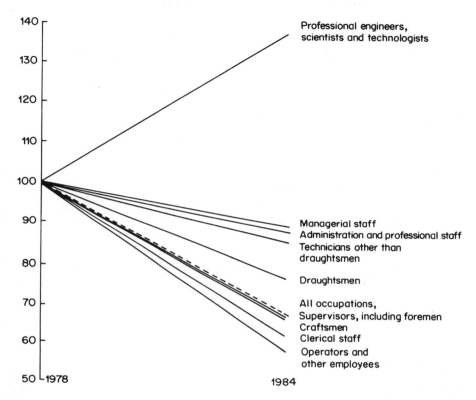

Figure 8.1   Changes in employment in different occupational categories in the engineering industry, 1978–84 (1978 = 100). Reproduced by permission of the Engineering Industry Training Board.

Indeed, the available evidence indicates that some of the most serious problems of education and training to meet industrial needs in Britain are generally at these levels, and not at the level normally addressed by vocational training. Statistically, as Prais (1981) has pointed out, the most important difference between West Germany and Britain in the education and training received by the labour force relates to vocational rather than professional training. But several detailed qualitative studies at a 'micro'-level have found serious deficiencies in British engineering and managerial skills. For example, in the mid-1970s, Bhattacharya (1976) found that only 5 per cent of the firms he examined had their numerically controlled machine tools running smoothly within 6 months of acquisition. In most cases this was mainly due to inadequacies in the machines and control systems delivered to them; but contributory factors were failures in education and training, particularly of management.

One conclusion which could be drawn is that management failed to realize the full implications of numerical control and computer numerical control, and had not implemented an appropriate organizational structure. Delays of up to 2 years in acceptance of new technology on the shopfloor were attributed to failure to educate and train work study and job evaluation engineers about the implications of NC and CNC. Subsequent research by Blumberg and Gerwin (1984) found that firms in several countries, including Britain, were having very great difficulties in evaluating and implementing the much more complex automated machining systems beginning to come into use in the early 1980s. They studied the experience of firms in West Germany, Britain, and America in adopting computer integrated manufacturing systems, and found that firms in all the countries studied, including West Germany, experienced considerable problems. The first function management has to discharge before purchasing such a system is to evaluate its costs and benefits. Firms had very great difficulty in performing this task, and particularly in making financial evaluations of the increased flexibility sueh systems offer. They had problems also in implementation, in relation to quality control, accounting, and maintenance. With the exception of maintenance, most of the key skills the firms lacked were at professional level, rather than at levels normally addressed by vocational training. Unfortunately, Blumberg and Gerwin did not include Japanese firms in their comparisons. There is, however, evidence elsewhere that Japanese firms deploy more and better-trained people at all levels in implementing such systems, and that the financial returns from Japanese firms' investment in such systems have been correspondingly greater (see, for example, Ingersoll Engineers, 1982).

There is evidence that this may reflect a general phenomenon. The in-house training of professional engineers may well be a significant factor in Japanese economic success. Rawle (1983) sees little to choose between the quality and relevance of engineering tuition and curricula in British and Japanese universities. On balance it seems that British engineering students work harder at their studies. But the initial training and continual retraining received by the Japanese engineer inside the company, which will normally employ him for the whole of his working lifetime, appears far superior to the training enjoyed by his British counterpart. Japanese firms have developed practices and procedures which enable them to produce high-quality products relatively cheaply.

Managements of Japanese firms devote considerable attention to ensuring that components and raw materials consistently attain very high standards. They also ensure that their own production workers are trained to give the highest priority to quality (Schonberger, 1982). Management training, which includes indoctrination in the need to accord high priority to training the whole workforce, plays an important part in Japanese economic success. In a very real sense the quality and effectiveness of Japanese vocational training results from the quality and effectiveness of the training they provide for managers and professional engineers.

In many ways the real need is for breadth, with the accompanying ability to apply different skills in flexible fashion. If we return to maintenance skills, then it is clear from work on robots, for example, that the new technology requires combinations of skills. As Fleck (1982) points out: 'the biggest challenge thrown up by robotics lies in the combination of electrical, electronic, mechanical, hydraulic (or whatever) and programming skills required, which cuts across traditional craft boundaries'.

Operator skills

Such flexibility and breadth is equally required at operator level (see Chapter 3). Here the pattern of work with AMT is approaching that already found in large-scale continuous plants like oil refineries, in which a small team has responsibility for a large amount of plant and is expected to be able to deal with various different sections and operations within it. Arrangements vary but examples can be found from small machine shops—in which skilled operators are responsible for CNC programming, planning, machining, quality control, and inspection—through to large-scale flexible transfer lines dealing with high volumes. An example of the latter case can be found in the automotive components sector, where one engineering firm has recently made extensive investment in flexible transfer lines, replacing a long sequence of discrete machining stages. Overall labour intensity has dropped dramatically, but those remaining operators now have full responsibility for the automated lines which produce at faster rates and with a much higher degree of flexibility than the original plant.

Once again the pattern extends across many sectors. In his study of major process industries, Cross (1984) reports that

despite the differences in detail in the processing technologies of the companies studied, the general direction in which an engineering craftsman's job is developing is common. In comparison with existing single trade craftsmen his 1980s and 1990s counterpart is more general . . . in many ways the old single trade base of most craftsmen is more of a limiting factor during a period of change because their core knowledge and understanding might bear no relation to the new and emerging ones.

Summarizing these trends we can surmise that the factory of the future might well differ from its contemporary ancestor in a number of important respects. These are set out in Table 8.1.

TRANSITIONAL PROBLEMS

In an ideal world the transition to the pattern on the right of Table 8.1 would be smooth. In practice it is not, and we need to consider a number of important issues regarding the transition to the factory of the future. Without question, the most serious is the ability of training provisions to cope with the rapidly escalating and broadening demands placed on them by the trend towards advanced manufacturing systems.

The response of many firms to skills problems is to buy them on the labour market. However, this is proving increasingly difficult because of the growing shortages,

Table 8.1   Patterns of work in present and future factories

Present pattern	Factory of the future
Single skills	Multiple skills
Demarcation	Blurring of boundaries
Rigid working practices	Flexible working practices
Operation mainly by direct intervention	Mainly supervision of advanced operations
High division of labour	Moves towards team-work
Low local autonomy	High local autonomy and devolution of responsibility
Training given low priority	Training and organizational development given high priority

particularly of graduate-level skills. At best these will be costly to obtain and difficult to retain in the face of tempting offers from would-be 'poacher' firms. At worst it may prove impossible to get hold of sufficient skills to support the moves into new technology. Thus firms are forced to look at alternatives, particularly sub-contracting and increasing emphasis on training in order to 'grow their own' skills.

Sub-contracting appears to be growing in importance, largely in specialist fields like maintenance where any problems beyond simple first-line diagnosis and repair are often carried out by the equipment supplier rather than the user. It is most effective in situations where the demand for skills is occasional rather than regular, and where the skills and equipment required tend to be of a specialized nature.

There are, however, a number of disadvantages (in addition to the relatively high cost of sub-contracting). First, there is a lack of sufficient training by service organizations of their own manpower. In their survey on contract maintenance, Brady and Senker (1984) found that three-quarters of service organizations relied on 'poaching' staff from in-house factory maintenance staffs. This means that when a machine breaks down the supplier may not have sufficient people available to provide a fast service.

Second, with rising capital costs, downtime becomes of critical significance. If equipment has been bought from suppliers located hundreds or even thousands of miles away then, even allowing for some kind of 'flying squad' service, it may take a long time for a service engineer to arrive and bring the machine back up into production.

Even when a service engineer does arrive, his familiarity usually extends only to the equipment supplied, not to the context in which it is now operating. Such local knowledge about environmental conditions, working practices, and so on is often an important element in fault-finding, and its absence may extend the time taken to complete the diagnosis of problems.

For these reasons firms are increasingly being forced to give a higher priority to training their own personnel. With the increasing pace of technological change it becomes uneconomic to recruit and train new blood for each new generation of equipment, and so more attention is now being given to retraining members of the existing workforce—often those whose present skill may no longer be required because of technological changes elsewhere in the plant.

Traditionally a dual system has operated in training with the external system (national education system, industrial associations, etc.) providing the bulk of training, and a few firms developing their own programmes in-house or using outside resources on a customized-course basis. However, with the cutback in investment on training in the external sector on the one hand, and the increasing requirements for local, company-specific skills on the other, the balance is beginning to shift towards more company-based training.

In either case there are a number of major problems confronting the training system as a whole. Perhaps the most serious is its ability to adapt its curricula rapidly and flexibly enough to keep pace with the demands posed by accelerating technological change. Despite the proliferation of alternative delivery systems, such as 'open learning', the problem remains that in many cases firms are unable to specify in detail exactly what skills, and in what combinations, they are going to require in the future.

One other problem should be mentioned. With the trend towards integration of manufacturing systems and functional areas comes a need for greater flexibility and mobility amongst the workforce and in working practices. Such flexibility, whilst essential to support the computer integrated facilities of the future, is often incompatible with the demarcation patterns of the present. We have already mentioned the need for multi-skilled personnel in areas like maintenance. It would clearly be most efficient for one person to be responsible for diagnostics and repair on a single machine. In practice, however, the UK tradition has split the maintenance activity into a number of trades and thus any attempt to move to multi-skilled working, and particularly towards what Cross (1984) calls 'the flexible craftsman', must raise industrial relations issues regarding demarcation.

Both management and trade unions have become increasingly aware of this problem, and there have been attempts from both sides to provide a suitable resolution. For example the TUC, in its guidelines for negotiating New Technology Agreements, acknowledges the need for inter-union co-operation on manning and skills distribution (TUC, 1979). On the management side attempts have been made to negotiate new working practices, but not always successfully. A good description of such an attempt can be found in the case of the Metro line at Longbridge (Willman and Winch, 1985).

RESPONDING TO THE CHALLENGE

As was suggested in the introduction to this chapter, getting the best out of advanced manufacturing technology will depend critically on securing the necessary skills. So far it must be said that the UK experience has not been particularly impressive. Since 1979 there have been regular reports expressing (with mounting urgency) the fear that the 'revolution' in manufacturing is being held back by a lack of suitable skills. The Policy Studies Institute have conducted a series of surveys of users and potential users of the new technology, and have found repeatedly that, with the exception of the shortage of funds for investment, the most frequently reported problem preventing firms from moving into this technology, or exploiting it as fully as they would like, is a shortage of suitable skills (Northcott and Rogers, 1985).

A recent House of Lords Select Committee Report (1985) suggested that 'technological progress in the UK is hampered by failure to develop the human resources of the nation'. The committee 'doubted whether there is a more serious challenge facing British industry than the adequate provision of people properly qualified and trained to exploit effectively the new technologies as they emerge'. They quoted the EITB's 1983/4 Annual Report: 'Training activity in the engineering industry—whether through apprenticeships, government schemes or in-house initiatives by companies—stands at its lowest level for 20 years.' But the Committee found some encouraging signs: publicity by electronics and engineering firms drawing attention to their inability to recruit sufficient people with the necessary skills; and the setting up of the Butcher Committee in spring 1984 to investigate IT sector skill shortages. (The Butcher Committee subsequently published two reports on graduates and on technicians.)

As the House of Lords Select Committee suggest, the picture is not all gloom. A number of initiatives have been taken to try and deal with the problem. Although some have been criticized, others, such as the concept of 'open learning' (exemplified recently by the Open Tech and its predecessor, the Open University), appear to have worked well. As John Stretch, the training manager for Austin Rover, put it recently,

> measured against our objectives—to deliver training at the right time, place and pace and to encourage self-development—open learning is an unqualified success here. In terms of cost effectiveness we expect to break even against using external and internal courses . . . what we cannot measure is what the cost would have been of not training those people whose opportunity to learn has come about because of our project (*Works Management*, October 1984).

Of course, the problems facing the UK are not unique. Nevertheless, it appears that other countries do not suffer to the same extent from the 'feast and famine' cycles of skills availability which have historically dogged British industry. A number of commentators have suggested that the economic success of countries like Japan and West Germany derives in part from the efficient way in which skills are provided and used, and it is worth looking briefly at some lessons which might be drawn from their experience.

Comparisons between Britain and West Germany certainly lend support to the view that a labour force containing a high proportion of people with nationally recognized technical vocational qualifications is likely to be effective in achieving economic growth. A crude but relevant indicator of a country's economic success is its share of world export markets for manufactured goods. In these terms, West Germany's share had already recovered to 15.5 per cent in 1955 after the ravages of World War Two. At that time the UK share was 20 per cent. By 1960 West Germany had achieved about the same level as the UK had held in 1955 and, with minor fluctuations, has sustained its share of world markets at around this level ever since. In contrast, the UK's share fell steadily to around 10 per cent in 1970, since when it has been more stable, drifting down to a current level of between 8 and 9 per cent. The reasons for West Germany's superior economic performance relative to Britain's are complex, but it has been widely suggested that German investment in vocational training has been one very significant factor.

The German system of vocational training varies somewhat from area to area. Broadly speaking, however, it requires all pupils not otherwise continuing in full-time education to attend 1 day per week for the following 3 years at a vocational school associated with their job, and to take examinations related to their studies and to practical aspects of their job. By no means all Germans actually acquire vocational qualifications, because there is a significant proportion of 'failures' at full-time secondary school and during vocational training (Prais, 1981). The system is employer-dominated, in so far as employers control and administer the largest and most important parts of training (Taylor, 1981).

Prais has pointed out that 'the essential difference between Britain and Germany lies not in the proportions [of the labour force] with university degrees or their equivalents, but in the proportions with intermediate qualifications, such as apprentice-ships, City and Guilds certificates, or full secretarial qualifications'. His statistics show that 'two-thirds of the British labour force have no vocational qualifications, or have only non-vocational school-leaving qualifications such as GCE or CSE, compared with a third in Germany'.

Prais argues that his detailed comparisons lead to the conclusion that the British system of on-the-job training is no longer adequate:

> in a world of more rapid technological progress, and faster economic change, the balance of advantage has shifted towards systems which provide a much greater stock of 'transferable' skills, in which formal training and external examinations—of both theoretical and practical aspects—play predominating roles.

This is a very interesting conclusion, in the light of the fact that the only major industrial country which has managed to challenge West Germany's pre-eminence in world trade, that is Japan, has no such national system of vocational training. In 1955 Japan accounted for scarcely more than 5 per cent of world trade in manufacturing—a quarter of Britain's share, and a third of West Germany's. In the past few years the Japanese share of world markets has risen to about the same level (20 per cent) as West Germany, and twice that of Britain.

There is, indeed, evidence that substantial resources are devoted to vocational education in Japan. But most of this effort is initiated and controlled by firms, mainly large ones who set their own standards. Reporting on a visit to Japan in 1979, Ball concluded that investment in training facilities by large firms is massive, as witnessed in Hitachi, Sony, NEC and Matsushita. Since Japanese companies regard technically qualified people as their most valuable asset, no effort is spared in ensuring that they are properly equipped to carry out their tasks. Companies, therefore, have a very serious commitment to provide adequate industrial training. Relevant and well-researched courses are provided for the special needs of particular groups within the company, from the 'blue-collar' on the production line to the most senior manager. Japanese companies are normally not happy to entrust this training to outside bodies. They much prefer to do it in-house and the instructors who teach in company education departments are usually doing so on secondment. They are key people occupying strategic positions within the company who are taken off the job and attached for short periods to the training department (Ball, 1980).

In an age of relatively slow technical change the rate of training curricula change can be modest: trainers need to retrain fairly infrequently; and the equipment on which trainees are taught only needs to be changed infrequently. In such an environment, education and training establishments independent of firms can hope to provide students with reasonably up-to-date vocational training. As the pace of technological change increases, so do the advantages of in-house training undertaken by firms near the leading edge of technology.

When technology is changing relatively slowly, most training can be carried out at the beginning of a person's working life, effectively as a continuation of full-time education. When technology changes more rapidly, needs for retraining during working life, as and when needed, tend to grow, and this also favours in-house training.

But firms only have incentives to invest in training and retraining if they can be reasonably sure that they themselves are able to appropriate the benefits arising from the exercise. If a firm makes an investment in capital equipment it can obtain the benefits, in terms of enhanced productivity, etc., which derive from that investment. If a firm makes an invention, patent laws are available which offer the firm some prospect of getting at least some of the benefits arising from the invention. If, however, a British firm invests in training its staff, nothing prevents the employee from leaving his or her firm immediately on completion of the training. Further, some training leads to the acquisition of qualifications which offer transferable skills readily recognizable by other employers. Thus there is a strong incentive for British firms to forgo the expense, and to hope that it will be able to acquire a fully trained person with a recognized transferable skill from the labour market. Indeed, this was noted by the British government in its New Training Initiative White Paper, which commented that in some occupations 'virtually the whole cost is borne by the individual firm. Yet the individual firm has no guarantee of a return on this investment since the trainee is under no legal obligation to stay once his training is complete.'

In Japan, too, the trained employee has no legal obligation to remain with the firm which trained him (very few women are trained by large Japanese firms). In practice, however, large Japanese firms can be sure that the overwhelming majority of those whom they train will, in fact, remain loyal to the company. Japanese companies recruit most of their employees straight from school or further education. In large manufacturing companies an average of about half the employees are, in effect, guaranteed lifetime employment from the time when they are recruited, and form a corps of 'permanent' workers on which most training and retraining is lavished. Pay is based mainly on the number of years spent in the company and the age and level of education on joining it.

As one group of commentators put it:

> Lifetime employment creates a high degree of employee stability and, coupled with other management practices and personnel policies, generates tremendous employee loyalty towards the company, with all that it entails. A company can invest money in the training of an employee, confident in the belief that once he is trained, he will not be lured away by a competitor. A Japanese enters a company right after graduation from his school and stays in the company until the official retirement age of between 57 and 60. His job security is virtually guaranteed unless he is accused of misconduct (Sethi, Namiki, and Swanson, 1984).

But it is important to note that the well-trained Japanese worker's skills are not 'transferable'. Large Japanese companies recruit virtually no permanent staff members from other companies. Mobility between firms is virtually non-existent. The on-the-job training received by Japanese workers is specific to the individual company and not recognized by other companies. And, outside the charmed circle of permanent employees of large firms, most Japanese workers are either temporary workers in large firms, or working in the small firm sector in which 'the large majority of workers toil for substandard wages, and work under unsafe conditions' (Sethi *et al.*, 1984).

Nevertheless, permanent workers in large Japanese companies are frequently retrained in a variety of jobs and skills. At all levels they are rotated frequently between jobs. They are loyal to the firm rather than to any particular trade or craft, and they are receptive to organizational changes and the introduction of new technology and machinery, largely because these are not seen as threats to their job security.

This flexibility is in contrast to the typical situation in British factories. British maintenance workers are trained in a number of separate crafts: millwrights, machine tool fitters, pipe-fitters, electricians, and so on. Modern automated production equipment embodies diverse technologies such as electronic control systems, hydraulic actuating systems, electric motors, and mechanical clutches. Ideally, the person responsible for diagnosing faults in such systems should have knowledge of a diverse range of technologies. In Japan there is no barrier to training individuals in-house in all aspects of the specific equipment the company happens to have installed. In Britain, with greater emphasis on national training standards, and with demarcation between trades, this is much more difficult. Considerable progress has been made, for example, in eliminating demarcation within mechanical trades. But demarcation between mechanical and electrical/electronic skills persists (Senker *et al.*, 1981). Further, in Japanese factories (and in West German ones), it is normal for relatively simple faults to be corrected by the operators themselves. In Japan it is normal to give operators the training required for basic preventive maintenance and fault-finding (Schonberger, 1982). In West Germany the higher proportion of non-professional workers who are given significant training also results in operators being capable of first-line maintenance (Warner and Sorge, 1980).

It is always dangerous to try and transplant ideas from one culture to another without modification. Differences in context are likely to mean that such attempts are unlikely to succeed. Nevertheless, we believe that a synthesis of the kind of experience described above, and of the better parts of the existing British approach, might provide valuable guidelines for future policy regarding the skills question. Elements of this would include: expanded investment in the vocational training system; greater direct involvement of employers in both curriculum development and specification and in implementation of training; and, within firms, greater use and development of existing resources through job rotation, staff training, and development. In addition, attention should be paid to issues such as exploration of alternative patterns of work organization and design to obtain a good fit between technological and human resources; provision for updating and broadening training via novel delivery systems such as open learning; and increased emphasis on management training for engineers.

Planning AMT systems requires deep technical knowledge and therefore an engineering background. It also requires broad knowledge of financial analysis, training, and industrial relations. Business schools in the UK and the USA have generally concentrated on training financial personnel for highly remunerative careers in fields such as merchant banking. More mundane areas such as manufacturing management have received less attention, although institutions such as Cranfield Institute of Technology and Imperial College have now recognized such needs and initiated suitable courses. Both NEDO and the EITB have recently initiated schemes for training systems engineers. This is an encouraging trend, but more is needed.

One other clear need is for institutional mechanisms which encourage firms to devote more resources to training and retraining. In particular, in an economy with an active labour market such as Britain's, retraining an employee in information technology skills represents an invitation to 'poach' to labour market competitors. Removal of this deterrent to training is a very high priority. At least two alternative sets of policy are conceivable. The first is to reduce or eliminate the costs to employers of training—for example by meeting such costs as a public investment in the nations' skills. The second is to create deterrents to trained employees leaving the companies which trained them—for example, by imposing the cost of training on employees who desert their firms. Which philosophy to adopt raises questions of political ideology and industrial relations beyond the scope of this chapter. All that we claim here is that urgent, and inevitably expensive, action is needed to remove pervasive and damaging deterrents to training, which is essential to the nation's economic future.

Above all it is essential that realistic policies for dealing with the skills problem are developed quickly, since the lead time for their implementation is, by its nature, long. If, as we are repeatedly being told, the UK cannot afford to miss the boat of advanced manufacturing technology, then it is important to make sure that we have a crew to man it!

CONCLUSIONS

This chapter has focused particularly on one aspect associated with the move to widespread use of AMT—that is the challenge of providing appropriate skills. Similar challenges will have to be met, not only in manufacturing but also in services, and on a broad front, if the UK is to benefit from the considerable technological opportunities now available.

As was suggested earlier, the nature of the challenge is one of managing transition from the present pattern, which is essentially one of using new technology to substitute for old, and of doing what we have always done a little bit better, to one in which entirely new possibilities are opened up. We know from forecasts and informed commentary a little about the likely shape of this 'tomorrow's world' and about the kinds of changes which it might involve. For example, it is likely to be a highly networked society, both within the factory and beyond. Developments like the ISDN (integrated services digital network) will mean that a vast amount and range of electronic traffic can be carried. This in turn will change the organization and structure of much business. In particular two trends are likely to emerge: on the one hand towards greater integration and concentration; and on the other towards greater decentralization (see Chapter 6).

Amongst issues on the integration side will be considerable change in industrial structures, with a blurring of conventional boundaries between sectors and activities, and increasing concentration of ownership and control. This will be accompanied by a change in the mix of factors of production, with an increasing emphasis on very high levels of capital investment, often in individual plants. As we have already seen, such shifts in capital intensity will be accompanied by considerable changes in skill structures, working practices, and employment levels. Lastly, there is likely to be increasing linkage between users, suppliers, and markets which may also lead to increasing concentration of ownership and control.

At the same time there are trends towards increasing differentiation, and the emergence of decentralized patterns of organization and operation. Amongst the most significant of these are the possible shifts which may take place in the pattern of scale of operation, with economies of scope (improved flexibility, etc.) which are possible for small firms to achieve, competing with more traditional economies of scale. At the same time the growing establishment of a communications infrastructure will facilitate shifts in the location of operations and industrial facilities and may lead to totally new patterns of working such as 'telecommuting'.

One other issue which emerges frequently in forecasts about the future is the way in which advanced manufacturing technology can increase the scope and range of choice available about how it is used. Whilst there may be widespread debate about whether, and how far, new technologies will increase or decrease the level of centralization in industrial structure or the quality of working life, there is general agreement that there is increased choice about these things made possible by the nature of the technologies. Far from there being a single 'best' way of handling these questions which leads directly from the nature of the technology, we suggest that the options are in fact extended by it. The question then becomes not so much one of technological determinism (where the technology is the centrepiece) as that of how technology is used.

This brings us back again to the problem of managing change. The foregoing discussion suggests that in both the specific case of skills, and in the general one of societal implications of advanced manufacturing technology, there is an increase in the range of choice which we have about how this technology is used. That implies that it should be easier to arrive at appropriate policies for handling the transition, but we must set against this the rapidly increasing pace of change. Although the policies which we should be developing need to take a long-term perspective, there is considerable urgency to begin their development before events overtake us and we lose our ability to exploit any choice at all.

REFERENCES

Arnold, E., and Senker, P. (1983). *Designing the Future: the Skills Implications of Inter-active CAD*. London: Engineering Industry Training Board.

Ball, G. (1980). *Report on Vocational Education and Training for Employment in Engineering in Japan*. London: British Council/EITB.

Bessant, J. (1985). The integration barrier: problems in the implementation of advanced manufacturing technology. *Robotica*, **3**, 97–103.

Bessant, J., Guy, K., Miles, I., and Rush, H. (1985). *IT Futures: Literature Review of Long-term Perspectives on the Social Implications of Information Technology*. London: National Economic Development Office.

Bhattacharya, K. (1976). *Penetration and Utilisation of NC/CNC Machine Tools in British Industry*. Department of Production Engineering, University of Birmingham.

Blumberg, M., and Gerwin, D. (1984). Coping with advanced manufacturing technology. *Journal of Occupational Behaviour*, **5**, 113–30.

Brady, T., and Senker, P. (1984). *Contract Maintenance: No Panacea for Skills Shortages*. Sheffield: Report prepared for the Manpower Services Commission.

Cross, M. (1984). *Towards the Flexible Craftsman*. London: Technical Change Centre.

Fidgett, T. (1983). *The Engineering Industry: Its Manpower and Training*. Watford: Report for the Engineering Industry Training Board.

Fleck, J. (1982). The employment effects of robots. In T. Lupton (ed.), *Human Factors in Manufacturing*. Kempston: IFS Publications.

Freeman, C., Clark, J., and Soete, L. (1982). *Unemployment and Technical Change: A Study of Long Waves in the Economy*. London: Frances Pinter.

Halevi, G. (1980). *The Role of Computers in Manufacturing Processes*. Chichester: Wiley.

Handky, G. (1983). Design and use of flexible automated manufacturing systems, In K. Rathmill (ed.), *Proceedings of First International Conference on Flexible Manufacturing Systems*. Kempston: IFS Publications.

House of Lords Select Committee on Science and Technology (1985). *Education and Training for New Technology, Volume One*. London: HMSO.

Ingersoll Engineers (1982). *The FMS Report*. Kempston: IFS Publications.

Kaplinsky, R. (1984). *Automation—the Technology and Society*. London: Longmans.

Khamis, C., Lawson, G., and McGuire, S. (1986). *Trends in Manpower and Training in the Engineering Industry since 1978*. Watford: EITB.

Northcott, J., and Rogers, P. (1985). *Microelectronics in British Industry*. London: Policy Studies Institute.

Prais, S. (1981). Vocational qualifications of the labour force in Britain and Germany. *National Institute Economic Review*, November, pp. 47–59.

Rawle, P. (1983). *The Training and Education of Engineers in Japan*. London: London Graduate School of Business Studies (February).

Schonberger, R. (1982). *Japanese Manufacturing Techniques*. London: Macmillan/Free Press.

Senker, P., Swords-Isherwood, N., Brady, T., and Huggett, C. (1981). *Maintenance Skills in the Engineering Industry: the Influence of Technological Change*. Watford: EITB (Occasional Paper No. 8).

Sethi, S., Namiki, N., and Swanson, C. (1984). *The False Promise of the Japanese Miracle*. London: Pitman.

Taylor, M. (1981). *Education and Work in the Federal Republic of Germany*. London: Anglo-German Foundation.

TUC (1979). *Employment and Technology*. London: Trades Union Congress.

Voss, C. (1985). Implementation: a key issue in manufacturing technology. Paper presented at ESRC Workshop on New Technology, Cumberland Lodge, Windsor, 28–29 May.

Warner, M., and Sorge, A. (1980). The context of industrial relations in Great Britain and West Germany. *Industrial Relations Journal*, **11**, 41–49.

Willman, P., and Winch, G. (1985). *Innovation and Management Control: Relations at BL Cars*. Cambridge: Cambridge University Press.

The Human Side of Advanced Manufacturing Technology
Edited by T. D. Wall, C. W. Clegg, and N. J. Kemp
© 1987 John Wiley & Sons Ltd.

CHAPTER 9

Research and Development into 'Humanizing' Advanced Manufacturing Technology

CHRIS CLEGG AND MARTIN CORBETT

INTRODUCTION

As a nation, we have developed a sense of the value of technology and of a scientific approach to it, but we have meanwhile taken people for granted. Our government appropriates hundreds of millions of dollars for research on new techniques in electrical engineering, physics, and astronomy. It supports the development of complex economic ideas. But almost no funds go to develop our understanding of how to manage and organize people at work (Ouchi, 1981, p. 4).

Ouchi was in fact characterizing American investment in research and development generally, and his comments were certainly not restricted to advanced manufacturing technology (AMT). But nevertheless, they apply—there has been precious little investment of research and development (R&D) effort, either by individual companies or on a national or international basis, into the human side of AMT, and this is as true of Europe and the rest of the world as it is of America.

This final chapter represents an argument for taking the human side of AMT more seriously, in part by increasing this investment. It makes some suggestions for adopting an R&D strategy that will enable social scientists to make a more significant impact on the future design and development of such technologies. In so doing, a number of unresolved questions are asked, serving to identify particular areas on which future work should concentrate. The chapter is organized in four major parts.

First, there is some justification for the claim that the human aspects of AMT are undervalued in practice, followed by a discussion of their significance for the design, implementation, and operation of such systems. Second, there is an analysis of the reasons for the lack of interest in, and consideration of, the human aspects of AMT design. Particular consideration is given to whether or not such factors will remain important as these advanced systems evolve and become increasingly 'automated', and to the problems social scientists have in making an impact in this area. Third, an R&D strategy is outlined which will contribute to this area. This involves the adoption of

173

methodologies incorporating an emphasis on prospective development work to complement traditional retrospective evaluation research, along with a much more determined effort on the part of social scientists to share their expertise and, where possible, to 'give it away' to practitioners working from other disciplines. The final section identifies some of the major areas on which R&D work should concentrate over the next few years. These include issues of process, content and outcomes, and the argument is for a multi-disciplinary and collaborative approach incorporating technical, cognitive and social psychological concerns.

THE SIGNIFICANCE OF THE HUMAN ASPECTS OF AMT

Three short stories illustrate the significance of the human aspects of AMT.

Scene 1. A business school seminar room

Some production engineers are on a short training course examining the possibilities of investing in AMT in their companies. In a problem-solving exercise they are split into small working groups to redesign a production system for making light bulb filaments. At present, continuous thin wire is fed to an operator who operates a machine which cuts it into small lengths. The operator picks up one piece of wire at a time, and attaches it to a small piece of metal by operating a forging machine which stamps down, pressing the two pieces together. Unfortunately, so far as the operator is concerned, the work is highly repetitive and very boring, but it requires concentration because of the need for care in picking up and accurately placing the materials. In addition, the environment is noisy and hot. The engineers are asked to redesign this process.

Whilst walking round the different groups of engineers, the tutor listens with interest to one group discussing the possibility of eliminating the operator's work by automating the process and including a robot. The wire could be fed to an automatic cutting machine, the robot could pick up and place the wire in position before automatically triggering the pressing machine. All that would be required would be some accurate sensing devices and a 'pick up and place' industrial robot.

Imagine the tutor's surprise then, at the reporting back session, when no mention was made of this AMT solution, the group preferring to keep the operator working on the equipment, with some modest changes to the surrounding environment.

'What happened to your idea with the robot?' he asked.

The group spokesman replied: 'Ah well, when we got down to it and analysed the production process more carefully, we realized how simple it all is. We decided not to use the robot because it seemed such a waste of its potential' (based on a story by H. H. Rosenbrock).

Scene 2. A steel mill

"In 1975 the Dutch steel company, Estel Hoogovens, installed a highly automated new hot-strip mill at its plant in Ijmuiden, on the coast near Amsterdam. Expecting productivity to be given a boost by this advanced equipment, the management was shocked to see the output of the mill actually fall. Consultants from the British Steel Corporation were called in. The journal *New Scientist* summed up their findings thus:

> The operators became so unsure of themselves that, on some occasions, they actually left the pulpits for control unmanned. The operators also failed to understand the control theory of the programs used in the controlling computer, and this reinforced their attitude of 'standing well back' from the operation—except when things were very clearly going awry. By intervening late, the operators let the productivity drop below that of plants using traditional control methods. So automation had led to lower productivity and operator alienation simultaneously.

Matters were made worse by the fact that, in the new design, the path of the steel strip had been enclosed, so the operators could not even see the material they were supposed to be working on. The consultant's report asserted that, among other things, the operators had to be put in closer touch with the process, and that information displays should help them understand the decisions taken by the automation, instead of just indicating the state of a process" (see Michie and Johnson, 1985, pp. 58–9).

Scene 3. A small batch engineering company

This company employs over 1,000 people and has MOD quality approval. A large CNC machining centre is under investigation because doubts have been raised about its performance. The machine has a cubic metre cutting space and a magazine that can hold up to 60 tools. To see how this machine performs, one particular batch is studied in some detail. It involves manufacturing 19 'gronts'. Each product is very complex, having 62 steps in the program and requiring the use of 50 different tools. The program is not new but it has been modified since it was last run. Each gront is machined in two parts, with one side machined first, then the other, with the workpiece re-set in between. However, since there are two tables on the machine, it is possible to be working on one workpiece whilst preparing the next.

The total allowed time for the batch is 77.25 hours, including initial setting up of the program and tools. The planners produce a list of tools for the tool-setters, who supply them to the operator, indicating the length of each tool to be entered by the operator into the machine, which then automatically calculates the offset required.

In this case the first operator began the batch at 1.30 p.m. It took him 24 minutes to load the tools into the magazine but some were missing, which took a further 32 minutes to sort out. He then spent 15 minutes changing tables on the machine. On checking the tool lengths into the computer he found some were not within permitted tolerances so he had to get new tools. This took until 7.40 p.m. that night— by which time his place had been taken by a colleague working the late shift.

By this time set-up had taken 6 hours 10 minutes rather than the 1 hour 15 minutes allowed. By 7 a.m. the next morning the night shift had machined both sides of the first workpiece, but no record was left explaining why a 4-hour machining job had in fact taken 11 hours. Once this first-off was completed, nothing else could be done until it had been inspected. With waiting time, this took 4 hours 30 minutes.

Work then began on the next gront. Thereafter the job proceeded in fits and starts. Switching tables sometimes took 1 minute, other times 15; a jammed tool took 20 minutes to sort out; a drill got stuck for 10 minutes; one complete shift was missed because the operator was absent; and so on.

In all, the total time for the job was 155 hours, almost exactly double the standard time allowed, on a machine which 'costs' approximately £56 per hour. The investigator reported that some of these organizational problems stemmed from very poor relations between management and the shopfloor, and also cited a complaint that the operators had had no say in which CNC machine had been purchased (see Dore, Dodgson, and Cross, 1986).

Unfortunately these three stories, set as they are in different environments, are not unusual. In each case there is inadequate recognition of the human aspects associated with technology, in which are included the design of the human–computer interface, and the wider management and organizational considerations. In the general development of AMT, many companies and individuals within them assume, and behave as if, it is simply and solely a technical innovation with associated technical problems and solutions.

Indeed, the common theme of many social science investigations is that too little regard is paid to the human aspects before, during, and after AMT is implemented. For example, Briefs, Ciborra, and Schneider (1982), along with many others, point to the need for user involvement in designing and procuring new systems, and Blackler and Brown (1986) stress the dominance of 'task and technology centred' (as opposed to 'organisation and end user centred') designs. Similarly, Clegg and Kemp (1986) report the prevalence of 'sequential design' processes (as opposed to 'parallel design') in which the technical aspects are designed first, with the human aspects considered too little and too late in the day. From their experience in a number of companies developing AMT systems, Clegg and Kemp (1986) suggest that it is not uncommon for organizations to devote at least 90 per cent of their resources (i.e. money, time, and commitment) to the technical side of AMT, such that any choices made about the human aspects get made by default, rather than on a planned basis according to some explicit strategy. Unfortunately, even when companies do recognize that there are human aspects of AMT, such considerations can be very limited—for example, to showing people a model of the proposed system, and giving operators on-the-job training once the technology is in place. Whilst both these activities are worthwhile in themselves, they represent a limited view of what the human aspects involve.

Indeed, whilst AMT is clearly a major technical issue, the rest of this book has amply demonstrated that the human aspects are wide-ranging and significant in their own right. This is true whatever AMT system is involved, whether stand-alone technologies like robots, CNC machine tools, and CAD work stations, or large integrated systems like FMS and CAD/CAM. Thus, any new system involves design and implementation; the change process needs managing; operators' jobs need designing; selection and training problems need addressing for all people interacting with the system (including managers, programmers, and maintenance engineers); supervisory and managerial roles require careful consideration; organizational structures and procedures are required to manage, organize, and support AMT; and industrial relations issues exist on many fronts. On a more macro-level of analysis there are national implications of the evolution and implementation of AMT generally, particularly with regard to skills provision, training needs, and manpower planning. To these one can add the problems of designing usable human – computer interfaces which promote understanding. And in all of these areas there are choices to make for the best way forward, both within individual factories and companies, as well as on a national basis (see Clegg and Wall, 1987; Piercy, 1984; and Winch, 1983).

In this context one major lesson to draw from the earlier chapters concerns the range of human aspects that are significant, embracing a number of psychological and organizational issues. Given, then, that they are wide-ranging, it is likely that there will be benefits from their careful consideration. Social scientists point to potential benefits in five main areas.

First, if the system users and managers are included in the design process, its design may be better, either because it suits their particular needs better, or because they have job-specific knowledge about the production process which should be included (Mumford and Henshall, 1979). We note with interest that many people believe that 'user participation' of this kind is a good thing because it makes people 'feel involved'—whilst this may be true in some instances, the rationale for such involvement should include the fact that the people using and managing the new technology will have knowledge and expertise that can usefully be incorporated in its planning.

Second, if the human – computer interface is difficult to comprehend, if operator jobs are poorly designed, if their training is inadequate, or if the support given by programmers and engineers is ineffective, then any system will be unable to perform to its potential. Thus, these and other human aspects need to be well designed to optimize the performance of AMT.

A third related point is that the human aspects need to be designed to promote a good quality of working life for the people working in the system. Thus, the aim should be to promote the skills of the people concerned, to allow them to derive some satisfaction from their jobs. This is important psychologically in its own right, since there is abundant evidence that people prefer complex skilful jobs rather than simplified deskilled ones. Furthermore, more complex jobs are usually psychologically healthier than simple ones (see Broadbent, 1986; Fraser, 1947; Karasek,

1979; Kornhauser, 1965; and Wall and Clegg, 1981). In addition there may be operational benefits to such an approach—for example, in terms of better quality and faster responses from operators when problems occur.

Fourth, if these human aspects are successfully managed, then it is likely that the system will reach its performance targets sooner than would otherwise be the case. This is particularly true in such complex areas as industrial relations where problems can significantly delay implementation. Furthermore, the experience of successfully managed change may promote confidence in a company's ability to cope with subsequent technical innovations.

Finally, the human aspects of the system need to be carefully designed to achieve the maximum competitive advantage. An example illustrates this point (see Clegg and Corbett, 1986). This case involves the progressive introduction of a flexible manufacturing system in a high-volume, high-quality, small batch precision engineering factory. Under the old, predominantly manual, method of working, the total production time for a batch was around 8 weeks (from receiving an order to its despatch), of which less than 8 hours represents machining time. (Such times are not unusual in small batch engineering companies.) This system of working is enormously flexible since people can stop work in mid-batch and change over to work on another, for example, if priorities change (i.e. poor production planning), if they run short of materials (i.e. poor materials control), or if their machine has a problem (i.e. poor maintenance engineering). It is also very inefficient. But, as the new FMS is phased in, these problems of planning, control, and engineering become much more visible. Rather than there being individual operators all over the factory performing below capacity, there is now a large expensive production facility either standing idle or operating well below its planned performance. Such problems are relatively easy to measure and this visibility creates energy for improvement. In this case, a major reason for the investment in the FMS, at least on the part of the General Manager, is that it promotes problem visibility, creates energy, and forces the rest of the organization to support the technology much better than in the past. In this view, AMT is a catalyst for more general organizational changes in production planning, materials control, and engineering support. With such efforts the company expects to reap much greater rewards than those simply arising from the technology itself. Thus, the aim is not to reduce the actual machining time, although this may happen; rather the objective is to improve information and control such that the lead times and delays can be significantly reduced. But these will only be achieved if the human organizational aspects of the FMS are carefully and correctly designed and managed.

TAKING PEOPLE FOR GRANTED

So far, this chapter has argued that the human aspects of AMT are often ignored in practice, even though they are wide-ranging and important. Why should it be then, in Ouchi's phrase, that we take people for granted? There are two possible reasons. It could be that, although the human aspects are important now, they will cease to be so as advanced systems become more fully 'automated'. Thus, the human factor will become irrelevant as AMT evolves. Alternatively, it could be that the human aspects are and will remain important, but this message has failed to get across. Each of these is examined in turn.

The first explanation looks to the attitudes and aspirations shared by many systems designers within the engineering community, where a vision persists of 'people-less' production systems (Rosenbrock, 1983). The explicit incorporation of the human aspect is a temporary and rather short-run problem becoming increasingly redundant.

Such a claim for the future of AMT should be taken seriously, and it is hard to answer since it is probably the case that the evolution of these new technologies will be somewhat haphazard and unpredictable. In part this is due to the uncertain nature of technical innovation during rapid periods of change. But it is also due to the inevitable uncertainties concerning the diffusion of such technical changes. Nevertheless, one can make some reasonable predictions about the nature of change and speculate on whether or not, in the foreseeable future, the sorts of human aspects identified above will remain relevant.

Are we then progressing towards a generation of fully automated 'people-less' factories in which there will be few if any human problems? A number of trends can be discerned from the current pattern of change (see, for example, Attenborough, 1984; Bessant *et al.*, 1985; Northcott and Rogers, 1982, 1984).

First, all commentators agree that the introduction of stand-alone technologies such as CNC machine tools, CAD work stations, and industrial robots will continue to accelerate. These will continue to be the most common forms of AMT for the immediately foreseeable future. But, at the same time, more and more companies will experiment with, and introduce, integrated systems such as FMS and CAD/CAM, and these will have a dramatic impact not just on performance but also on the organization's ability to co-ordinate its activities through improved information and control. Considerable effort will also go into developing computer integrated manufacturing systems but, except in R&D cases and in some instances of highly predictable production environments, these will not extend to fully automated 'people-less' factories on any widespread basis. In large part this is because reliable enabling technologies are not yet in place, and furthermore, most companies are simply unable to address the complexities involved, to say nothing of expense, particularly in the field of systems integration. However, computer based management information systems, already relatively popular, will become more widespread and will continue to improve the opportunities for companies to integrate the co-ordinate their efforts. Overall, such new systems as do evolve, particularly those with integrating potential, will get larger and, so far as both the designer and the user are concerned, more complex.

As Wall and Kemp point out in Chapter 1, these opportunities will probably be greatest in small and medium batch production firms, which account for around 70 per cent of engineering industrial output (NEDO, 1985) and where there is huge potential to improve overall performance by better information and control. Such innovations as are implemented will, in most cases, be operated in the midst of relatively old technologies such that there will be 'islands of automation' amongst traditional technologies (see Wall, 1985). And because the performance of such new technologies will be influenced by the working practices for the old, it will probably be increasingly common for large organizations to try to side-step some of these difficulties by implementing their most advanced systems in small separate production units set up on green-field sites.

It will also be the case that companies use the new technologies to be more competitive by cutting down on their production throughput times. This will make them more responsive to customer needs. As such, AMT will be used to gain a competitive edge by encouraging customers to demand more choice and better service. Accordingly, products in such markets will become more differentiated and be ordered in smaller batches. In this view AMT will increase the levels of uncertainty in such markets.

The argument, then, is that the human aspects of AMT will remain important for the foreseeable future. In particular, as AMT systems get larger, more sophisticated, and more complex, they will need well-trained, well-managed, and well-co-ordinated support from operators, engineers, planners, programmers, and managers. They will also need to be designed so that they are comprehensible to the operators if performance levels are to be satisfactory. Furthermore, as such systems are increasingly applied to, and indeed themselves encourage, uncertain production environments, then problem solving abilities and skills will be at a premium, as will be the capacity to apply them flexibly, and organize them effectively (see Clegg, 1986). In addition, the emerging emphasis on integrated systems that cut across existing organizational structures will lead to greater interdependence (see Cummings and Blumberg, Chapter 3), and tighter coupling between activities (see Weick, 1976; Perrow, 1984; and Corbett, 1987). But the opportunities this affords for significant improvements in performance will only come about if the organizational structures and systems are designed to foster better information flows and control.

The conclusion is that, far from making the human aspects less important, the likely emerging trends in the development of AMT, make it essential that they are carefully considered and consistently designed. The advanced technologies of the foreseeable future will not design, run, support, and manage themselves, any more than did their simpler predecessors.

The second possible explanation for 'taking people for granted', focuses on the failure to communicate the importance of these human aspects. This explanation incorporates a number of interrelated factors. For example, some people believe our educational system is unduly specialized in its emphasis and curricula, such that relatively few engineers have strong social science components to their training, either at university or once joining a company. And even fewer social scientists are exposed to the disciplines and problems of engineering. There is little in our education and training that encourages contact and mutual learning. Nor is this encouraged by research funding bodies which tend to support excellent work within disciplines, rather than fund collaborative endeavours across disciplinary boundaries. There are some exceptions in the area of IT research, but even here a typical response to attempts to include a human component to technical research is that such concerns are a matter for the companies themselves after the technology has been implemented, rather than an issue for research funding, which is a particularly scarce resource.

At present, in the UK, there is relatively little social science research taking place into the human aspects of AMT (see, for example, Kemp, 1985), and this is probably due to three interrelated factors, namely a shortage of funding for social science research generally, the lack of recognition of its importance, and a shortage of skills in this area.

Within individual companies the picture is scarcely any better. Many engineers are loth to adopt more psychological and organizational views of their work, especially when these extend into areas which are difficult to quantify. At the same time, other professional groups, such as line managers, general managers, and personnel and industrial relations specialists, are reluctant to adopt more proactive roles in the development and introduction of AMT, preferring to leave these issues to the technical specialists (see Clegg and Kemp, 1986). Similarly, eventual users and their representatives rarely put these items high on their agendas, perhaps because their interest in new technology is dominated by whether or not it affects their job security and job prospects.

For all these understandable difficulties, however, it has to be said that social scientists themselves have substantially contributed to their own lack of influence. Social scientists have failed to persuade others of the legitimacy and significance of the human aspects of AMT. The case has not been demonstrated. These failures on the part of social scientists are partly matters of research goals, emphasis, and style, and this view prompts us to specify a strategy for research and development work which will make a contribution to this area.

One paradox deserves mention here. People, in this context, may well be their own worst enemies. In practice, many technologies and production systems were, and continue to be, designed on the premise that the human component in the system is inflexible and stupid, and that, where possible, the potential for human contribution should be minimized and designed out of the system (see Taylor, 1911; and Taylor, 1979); whereas, in practice, it is often people's flexibility and intelligence that allow reasonable levels of performance out of poorly designed systems.

RESEARCH AND DEVELOPMENT STRATEGY

Most social science research into AMT involves retrospective evaluation studies of its impact on a range of human issues, such as operator responsibilities, skill use, job satisfaction, social attitudes, and industrial relations. A dominant theme within such enquiries has been whether or not new technologies serve to deskill the jobs of people working within production systems, either as a result of the technology *per se*, or because of the way it is managed, supported, and operated. (See, for example, Blumberg and Gerwin, 1984; Buchanan and Boddy, 1983a,b; Mueller *et al.*, 1986; Scarbrough, 1984; Wall *et al.*, 1987.) Indeed this retrospective methodological bias is reflected in this book.

Such research is usually undertaken by people with expertise in a particular area, such as industrial relations, skills analysis, or job design. Because of the shortage of expertise, it tends to be rather infrequently undertaken and, when it is done, it is usually partial in its focus, rarely considering a wide range of human aspects, and even more rarely incorporating important technical, operational, and financial considerations. For example, the authors know of no cases of empirical evaluation of AMT systems that embrace its organizational impacts, the job designs and views of the operators, the usability of the human−computer interface, and the overall effectiveness of the system.

Whilst such monitoring and evaluation work is an essential part of the process of learning about the human aspects of AMT and should be extended, it remains the case that its practical use for the companies concerned has a medium-term focus. Thus, organizations in which such evaluations are conducted may feel they can make minor adjustments to their current systems, but otherwise are learning for their next investment. And where the findings from such studies are generalizable to other situations, such transfer of knowledge is exceptionally difficult to manage and can involve a slow dissemination process—for example, through conferences, publications, and professional meetings. Furthermore, what social scientists learn through such endeavours concerns the impact of AMT, rather than how these outcomes come about. From a practitioner's point of view, in particular, this last point is crucial— since engineers, managers, and trade unionists need knowledge not just concerning what they are trying to achieve and avoid in the way of human aspects, but also how they can set about it.

Thus, there are two general criticisms of social science work in this area. First, it is too specialist an activity, too focused and partial in its emphasis, and too rarely undertaken: accordingly, social scientists should be trying to pass on their evaluation knowledge and skills to people with different knowledge and skills and with other expertise to contribute. And second, most work in this area is too limited in its application because of its retrospective focus: social scientists should therefore be trying to input their ideas during the design of new systems so that they incorporate human considerations from the outset. If possible, these skills too should be passed on to non-specialists in these areas. Since little of this kind of work has been undertaken to date, the argument is illustrated using examples from our own research.

Retrospective evaluation work

Whilst some evaluation aids exist in some of the human areas identified in this book (see, for example, Hackman and Oldham, 1975; Cook *et al.*, 1981), these are exceptions. There are no well-known evaluation tools currently available for non-specialists to use in undertaking relatively systematic and broad-ranging evaluations of their own experiences with information technology. For this reason, the first author of this chapter, in conjunction with Thomas Green (of the Medical Research Council Applied Psychology Unit in Cambridge) and seven other psychologists (see note 1), are undertaking a project entitled 'Evaluation of information technology in organizations, including the man – machine interface'. It is part-funded by the UK Alvey Directorate within its Man – Machine Interface Programme. The objectives of the exercise are to identify a set of human aspects requiring evaluation when information technology, such as AMT, is introduced into an organization; and to design, pilot, and make available a set of measurement tools which organizations can use to undertake their own evaluations of it.

The project is based on three premises: first, that organizations are rather bad at assessing the human and organizational impacts of IT, in part for the reasons described earlier; second, that such evaluation needs to be broad-ranging, covering cognitive, social, and organizational factors; and third, that evaluation tools are needed that are of immediate use to engineers, managers, trade unionists, and others in organizations, so that they can evaluate their own experiences in relatively systematic and broad-ranging ways. The intention is that the results of such internal evaluations will identify specific problems and promote actions for their solution.

The end product of the project will be in the form of a published 'easy-to-use' manual. To date, the project group has identified five main areas requiring evaluation. These are: the technology itself; the human – computer interaction; the job designs; the wider organizational aspects; and the management of change. Major issues and problems for evaluation have been identified within each of these areas. For example: is the technology compatible with other technologies in the organization so that 'adding on' and integration are straightforward tasks?; during interactions with the computer, does the user make serious errors, such as losing data files, as a result of simple slips?; has the new technology created repetitive jobs that users find unsatisfactory and which may reduce performance?; in the wider organization, has the introduction of new technology led to problems with pay relativities and/or career progression?; and has adequate training and documentation been provided for operators to allow for the effective introduction of the new system?

These and many other issues form the core of the manual, and a set of measurement tools is currently being developed for their systematic evaluation. These tools will be based around a set of questions and may take the form of items for group discussion, structured interviews, questionnaires, and more formal experimental assessment procedures. The project will be completed in 1987.

Prospective research and development work

This method of working involves explicit consideration of the human aspects of a system from the beginning of its design. Whilst psychologists have had very little involvement in work of this kind, some notable efforts have been made. (For a European example within the newspaper industry see Ehn, Kyng, and Sundblad, 1983.) Within the UK, the best-known example is that based at UMIST under the leadership of Rosenbrock (1983). This project involved the development of a 'flexible manufacturing system in which operators are not subordinate to machines'. It consisted of an NC lathe, a milling machine, and a robot, and included the second author of this chapter as a social scientist in the design team. In practice, much of the work focused on developing 'user-friendly' software for the lathe. The results included the preparation of a set of software which was designed to embrace a number of 'good human' criteria, which are intended to generalize to other manufacturing environments (see Corbett, 1985). This work is currently being extended by funding under the auspices of ESPRIT (the European Strategic Programme for Research and Development into Information Technology).

The authors of this chapter, along with colleagues at SAPU (see note 2), are partners in a separate ESPRIT project, within the computer integrated manufacturing (CIM) programme of work. This provides another example of prospective R&D work. In this case, we are one of five partners designing and developing a flexible assembly system, which will be used for the automatic assembly of complex engineering products. The product is funded for 5 years and is now 18 months old. The objectives are to include human factors considerations in the design of the system, to evaluate the eventual system from a human factors perspective, and to develop a generalizable set of human factors criteria, and their means of applications, for use in other CIM environments.

A broad definition of 'human factors' has been adopted, incorporating six major areas of work; namely: the systems design process; the allocation of functions between humans and machines; job design; organization structure; hardware ergonomics; and software ergonomics. Health and safety issues are handled, as appropriate, within each of these areas.

Within each of these areas a preliminary set of design criteria has been developed which the designers and others should incorporate in their designs. Some examples of these criteria are given in Table 9.1. Such criteria are general and the next stage of work involves identifying particular examples of each so that the designers can apply them when working on specific applications. For the same reason, an outline model of the design process has been formulated and agreed, which fits specific areas into a design sequence (see Ravden *et al.*, 1987). The designers are happy to work with this model, and the next stage involves the identification of conflicts within these criteria, and also between the human factors considerations and engineering practice, since these are especially important as design choices are made. In the longer term, a set of methods will be developed for assessing these criteria in CIM environments more generally.

One key feature of this activity is attempting to make these criteria, along with their means of assessment, generalizable and applicable elsewhere, without extensive inputs from local human factors experts. Again the aim is to give such expertise away.

Table 9.1   Examples of design criteria

Area	Examples of criteria
Design process	*Participation:* the design process should be undertaken participatively; e.g. system users, supporters and managers participate at all stages in the design process.
Allocation of function	*Complementarity:* decisions on allocation of function should recognize that humans and machines may complement one another in synergistic ways; e.g. humans and machines both contribute to production scheduling.
Job design	*Control:* the operators should have some control over their jobs, which should include distinct areas of responsibility and decision making; e.g. operators are responsible for deciding the order in which tasks are undertaken.
Organization structure	*Boundary management:* supervisors and managers of the system should be responsible for managing its boundaries; e.g. supervisors provide operators with warning of alterations to work schedules.
Hardware ergonomics	*Safety and prevention of accidental operation:* the workstation and equipment should be safe and the workspace and the components within it should be designed/chosen and arranged so that accidental (possibly dangerous) operation is avoided; e.g. controls are guarded by recessing of buttons and switches.
Software ergonomics	*Informative feedback:* users should be given clear, informative feedback regarding where they are in the system, what actions they have taken, whether these actions have been successful, and what actions should be taken next; e.g. any error message or warning explains what it is, and how it can be corrected.

Psychologists and social scientists, generally, should invest more effort in undertaking prospective design and development work to complement their retrospective evaluations. This will be especially useful to companies anxious to incorporate good human factors during the design of new technologies. Such work also presents excellent learning opportunities for researchers, since they are faced with some new and challenging questions, some of which are discussed in the next section of this chapter. The need is for social scientists to be giving away both their old evaluation skills, and their new development skills, since there is an acute shortage of people with necessary skills and knowledge. The next obvious step will be for the development of expert systems in these areas. One advantage of this approach, for social scientists, is that it forces them to be clear and specific in what they say, and in its nature engages them in debate with experts from other disciplines and with other experiences. It must be stressed that we are not advocating that work of this kind replaces retrospective evaluation research—these are complementary strategies.

In summary, then, we propose that social scientists incorporate both research and development components in their work, where possible undertaking the design of new systems of AMT in collaboration with engineers, users, managers, and trade unionists. The aim is to incorporate good human factors alongside good engineering practice, in part to find out where conflicts between the two arise, and subsequently to evaluate how well the eventual systems meet their criteria. The emphasis should be on mutual influence and learning, and part of this process requires that social scientists develop evaluation tools and human factors design criteria that are generalizable to and usable elsewhere. In the immediate future, these tools and criteria will not in any sense be perfect, but a start should be made now!

RESEARCH AND DEVELOPMENT THEMES

This final section identifies three interrelated themes which are particularly important in this area of enquiry. They reflect the need for complementary studies of a prospective and retrospective kind on a multidisciplinary basis, and correspond to the distinctions between issues of process, content and outcomes.

Collaborative design process

As stated earlier in this chapter, most design processes are dominated by technical specialists, despite the occasional call for more 'participative' designs, by which people usually mean user involvement. The drive towards more collaborative design processes in part reflects an attempt to achieve optimal sociotechnical designs (see Eason, 1982) that are more effective because of the inclusion of the social or human aspects, and the broader expertise that has been incorporated. But, for some, it also reflects a drive towards the democratization of work, and of strategically important aspects of it. Because so little work of this kind has been attempted, one cannot confidently say that the benefits of better designs or of more democratic working practices accrue, although there are plenty of examples of horror stories arising from failures to incorporate the views of important groups.

Many believe that these intended benefits are at the cost of less efficient design processes. This is partly because the human issues are so broad, ranging from the design of jobs and the provision of training, through supervisory and managerial roles, to organization structures. To these one should add ergonomic considerations of any hardware, and the problems of designing usable interfaces. Relevant experts with potential contributions include line managers, supervisors, operators, engineers, programmers, personnel and industrial relations specialists, trade union representatives, and a range of cognitive and social psychological expertise.

The design of large advanced systems is difficult in itself, even without extensive collaboration; and few would relish the prospect of getting such a diverse group of people to form a design team, especially in large organizations that may be highly differentiated and have problems of integration. Nevertheless, one must question what the alternatives are, particularly remembering the fact that few technologically advanced systems perform to their potential.

What is required here is more knowledge of the design process. There is a need to study: the way in which design work is undertaken; who does what and according to what criteria; what decisions get made and when; which decisions get overlooked and/or taken by default; the political aspects of this process, arising from competition for scarce resources; and the contingencies affecting design decisions (see Kemp and Clegg, 1987). There is also a need to research the ways in which teams of experts can pool their knowledge and skills to collaborate in such designs; how collaborative work can be effectively organized and managed; what temporary project management structures can be created to allow experts, from different disciplines and representing different interests, to manage their differences and conflicts in effective ways; and to identify the kinds of training and education that are required to make the process effective.

Thus, social scientists should have an input to the design process as experts in their fields, but, just as importantly, should be studying the process itself to find ways of achieving effective and efficient collaboration (see Rosenbrock, 1983).

Choice, control, and constraint

Regarding the content of the new technologies, all agree that choices exist. Take the example of a CNC machine tool with an operating problem, such as an error in the software controlling machine speeds. When this problem occurs, should the machine cut out automatically and let the operator find the problem? Should the computer offer a diagnosis of the problem? Should it go further and suggest possible remedial actions? Or perhaps tell the operator exactly what to do? Or even solve the problem and tell the operator what it has done? Engineers and ergonomists stress that there are choices over what humans do and over what machines do in any automated system—a problem of 'allocating functions' between humans and machines. In a sense these are choices regarding the pattern and extent of automation.

For their part, cognitive psychologists point to the significance of these choices for the human in the system, usually in terms of performance effects, but also stress that there are choices for how the human and the machine interact *within* a level of automation. For example, if the operator is to make decisions on which of several actions is optimal, then what information must the computer provide, and in what form, to allow a good decision? And what understanding does the operator require of the work process and of the computer's representation of it, to be able to handle exceptions when they occur? Thus, there are choices for what can be called the surface characteristics of the human − computer interaction, and also for the deeper structure and modelling of the computer system.

Finally, organizational psychologists have identified the choices that exist after the above choices have been made. They stress that, with current and foreseeable state-of-the-art systems, there remain choices for who operates, supervises, programs,

edits, repairs, maintains, and manages the technology. This can be termed an 'allocation of responsibilities' problem between humans. For example, divisions of labour
with highly specialist responsibilities are defined in some organizations, whilst less
differentiated and more flexible structures are chosen in others, even for companies
working in similar markets, making similar products, and using similar technologies
(see Clegg and Kemp, 1986; Clegg and Corbett, 1986).

   The argument then is that choices exist for control at three different levels. They
are probably made successively in the order described above, and little is known
about the ways in which they influence and constrain one another. The choices are
summarized in Table 9.2. Research indicates that early choices on the allocation of

Table 9.2   Choices for control of AMT systems

Design level	Examples of choice
Allocation of function	1. Operators carry out those functions that cannot be automated.
	2. Operators themselves allocate functions depending on circumstances arising during production.
Human – computer interface	
Deep characteristics	1. Computer takes controlling decisions after operator enters data.
	2. Operator takes controlling decisions after computer displays data.
Surface characteristics	1. System status information is presented only in the event of machine malfunction. Information is restricted to specific machine.
	2. System status information is available on demand and includes information on all machines.
Allocation of responsibilities	1. Work is controlled by functional specialists, e.g. machine programming, maintenance, setting, quality control, and machine monitoring are carried out by individual specialists.
	2. Work is controlled by operators, e.g. operator is responsible for machine setting, programming, and monitoring.

function are made by engineering designers according to technical criteria, automating
whatever is feasible, and/or what they can afford. In this method the humans get
to do what is left (Brodner, 1982; Price, 1985). Ergonomists have promoted a more
balanced approach, arguing that machines are good at some activities, whilst humans
are good at others (see, for example, the Fitts list—Fitts, 1951). However, this has
been criticized as unduly comparative. What happens when machines and humans
are almost equally good or equally bad at something? Or when what is left, for the
humans, together adds up to a poorly designed and thereby sociotechnically sub-
optimal job? Some argue that the allocation of functions should be complementary

(see Jordan, 1963), seeking a symbiosis of technical and human benefits. Unfortunately, this is very difficult to achieve and, to date, social scientists have been unable to specify a procedure by which designers can meet these objectives. One approach to this problem has been offered by Corbett (1985), who uses the notion of uncertainty in production systems to identify those functions or tasks where a complementary approach is required.

Since such allocations determine the tasks left for the humans in the system, and logically must also influence the supporting roles required of them, it is important to know about the flexibility or rigidity of such choices. Thus, once a function has been allocated, is this fixed? There are some automated functions which an operator can override manually by turning it off; for example, automated loading and unloading of a machine. But can complex systems have flexible allocations designed and built into them? This is equivalent to building redundancy into a system. For example, in the ESPRIT project described earlier, the possibility of the flexible allocation of production scheduling is under discussion, whereby a human has the choice of whether or not the computer makes scheduling decisions. The human factors researchers argue that these choices could be made contingent upon local circumstances, such as the amount of work, the product mix, and the availability of key personnel. Interestingly, the designers' response to this idea has been that such flexibility builds in the prospect of inefficiency, since what they are seeking is a single most efficient method which is invariant. This, of course, assumes that there is one best way that can cope with all contingencies—something that must be doubted in certain production environments. On the other hand, it is certainly the case that such flexibility/redundancy is expensive; for example, in terms of the software required.

The design of the surface characteristics of the human–computer interaction influences how the operator receives and uses information, and it is this area that has dominated the research agendas of cognitive ergonomics. But, as Michie and Johnson succinctly put it, 'syntactic sugar is not enough' (1985, p. 72)—thus, good surface designs do not necessarily mean that the human–computer interface is satisfactory, since the model the user holds of a complex system is a critical factor influencing performance, particularly when unforeseen circumstances occur. Cognitive psychologists are increasingly turning to the study of the fit between users' and computers' representations of complex production environments (see, for example, Rouse, 1981). As yet, little is known of the impact of the computer system's representation of the production process on the behaviour of users and on their performance.

At the organizational level there has been much debate on the extent to which a choice of technology determines a method of organization. Is deskilling an inevitable consequence of the introduction of AMT? (see Wood, 1982). Few probably subscribe to this view in respect of the current generation of systems, and received wisdom has it that the impact of technologies depends on the organizational choices for how it is managed and supported. In our view, the technology determines the tasks people undertake, but not necessarily their roles, though these will be constrained by the technology (see Clegg, 1984). What then is the impact of the earlier choices described above?

These distinctions on the different choices made in the design and implementation of advanced systems are useful because they point to a number of R&D issues. For example, little is known of the ways in which allocation of function decisions influence the subsequent management and operation of large systems. How constrained are computer systems and their operation by earlier choices? (Rose *et al.*, 1986). How important are the designs of the structure and modelling of the computer system in influencing subsequent operation? How much choice is left for managers and other interested parties when it comes to organizing work within such systems? (see Bessant, 1983).

Unfortunately, most cognitive research has focused on the surface aspects of human — computer interactions, whilst most organizational psychologists have concentrated on the division of responsibilities once systems are designed. What is required is R&D work in the other areas, namely allocation of function and the match between the representation held by computer systems and their users of complex production environments, and, even more importantly, studies of the ways in which all these design choices influence and constrain one another.

Elsewhere, Clegg (1984) has argued that sociotechnical designs have rarely been undertaken in practice, since the technologies are usually accepted as given, the social efforts going into redesigning the organizational roles of operators to enhance satisfaction. True sociotechnical design will only take place when social scientists are actively involved in all areas of research identified above.

Cost — benefit outcomes

It was argued earlier that social scientists have failed to convince others of the legitimacy and significance of the human aspects of AMT. In part this is because the small amount of work that has been done has had a partial focus, concentrating on behavioural concerns to the exclusion of operational and financial issues. Indeed, Cascio (1982) argues that 'the time has clearly arrived for behavioural scientists to begin to speak the language of business' (p. 94) (i.e. money). One must have doubts that this is possible in the short term, and also some concern that it is desirable, but implicit in Cascio's argument is the criticism that outcome evaluation research has been too limited in scope. Here we heartily agree — research into AMT needs a more complex and comprehensive view of relevant outcomes.

However, in pleading the case for a wider-ranging perspective than currently prevails, it is important not to lose theoretical focus. As psychologists we advocate the inclusion of two important classes of variables in such evaluations—namely, performance and mental health. Under the heading of performance, the concern is with variables such as: individual problem-solving and effectiveness; system efficiency, utilization and productivity; and organizational flexibility, responsiveness, and effectiveness. By mental health is meant assessment of variables such as: psychological arousal; strain, neurosis, and anxiety; and demands, skill requirements, and job satisfaction. A critical research issue concerns the way in which these variables are affected by the choices described earlier in this chapter.

Two features of AMT, stressed throughout this book, concern its potential for integrating production systems both physically and through better information and control, along with its increasing application to uncertain production environments. The trend is towards greater interdependence and tighter coupling between constituent parts. Nor is this solely a technical trend. The same drive towards tighter coupling can be discerned in structural and procedural changes that are taking place in many companies, for example through 'just-in-time' inventory (see Clegg, 1986). The advantage of tight coupling is that work flows more smoothly and more quickly, inventories are lower, and control is easier. But there are risks, since problems in such systems propagate downtime both upstream and downstream. With their application in uncertain production environments, such production problems are inevitable. Given their size, expense, and potential, these issues of overall system performance and utilization are critical management concerns.

The current lack of technical sophistication in state-of-the-art sensing devices and error recovery software has led to a concentration of humans in monitoring and error recovery roles (Gerwin and Leung, 1980). The humans have been allocated tasks and roles which the machines cannot effectively perform. As such individual vigilance and responsiveness is critical to the performance of the such systems. Such operator roles are causing concern for some:

> The role of people in an environment which is to an increasing extent determined by computer systems which are outside their control will demand careful study by industrial management. The unsocial hours and the heavy work may well be left behind but what takes their place could be, in its own way, even less pleasant (Ingersoll Engineers, 1983, p. 49).

The psychology of control, which is well developed within developmental and environmental psychology (Corbett, 1985), is relevant here. Although some work has been carried out in process control industries (see Buchanan and Bessant, 1985), the social and cognitive aspects of control in AMT environments remain largely unexplored. It seems likely that the trend towards tight coupling in these systems will be associated with computer control of work pacing, and therefore the developing literature on machine pacing and occupational stress will be of relevance (see Salvendy and Smith, 1981). Indeed exploratory empirical work by Corbett (1987) suggests that tightly coupled production systems are accompanied by reports of relatively high strain.

In addition, advanced systems need other forms of support, especially in terms of engineering (e.g. maintenance), materials control, programming, and production planning. If these support activities are poorly organized, it is reflected in relatively poor performance of the system. It is for these reasons that senior managers have been heard to identify the major benefit of their new technology investment, in terms of its capacity to force the rest of the organization to give more effective support. These are matters of job design and organizational structure.

What is required is research which more carefully and comprehensively identifies the impact of the choices described earlier on these outcome variables. For example: what is the impact of the allocation of functions between machines and humans on system performance and on the mental health of the users? Can optimal allocations be identified? What is the impact of the chosen interfaces on the operators and on their performance? Does the computer system's representation match the user's model of the production process for control purposes? Can more 'humanized' computer representations be developed? And in what ways do choices of operator job designs and of supporting organizational structures influence performance and mental health?

Such evidence as is available suggests that there are positive links between performance and mental health, particularly in the application of advanced systems to uncertain production environments. Thus, Cummings and Blumberg (Chapter 3), Clegg and Wall (1987), Jones (1984), and Gerwin and Leung (1980) all propose that performance is likely to be optimized by providing operators with the skills and responsibilities to solve problems as they occur, as proposed by sociotechnical theory under the rubric of controlling variances at source. Fortunately these methods of organization are also likely to incorporate and promote the sorts of job designs and organizational structures that many believe provide for good mental health. Perhaps AMT provides an excellent opportunity to break the pattern of deskilling within production systems. To summarize, outcome evaluation of AMT requires consideration of a range of performance and mental health variables. We advocate the adoption of a cost−benefit approach involving the use of a methodology which is systematic and rigorous, as well as being comprehensive, plural, and multi-disciplinary.

CONCLUSION

To date, AMT has been evolving quickly, and there is every indication the process will continue since there are many advantages in its development and adoption. This chapter, and indeed all of this book, has argued that the human side of such technologies is important, but unfortunately is largely ignored in practice. Nor should we relax, fondly hoping perhaps that the future of AMT will be so automatic as to render the human aspects irrelevant. If anything, quite the reverse; these human and organizational issues will get more important. Indeed, Michie and Johnson (1985) have gone so far as to claim that 'the greatest social urgency attaches not to extending automation, but to humanizing it' (p. 72).

This chapter has argued that one of the main reasons for the relative exclusion of such human aspects from debates on new technologies can be found in social scientists' own failures to demonstrate their case. In part, this is due to the style of work that has been undertaken, and the argument is for a much greater emphasis by social scientists on an R&D strategy which incorporates both retrospective research and prospective development work. At the same time, more effort is required to share knowledge and skills through the provision of generalizable criteria and tools for use by engineers, managers, trade unionists, and users. Three areas of particular importance have been identified for future R&D work, corresponding to issues of process, content, and outcome. As befits a chapter on future work, a large number of questions have been asked. A multi-disciplinary approach is advocated which incorporates technical, cognitive, and social issues. Collaborative work of this kind will be enormously difficult and challenging, placing heavy demands on social scientists' ability to learn and co-operate. But without such efforts there is a real danger that the new generations of high technology will pass us by, to everybody's disadvantage.

NOTES

1. Other collaborators are Gordon Allison, Ian Cole, Nigel Kemp, Mark Lansdale, Andrew Monk, Colin Potts, and Peter Warr.
2. Colleagues are Sue Ravden and Toby Wall.

REFERENCES

Attenborough, N. G. (1984). *Employment and Technical Change: the case of microelectronic-based production technologies in UK manufacturing industry*. London: Department of Trade and Industry.
Bessant, J. (1983). Management and manufacturing innovation: the case of information technology. In G. Winch (ed.), *Information Technology in Manufacturing Processes*. London: Rossendale.
Bessant, J., Guy, K., Miles, I., and Rush, H. (1985). *IT Futures*. London: National Economic Development Office.
Blackler, F., and Brown, C. (1986). Alternative models to guide the design and introduction of the new information technologies into work organisations. *Journal of Occupational Psychology*, **59**, 287–314.
Blumberg, M., and Gerwin, D. (1984). Coping with advanced manufacturing technology. *Journal of Occupational Behaviour*, **5**, 113–30.
Briefs, U., Ciborra, C., and Schneider, L. (eds) (1983). *Systems Design For, With, and By the Users*. Amsterdam: North-Holland.
Broadbent, D. E. (1986). The clinical impact of job design. *British Journal of Clinical Psychology*, **24**, 33–44.
Brodner, P. (1982). Humane work design for man–machine systems: a challenge to engineers and labour scientists. In *Proceedings of Conference on Analysis, Design and Evaluation of Man–Machine Systems*. Baden-Baden, pp. 179–85.
Buchanan, D., and Bessant, J. (1985). Failure, uncertainty and control: the role of operators in a computer integrated production system. *Journal of Management Studies*, **22**, 292–308.
Buchanan, D., and Boddy, D. (1983a). *Organisations in the Computer Age: technological imperatives and strategic choice*. Aldershot: Gower.
Buchanan, D., and Boddy, D. (1983b). Advanced technology and the quality of working life: the effects of computerised controls on biscuit-making operators. *Journal of Occupational Psychology*, **56**, 109–19.
Cascio, W. F. (1982). *Costing Human Resources: the financial impact of behaviour in organisations*. New York: Van Nostrand Reinhold.

Clegg, C. W. (1984). The derivation of job designs. *Journal of Occupational Behaviour*, **5**, 131−46.

Clegg, C. W. (1986). Trip to Japan: human resources and synergy. *Personnel Management*, August, pp. 35−9.

Clegg, C. W., and Corbett, J. M. (1986). Psychological and organisational aspects of computer aided manufacturing. *Current Psychological Research and Reviews*, **5**, 189−204.

Clegg, C. W., and Kemp, N. J. (1986). Information technology: personnel, where are you? *Personnel Review*, **15**(1), 8−15.

Clegg, C. W., and Wall, T. D. (1987). Managing factory automation. In F. Blackler and D. J. Oborne (eds), *Information Technology, and People: designing for the future*. Leicester: British Psychological Society.

Cook, J. D., Hepworth, S. J., Wall, T. D., and Warr, P. B. (1981). *The Experience of Work: a compendium and review of 249 measures and their use*. London: Academic Press.

Corbett, J. M. (1985). Prospective work design of a human-centred CNC lathe. *Behaviour and Information Technology*, **4**, 201−14.

Corbett, J. M. (1987). A psychological study of advanced manufacturing technology: the concept of coupling. *Behaviour and Information Technology* (In press).

Dodgson, M. (1985). *Advanced Manufacturing Technology in the Small Firm*. London: Technical Change Centre.

Dore, R., Dodgson, M., and Cross, M. (1986). *Best Practice in Skill Packaging for CNC Machines: interim report*. London: Technical Change Centre.

Eason, K. D. (1982). The process of introducing new technology. *Behaviour and Information Technology*, **1**, 197−213.

Ehn, P., Kyng, M., and Sundblad, Y. (1983). The Utopia project. In V. Briefs, C. Giborra, and L. Schneider (eds), *Systems Design For, With and By the Users*. Amsterdam: North-Holland.

Fitts, P. M. (ed.) (1951). *Human Engineering for an Effective Air Navigation and Traffic Control System*. Washington, DC: National Research Council.

Fraser, R. (1947). The incidence of neurosis among factory workers. Report No. 90, Industrial Health Research Board. London: HMSO.

Gerwin, D., and Leung, T. K. (1980). The organisational impact of FMSs: some initial findings. *Human Systems Management*, **1**, 237−46.

Hackman, J. R., and Oldham, G. R. (1975). Development of the Job Diagnostic Survey. *Journal of Applied Psychology*, **60**, 159−70.

Ingersoll Engineers (1983). *The FMS Report*. London: IFS Publications.

Jones, B. (1984). Factories of the future, conflicts from the past. Paper presented at the Technology Innovation and Social Change seminar, University of Edinburgh.

Jordan, N. (1963). Allocation of functions between man and machines in automated systems. *Journal of Applied Psychology*, **47**, 161−5.

Karasek, R. A. (1979). Job demands, job decision latitude and mental strain: implications for job redesign. *Administrative Science Quarterly*, **24**, 285−308.

Kemp, N. J. (1985). *A Directory of Psychologists and Information Technology Research*. Leicester: British Psychological Society.

Kemp, N. J., and Clegg, C. W. (1987). Information technology and job design: a case study in CNC machine tool working. *Behaviour and Information Technology* (In press).

Kornhauser, A. (1965). *Mental Health of the Industrial Worker*. New York: Wiley.

Littler, C. (1983). A history of 'new' technology. In G. Winch (ed.), *Informtion Technology in Manufacturing Processes*. London: Rossendale.

Michie, D., and Johnson, R. (1985). *The Creative Computer: machine intelligence and human knowledge*. Harmondsworth: Pelican.

Mueller, W. S., Clegg, C. W., Wall, T. D., Kemp, N. J., and Davies, R. T. (1986). Pluralist beliefs about new technology within a manufacturing organisation. *New Technology, Work and Employment*, **1**, 127 – 139.

Mumford, E., and Henshall, D. (1979). *A Participative Approach to Computer Systems Design*. London: Associated Business Press.

NEDO (1985). *Advanced Manufacturing Technology: The impact of new technology on engineering batch production*. London: National Economic Development Organization.

Northcott, J., and Rogers, P. (1982). *Microelectronics in Industry: what's happening in Britain*. London: Policy Studies Institute.

Northcote, J., and Rogers, P. (1984). *Microelectronics in British Industry: the pattern of change*. London: Policy Studies Institute.

Ouchi, W. (1981). *Theory Z*. Reading, Mass.: Addison-Wesley.

Perrow, C. (1984). *Normal Accidents: living with high risk technologies*. New York: Basic Books.

Piercy, N. (ed.) (1984). *The Management Implications of New Information Technology*. Beckenham: Croom-Helm.

Price, H. E. (1985). The allocation of functions in systems. *Human Factors*, **27**, 33 – 45.

Ravden, S. J., Johnson, G. I., Clegg, C. W., and Corbett, J. M. (1987). Human factors in the design of a flexible assembly cell. In P. Brodner (ed.), *Skill-Based Automated Manufacturing*. Oxford: Pergamon Press.

Rose, H., McLoughlin, I., King, R., and Clark, J. (1986). Opening the black box: the relation between technology and work. *New Technology, Work and Employment*, **1**, 18 – 26.

Rosenbrock, H. H. (1983). Social and engineering design of an FMS. In E. A. Warman (ed.), *CAPE '83*. Preprints, part 1. Amsterdam: North-Holland.

Rouse, W. B. (1981). Human – computer interaction in the control of dynamic systems. *Computing Surveys*, **13**, 17 – 31.

Salvendy, G., and Smith, M. J. (eds) (1981). *Machine Pacing and Occupational Stress*. London: Taylor & Francis.

Scarbrough, H. (1984). Maintenance workers and new technology: the case of Longbridge. *Industrial Relations Journal*, **15**, 9 – 16.

Taylor, F. W. (1911). *The Principles of Scientific Management*. New York: Harper.

Taylor, J. C. (1979). Job design criteria twenty years on. In K. Legge and E. Mumford (eds), *Designing Organisations for Satisfaction and Efficiency*. London: Gower.

Wall, T. D. (1985). Information technology and shopfloor jobs: opportunities and challenges for psychologists. *Occupational Psychology Newsletter*, **19**, 3 – 10.

Wall, T. D., and Clegg, C. W. (1981). A longitudinal field study of group work redesign. *Journal of Occupational Psychology*, **51**, 183 – 96.

Wall, T. D., Clegg, C. W., Davies, R. D., Kemp, N. J., and Mueller, W. S. (1987). Advanced manufacturing technology and work simplification: an empirical study. *Journal of Occupational Behaviour* (In press).

Weick, K. E. (1976). Educational organisations as loosely coupled systems. *Administrative Science Quarterly*, **19**, 1 – 19.

Winch, G. (ed.) (1983). *Information Technology in Manufacturing Processes*. London: Rossendale.

Wood, S. (ed.) (1982). *The Degradation of Work?* London: Hutchinson.

Author Index

197

Subject Index